# International Exchange of Information in Tax Matters

# International Exchange of Information in Tax Matters

Towards Global Transparency

Xavier Oberson

*Professor of Law, University of Geneva, Switzerland*

Edward Elgar
PUBLISHING

Cheltenham, UK • Northampton, MA, USA

Published by
Edward Elgar Publishing Limited
The Lypiatts
15 Lansdown Road
Cheltenham
Glos GL50 2JA
UK

Edward Elgar Publishing, Inc.
William Pratt House
9 Dewey Court
Northampton
Massachusetts 01060
USA

A catalogue record for this book
is available from the British Library

Library of Congress Control Number: 2015930140

This book is available electronically in the **Elgar**online
Law subject collection
DOI 10.4337/9781784714727

ISBN   978 1 78471 471 0   (cased)
ISBN   978 1 78471 472 7   (eBook)

Typeset by Columns Design XML Ltd, Reading
Printed and bound in Great Britain by T.J. International Ltd, Padstow

# Contents

# Abbreviations

| | |
|---|---|
| AEOI | automatic exchange of information |
| AML | anti-money laundering |
| Archives | Archives de droit fiscal suisse (ASA) (periodical) |
| ATF | 'Arrêt du Tribunal fédéral' |
| CAA | competent authority agreement |
| CDFI | Cahiers de Droit Fiscal International |
| CMAAT | CoE/OECD Multilateral Convention on Administrative Assistance in Tax Matters |
| CoE | Council of Europe |
| CRS | common reporting standard |
| DoJ | United States Department of Justice |
| DPD | Data Protection Directive |
| DRC | EU Directive on recovery of tax claims |
| DTC | double taxation convention |
| DTT | double taxation treaty |
| EATLP | European Association of Tax law Professors |
| ECHR | European Convention/Court on Human Rights |
| ECJ | European Court of Justice |
| ECOFIN | Economic and Financial Affairs Council |
| EID | Exchange of Information Directive |
| EOI | Exchange of Information |
| ET | European Taxation (periodical) |
| EUDAC | EU Directive on Administrative Assistance |
| EUSD | EU Savings Directive |
| FAC | Federal Administrative Court |
| FATCA | Foreign Account Tax Compliance Act |
| FATF | Financial Action Task Force |
| FFI | foreign financial institution |
| FIU | Financial Intelligence Unit |
| FStR | IFF Forum für Steuerrecht (periodical) |

| | |
|---|---|
| GIIN | Global Intermediary Identification Number |
| Global Forum | Global Forum on Transparency and Exchange of Information for Tax Purposes |
| G5 | Group of five |
| G8 | Group of eight |
| G20 | Group of twenty |
| IAAT | Swiss Federal Law on Administrative Assistance in Tax Matters |
| IBFD | International Bureau of Fiscal Documentation |
| IFA | International Fiscal Association |
| IGA | intergovernmental agreement |
| IMAC | International Mutual Assistance in Criminal Matters |
| Intertax | International Taxation (periodical) |
| IRC | Internal Revenue Code (USA) |
| IRS | Internal Revenue Service (United States) |
| KYC | 'know your customer' |
| LDF | Liechtenstein Disclosure Facility |
| LoN | League of Nations |
| MFN | most favoured nation |
| MoU | Memorandum of Understanding |
| NFE | non-financial entity |
| NFFE | non-financial foreign entity |
| OECD | Organisation for Economic Co-operation and Development |
| OECD Model | OECD Model Double Taxation Convention on Income and on Capital |
| OJ | Official Journal of the EU |
| QI | Qualified Intermediary |
| TFEU | Treaty on the Functioning of the EU |
| TIEA | Tax Information Exchange Agreement |
| TIEA Model | Model Agreement on Exchange of Information in Tax Matters |
| TIN | Taxpayer Identification Number |
| TNI | Tax Notes International (periodical) |
| UCI | undertakings for collective investment |
| UCITS | undertakings for collective investment in transferable securities |

# 1. General introduction

The power to levy taxes is one of the key features of the Sovereignty of States. At the beginning, taxes were levied on a territorial basis, focusing on the place of situation of the assets or the location of transfers of goods. Later, with the development of industrial States and the need to finance global infrastructures and social services, modern States tended to move towards more global systems of taxation, notably on worldwide income tax. This major development led to a need to combat double international taxation (with rules such as exemption or credit methods) and, as a consequence, exchange of information. Indeed, in order to insure a fair international level of tax, each State has to be able to verify the global position of any relevant taxpayer.

Parallel to this development, globalization led to an effort to develop instruments to combat international tax fraud and evasion. Sophisticated taxpayers, such as multinational companies, could try to use the international legal framework, typically double taxation treaties (DTT), in order to insure double non-taxation. Other taxpayers, including individuals, were developing schemes of tax evasion through the use of offshore or complex structures. The transfer of the place of residence to tax favourable countries also started to develop.

As a consequence, international organizations and governments entered into exchange of information networks around the world with a view to fostering global transparency.

In fact, the need for international agreement in tax matters is the result of a conflict, based on international public law, between the principle of universality in taxation, on the one hand, and the principle of territoriality for the implementation of the tax rules, on the other hand.[1] Indeed, it is generally recognized that states have the right to tax persons (individual or entities) globally (universally), so long as there is a personal connection with that state (universality). By contrast, states are usually locked inside their territory in order to implement or enforce their tax rules. States therefore need international treaties, bilateral or multilateral, in

---

[1]  Seer/Gabert (2009), p. 23.

*1*

order to solve this conflict and in particular obtain information or collection measures to ensure a fair and global taxation of their tax-payers.

While the trend towards exchange of information in tax matters started a long time ago, namely during the works of the League of Nations in 1919, it really developed globally after the publication of the various OECD Models of double taxation convention, as of 1963, and took another impetus, following the publication, in 1998, of the OECD Report against harmful tax competition.

Following the financial crisis of 2008, a major acceleration of the movement took place in the 'big bang' of 2009. This led to the renegotiation of hundreds of double taxation conventions based on the OECD Model Double Taxation Convention (DTC) around the world and the signature of tax exchange of information agreements (TIEA) with tax haven countries in an unprecedented way. The United States, with the enactment of FATCA in 2010, was pushing towards a global standard and has succeeded in designing a system, which is now adopted around the world, notably through the mechanism of the intergovernmental agreements.

Countries started to exchange information around the world like never before. In 2013, a step further was reached: the global consensus towards the automatic exchange of information as the new global standard. This tremendous development toward exchange of information, and more generally administrative assistance in tax matters, with its constant and rapid evolution, raises of course many issues. Different, sometimes conflicting, rules and models have been developed in parallel by different institutions and governments. There is therefore a need for coordination and consultation among the various actors. In addition, while the focus relied on the efficiency and global acceptance by countries of the rules of the exchange of information, the legal positions of the persons involved, the taxpayers, have remained of less concern. In fact, their situation remains mostly a question of domestic law, with all the potential differences that this may cause.

The purpose of this book is therefore to describe the main developments in the area of exchange of information in tax matters, the various existing instruments, their interaction and the position of the persons involved during the process.

We will thus start by describing the historical development towards a mechanism of global exchange of information in tax matters. Then, we will focus on an analysis of the main instruments providing for international exchange of information in tax matters. This includes double taxation treaties, TIEAs, the CoE/OECD Multilateral Convention on

Mutual Administrative Assistance in Tax Matters (CMAAT), European Directives, the Swiss Rubik models and the FATCA regime. We will move on to the development of a global model of international automatic exchange of information. There are already various systems in force, which could serve as models. The proper design of this new system has therefore to take into account the complexities of the existing models and try to coordinate them. Moving towards automatic exchange of information also requires taking a look at potential solutions for solving the past.

Finally, after having analysed in detail the various systems of international exchange of information, their interaction and complexities, we will then move on to look at the position of the taxpayers involved. This should lead us to define more precisely the level of protection of the taxpayers, during the whole exchange of information process, and the existing rights that may be challenged during it. More precisely, we will distinguish between substantive rights, such as human or constitutional freedoms, which cover essential rights of protection of human features (privacy, possession, data protection, etc.), and procedural rights, namely rights of defence in the process as such.

# 2. Historical development of international exchange of information rules

## I. FIRST MODELS

It appears that the first exchange of information rules took place in the framework of double taxation treaties concluded between Belgium and France (1843), and Belgium and the Netherlands (1845).[2]

The starting point of a model providing for the obligation to exchange information under a bilateral convention can be traced back to the works of the League of Nations.[3] Indeed, in 1927, the League's Committee of Technical Experts on Double Taxation and Tax Evasions issued a general report, that presented four separate model tax conventions.[4]

One year later, the committee and experts published the 1928 model double taxation treaty that would form the basis of bilateral treaties, which under the following works of the OECD, would form the basic structure of the international tax regime.[5] As Dean has demonstrated, the fate of the four models presented by the League of Nations would however be quite different.[6] Indeed, the Model designed against double taxation would clearly prevail over the others. Later on, the League of Nations issued two model tax treaties, the so-called Mexico drafts, in 1943, and the London drafts, in 1946, which included a model double

---

[2] Gangemi (1990), p. 19.

[3] Dean (2008), p. 35.

[4] See Reports Presented by the Comm. of Technical Experts on Double Taxation and Tax Evasion, League of Nations Doc. C.216M.85 1927 II (1927 Report); Dean (2008), p. 35.

[5] In this sense, Dean (2008), p. 35, who refers also to Avi-Yonah (1996), p. 1306.

[6] Dean (2008), p. 38.

taxation treaty and a model for the establishment of reciprocal administrative assistance in the field of taxation.[7] Finally, the two distinct drafts would be combined into a single model treaty.[8]

The Organisation for European Economic Co-operation (OEEC) published its recommendation concerning double taxation, on 25 February 1955, and its successor, the OECD, adopted in July 1963, a Draft Double Taxation Convention on income and capital. Article 26 of the OECD Draft would later become one of the leading frameworks for international exchange of information in tax matters. The essential feature of this type of exchange of information corresponds to an exchange of information upon request. In addition, it covers information relevant to carry out the provisions of the convention or to implement the domestic law of the requesting State. In the first case, we refer to a 'minor exchange' and, in a second case, to an 'extended exchange' clause.

At this stage, some countries, like Austria, Belgium, Luxembourg and Switzerland, were more in favour of granting a restricted exchange of information in tax matters. For instance, Switzerland, under the so-called 'traditional approach', would only accept a treaty with a minor exchange of information clause, limited to the information necessary to carry out the provisions of the treaty.[9] Therefore, Switzerland would not grant exchange of information about a taxpayer, resident in the requesting State, who did not claim any benefit from an applicable DTT, typically in order to obtain a reduced tax at source from Swiss source dividends, interests or royalties.

In 1979, the Council of Europe and the OECD issued in Strasbourg a Multilateral Convention on Mutual Administrative Assistance in Tax Matters (CMAAT), which was approved in 1987. It was open to signature first for OECD Members in 1988 and entered into force on 1 April 1995, after ratification from five States (United States, Denmark, Finland, Sweden and Norway).

---

[7] Fiscal Comm., London and Mexico Model Tax Conventions: Commentary and Text, League of Nations Doc. No. C.88.M.88.1946.IIa.; Dean (2008), p. 39.

[8] Dean (2008), p. 40.

[9] It should be noted that this position already evolved in 1996, under a new income tax treaty with the United States, where Switzerland was ready to exchange information in cases of 'tax fraud and the like'. This concept, derived from domestic Swiss law, corresponds to a tax evasion combined with fraudulent behaviour of the taxpayer, such as manoeuvres, 'schemes of lies' designed to deceive the tax administration; see infra p. 41.

## II. THE DEVELOPMENT OF THE INITIATIVE AGAINST HARMFUL TAX COMPETITION AND ITS IMPACT

The year 1998 remains a landmark moment in the path towards global transparency. On that date, the OECD published the famous report against harmful tax competition. It sets a pattern to identify tax havens and harmful tax regimes of countries with a comprehensive tax system. Looking at this report in retrospect, it is interesting to note that most of the changes that would occur later in the area of exchange of information were already announced ten years before, albeit not in such an extensive and comprehensive form. Among the criteria to identify both tax haven and harmful tax regimes, the lack of effective exchange of information plays a key role. At that time, Luxembourg and Switzerland abstained from approving the report. Both countries however continued to participate in the works of the OECD on these matters.

The pressure started to grow notably against identified tax havens, which were further divided into two categories: cooperative and non-cooperative. In 2000, the OECD issued a report entitled Improving Access to Bank Information for Tax Purposes.[10] This time, both Switzerland and Luxembourg approved it. Retrospectively, it can be seen as a compromise because it only provides for a minimum standard of an exchange of information upon request, and subject to tax fraud, as defined according to the law of the requested State.[11] For a while, due notably to a public statement of the United States in early 2001,[12] the focus was less on the harmful features of corporate taxation than on exchange of information as such. The pressure however kept going on.

As a result of the works of the Global Forum on Transparency and Exchange of Information, which was created in 2000, the OECD issued in 2002 a model tax information exchange agreement (TIEA). The OECD presented both a multilateral and a bilateral model, which provided for exchange of information upon request, without the possibility for the requested State to oppose bank secrecy rules. Indeed, the

---

[10]   OECD, Improving Access to Bank Information For Tax Purposes (OECD 2000), International Organizations Documentation IBFD.

[11]   The approval of the 2000 OECD Report, and the later introduction of the EU Saving Directives, led Switzerland to modify its position in favour of an exchange of information in case of tax fraud according to the law of the requested State, see infra p. 23.

[12]   See, US Treasury Department, Statement from Treasury Secretary O'Neil on OECD Tax Havens, of 10 May 2001.

request was based on the conditions set forth under the rules of the requesting States. While it appears that TIEAs had already been concluded in the past, notably between the United States and Caribbean countries, the OECD Model TIEA however represents a major development providing for a global framework, still based on exchange of information upon request. At first, the progress of TIEAs was rather slow; only a dozen of such agreements were signed, notably with the United States. Time would however show the success of these models, namely seven years after.

In 2005, strongly influenced by the works of the Global Forum and the adoption of the Model TIEA, the OECD Model DTC, and its Commentary, were modified in order to comply with the global standard. A new par. 5 to Art. 26 was adopted. It provides, in particular, that the requested State cannot decline to supply information solely because it is held by a bank, other financial institution, or because it relates to the ownership interests in a person.

## III. DEVELOPMENTS AT THE EU LEVEL

At the EU level, actions were also being undertaken in order to fight against tax evasion and develop exchange of information. Significant instruments have been put in place, notably in the area of VAT and various excise duties. On 27 January 1992, the Council Regulation (218/1992) on administrative cooperation in the field of indirect taxation (VAT) was adopted, followed later by a new Council Regulation on 7 October 2003. In the field of direct taxes, the first Directive on exchange of information (77/799) was adopted on 19 December 1977. This Directive would then be modified many times in the future.

On 3 June 2003, the Directive 2003/48/EC on the taxation of savings income in the form of interest payments was adopted.[13] It entered into force on 1 July 2005. At the same time, bilateral agreements with equivalent rules were adopted between the EU and third States, namely Switzerland, Andorra, Monaco, Liechtenstein and San Marino.

---

[13] Council Directive 2004/48/EC of 3 June 2003 on the taxation of savings income in the form of interest payments, OJ L 157 of 26 June 2003, p. 38 ff.

## IV. THE 'BIG BANG'

The year 2007 will remain the year of the last pause before the storm. It all started in Liechtenstein. A gentleman by the name of Kiefer was able to transfer a CD with clients' names from an accounting firm in Vaduz to Germany. The CD did contain a list of noncompliant German taxpayers. Without knowing it Mr. Kiefer provoked a major political crisis, resulting in the resignation of a top German politician involved in the fraud and put the issue at the forefront of the political agenda and in the media. Shortly after, in 2008, the UBS scandal started in the United States with thousands of undeclared bank accounts of US taxpayers under investigation.

The economic crisis of 2008, although not directly linked with the issue of bank secrecy and offshore accounts, gave a further impetus in favour of global transparency and put more pressure on tax havens. International organizations (such as the UN or the OECD), and notably G20 countries called for action in this field. As of 2008, the implementation of global standards of transparency and exchange of information has been at the top of the agenda of the G20 meetings in Washington, London and Pittsburgh.[14]

The Leader's statement of the London G20 meeting of 2 April 2009, stated:

> We agreed to take action against non-cooperative jurisdictions, including tax havens. We stand ready to deploy sanctions to protect our public finances and financial systems. The era of bank secrecy is over. We note that the OECD has today published a list of countries assessed by the Global Forum against the international standard for exchange of information of tax information.

Indeed, the G20 meeting of 2009 introduced white, grey, or black lists of countries, according to their level of implementation of a sufficient network of exchange of information treaties. The 'rule of 12' became reality. In order to belong to the white list, a country had to sign a minimum of 12 DTCs, with an extended exchange of information clause corresponding to the OECD Model, or of 12 TIEAs. This time the pressure from the world community was too strong. On 13 March 2009, a 'big bang' occurred: Austria, Belgium, Luxembourg and Switzerland, in particular, announced their willingness henceforth to apply the standard defined in Article 26 of the OECD Model DTC within the framework of new tax treaties. Those countries, during the London G20 summit on 2

---

[14] Cannas (2013), p. 28.

April 2009, were still on a 'grey' list, which refers to states that had committed to implementing the international standard without having done so in substance.[15] By September 2009, they had been moved to the white list.[16] March 2009 would further lead to negotiations of tax treaties, with extended exchange of information clauses, and of TIEA, all around the globe, like never before, including notable tax haven countries.

The Global Forum started to implement a 'peer review' process, in order to verify the level of implementation of the global standard. The *first phase* started in 2010. Some countries already had to modify their legislation, which could be viewed as too restrictive in view of the requirement of the generally accepted standard. The *second phase* of the peer review concentrates on the effective practices of the member states. It is still underway but important progress has generally been implemented globally.

According to the Global Forum, the *international standard*,

> which was developed by the OECD in co-operation with non-OECD countries and which was endorsed by G20 Finance Ministers at their Berlin Meeting in 2004 and by the UN Committee of Experts on International Cooperation in Tax Matters at its October 2008 Meeting, requires the exchange of information on request in all tax matters for the administration and enforcement of domestic tax law without regard to a domestic interest requirement or bank secrecy for tax purposes. It also provides for extensive safeguards to protect the confidentiality of the information exchanged.[17]

In the United States, major developments also occurred. As of 2001, the 'Qualified Intermediary' (QI) agreements were implemented. They allow foreign financial institutions (FFI) to enter into QI agreements, which provide for determining the identity of their US clients, and levy a withholding tax of 30 per cent on US source income (dividends, interest, gross proceeds from sale). Under the QI, however, the FFI did not have to disclose the names of their US customers.

The UBS case, including the Birkenfeld whistleblowing,[18] drew a lot of attention from the media, and political pressure grew against the use of offshore structures, with the participation of banks or FFI to evade taxes. As a consequence, the United States introduced the Foreign Account Taxpayer Compliance Act (FATCA) in 2010. Under FATCA, foreign FFI

---

[15]   OECD Global Forum, Progress Report, 2 April 2009.

[16]   OECD Global Forum, Progress Report, 28 September 2009.

[17]   OECD, Tax Co-operation 2010: Towards a Level Playing Field (2009); see also Malherbe/Beynsberger (2012), p. 125.

[18]   For a description of the UBS saga, see infra p. 43 ff.

must identify and report to the IRS US account holders and non-US account holders with substantial US owner. Participating FFIs are also required to levy a 30 per cent withholding tax on certain payments of recalcitrant account holders.

In 2011, the Joint CoE/OECD CMAAT of 1988 was further amended.[19] It was opened for signature by non-OECD Member countries. The rules were adapted to the current standard on exchange of information. In particular, similar to Article 26, paragraph 5 of the OECD Model DTC, information held by banks or relating to the ownership must be exchanged. Increasingly, in parallel to the bilateral network of double taxation treaties, a multilateral form of cooperation was fostered. While on 27 May 2010, the new Protocol CMAAT had been signed by 15 countries, it has nowadays been signed by more than 65 countries.

The same year, at the EU level, the Directive 2011/16/EU on administrative cooperation in the field of taxation, replacing Directive 771/799/EEC, was adopted.[20] It provides for the exchange of information upon request or spontaneously, and for an automatic exchange of information, as from 1 January 2015, that is available on the following five specific categories of income and capital: employment income, director's fees, life insurance products, pensions and ownership and income from immovable property. It should be noted that there is already a pending proposal to extend such automatic exchange to dividends, capital gains, and other income held in specific financial accounts.

In the same period, Switzerland started to implement an alternative model, the so-called 'Rubik' agreements. In a nutshell, the model is based on a withholding tax on Swiss source income to foreign residents in Contracting States, which is then transferred to that state, while preserving anonymity of the taxpayer. The rate corresponds to the state of residence. Withholding tax agreements have been signed by Switzerland in 2012 with the United Kingdom, Austria and Germany (but the latter was finally not ratified).

A further development took place in 2012. On 17 July 2012, the OECD updated its Commentary on the OECD Model and confirmed the admissibility of so called 'group requests' in the context of exchange of information.[21] It means that a request may not only refer to a single identified taxpayer but also pertain to a specific group of taxpayers, who

---

[19]   See in particular, Pross/Russo (2012), p. 381.

[20]   Council Directive 2011/16/EU on administrative cooperation in the field of taxation of 15 February 2011, O.J. L 64/1 of 11.03.2011.

[21]   See, notably, OECD Model Tax Convention on Income and on Capital: Commentary on Article 26, para. 5.2. (22 July 2010).

are in a similar situation. The prohibition of fishing expeditions still applies under the standard, so that the group must be sufficiently related to a specific and joint 'pattern of facts'.[22]

In the same year, the Financial Action Task Force (FATF) adopted a revision of its guidelines. According to the FATF Recommendation No 3 of February 2012, serious tax crimes (direct or indirect), a concept to be defined under domestic tax law, becomes a predicate offence for criminal money laundering prosecution. This rule, which was already implemented by many States, namely in Europe, became thus a global standard. Following that trend a proposal of a new EU Directive on the prevention of the use of the financial system for the purpose of money laundering and terrorist financing of February 5 2013 (COM (2013) 45 final) is under analysis.

The development of money laundering rules in the tax area has a direct impact on exchange of information. Indeed, coordination between criminal and tax rules will foster such exchanges. In addition, criminal rules on identification of the beneficial owner of complex structures, implemented for anti money laundering purposes, may be used as additional tools in the tax area, in order to identify beneficial owners or controlling persons.

## V. TOWARDS AUTOMATIC EXCHANGE OF INFORMATION

While most observers were thinking that giant steps had already been achieved in the area of exchange of information, a major development, somewhat comparable to the 'big bang' of 2009, again took place in 2013: the move towards automatic exchange of information.

In fact, the movement can already be traced back to 2012. In particular, in February 2012, five European countries (France, Germany, Italy, Spain and the United Kingdom) announced their intention to develop a system of multilateral automatic exchange of information with the United States, in order to implement the FATCA rules. This agreement forms the basis of the so-called Model 1 IGA. This development can be described as a 'turning point' toward the global standard of automatic exchange of information.[23] Indeed, the FATCA system of global reporting started to

---

[22] For an example of a group request, see Federal Administrative Court (FAC), of 5 March 2009 ('case UBS I'), Archives 2009, p. 837; see infra p. 43.

[23] See also Tello/Malherbe (2014), p. 1; Grinberg (2014), p. 333ff; Grinberg (2012), pp. 305, 375; Morse (2012), p. 529 ff.

be implemented globally and endorsed as a potentially reciprocal standard under the Model 1 IGA.

On 19 April 2013, the meeting of G20 Finance Ministers and Central
Bank Governors endorsed automatic exchange of information as the
expected new standard,[24] followed by a commitment of the G20 Leaders,
on 6 September 2013, in favour of this standard. In February 2014, the
G20 Finance Ministers and Central Bank Governors endorsed the Common Reporting Standard for automatic exchange of information. By May
2014, more than 60 jurisdictions had committed to implement the
Common Reporting Standard of automatic exchange.[25] Finally, on
29 October 2014, during the meeting of the Global Forum in Berlin, 49
countries, the 'early adopters', agreed to sign a multilateral competent
authority agreement implementing the global standard. The first automatic exchanges are expected to take place as of 2017. Other countries
have already announced that they should follow one year later.

It is interesting to note the acceleration of the developments of the
rules of international exchange of information. In less than five years, the
standard, applied globally, has evolved from exchange of information
upon request (2009), to group requests (2012) and further automatic
exchanges (2013). Such acceleration towards a global consensus may be
explained by the following factors.

First, as of 2008, following the financial crisis, the subject was put on
the agenda of many international organizations and most countries
around the world. While the standard of exchange of information was
developed, an ongoing series of scandals related to transnational frauds,
such as the UBS case, the Cahuzac case of a French Minister with
undisclosed bank accounts, the Falciani case, providing listing of clients
at HSBC in Geneva, or the Hoeness indictment in Germany, contributed
to growing media and public attention and blame. Non-governmental
organizations, such as the Tax Justice Network, press and media around
the world, including social networks, also contributed to fostering stricter
rules against tax evaders.

Second, rules of automatic exchange of information started to be
implemented with a growing consensus among states, the EU and
international organizations, such as the OECD or the UN. This is notably
the case of the EU Savings Directive, providing as of 1 July 2005, for
automatic exchange of information on savings interest (subject to the

---

[24]   OECD, Standard for Automatic Exchange of Financial Account Information in Tax Matters, 2014, n. 3 ad Introduction.
[25]   OECD, ibid.

transitory regime), followed by the EU Directive on Administrative collaboration of 2011. The development of the CoE/OECD CMAAT should also be mentioned here. By opening signatures to non-OECD countries in 2011 with high standards of international exchanges, the multilateral conventions opened the gate towards a multilateral framework that can serve as a legal basis for many countries implementing automatic exchanges.

Third, the impact of FATCA, in this ongoing process, cannot be underestimated. Indeed, the unilateral features of the domestic FATCA regime, adopted in 2010, led many countries to develop more balanced and reciprocal forms of cooperation, notably under IGAs.[26]

Fourth, the suggested alternative model of withholding tax, the so-called 'Rubik' Model, as presented by Switzerland, did not reach a global consensus. The system is rather complex to be implemented as a global standard. In addition, the anonymity of the taxpayer seems to be rejected as a matter of principle by some states. This system however still remains as an interesting alternative for states which would have difficulties in implementing an automatic exchange of information system.

The implementation process of the automatic exchange of information is under way. While the principle seems to be of global consensus many issues remain open. We are going to analyse them in more detail in the following chapters.

---

[26]    Blank/Mason (2014), p. 5.

# 3. Exchange of information under Double Taxation Conventions (DTC)

## I. TOWARDS A MODEL DTC

### A. Introduction

So far, exchange of information in tax matters has developed mostly within the framework of DTC. While the purpose of a DTC is to fight against international double taxation, it also serves as a tool to combat tax evasion and avoidance.[27] In this respect, the exchange of information under a treaty fulfills double functions. First, it ensures the proper implementation of the treaty, especially for the country of residence, which applies a system of worldwide taxation. Second, it helps the fight against international tax avoidance and evasion by providing to each Contracting State, information relevant to the application of their domestic laws. The development and global success of DTC, which is one of the major achievements of international law,[28] corresponds to the global acceptance of models of double taxation conventions around the globe.

Today, the leading standard on exchange of information in the framework of DTC is based on the OECD Model DTC (including the UN Model). In particular, Art. 26 of the OECD-MC represents the most relevant legal basis for the international exchange of information.[29] The path that led to this achievement was started by the works of the League of Nations in 1918, after the First World War.

### B. The Drafts of the League of Nations

The starting point of the obligation to exchange information under a bilateral convention is the result of the work of the League of Nations.[30]

---

[27]   OECD, Model DTC Commentary, n. 7 ad Art. 26.
[28]   Avi-Yonah (1996), 1301 ff.
[29]   Fort/Hondius/Neugebauer (2012), p. 88.
[30]   Dean (2008), p. 35.

Out of the four separate models that were presented in 1927,[31] one focused on administrative assistance in tax matters.

The Draft Convention on Administrative Assistance in Matters of Taxation, issued by the League of Nations, can be seen as the first model to cover the issue of exchange in tax information among States. That model was structured as a bilateral agreement between two countries, under which each government would be obligated to provide extra-territorial information both (i) upon request and (ii) automatically for enumerated categories of information.[32] The draft mentioned the information regarding natural or juristic persons that was to be supplied automatically. The information had to include: the names and residence of the persons concerned, and their family responsibilities, if any.[33] Automatic exchange of information had to be provided on: (i) immovable property; (ii) mortgages; (iii) industrial, agricultural and commercial undertakings; (iv) earned income and director's fees; (v) transferable securities and (vi) estates.[34] The model also included procedural rules and clarified that each country had the right to refuse to provide information, if such supply would be contrary to public policy.[35] Finally the model confirmed that administrative assistance had to be 'given without payment'.[36]

As we have seen above, out of the four models published, the draft model focusing on administrative assistance would not be further implemented as such. In 1928, the League of Nations would publish a model double taxation treaty that would form the basis of future bilateral treaties. This resulted in the drafting of the Mexico Model of 1943, followed by the London Model of 1946.[37] Both models included a model double taxation treaty and a model for the establishment of reciprocal administrative assistance in the field of taxation.[38]

---

[31]  See Reports Presented by the Comm. of Technical Experts on Double Taxation and Tax Evasion, League of Nations Doc. C.216M.85 1927 II (1927 Report); Dean (2008), p. 35.

[32]  Dean (2008), p. 35; 1927 Report, p. 22.

[33]  1927 Report, p. 22.

[34]  1927 Report, p. 22; Dean (2008), p. 37.

[35]  1927 Report, p. 23; Dean (2008), p. 37.

[36]  Ibid.

[37]  Dean (2008), p. 39; Vogel (1998), n. 18 ad Introduction.

[38]  Fiscal Comm., London and Mexico Model Tax Conventions: Commentary and Text, League of Nations Doc. No. C.88.M.88.1946.IIa.; Dean (2008), p. 39.

## C. The OECD Model DTC

The development of a Model DTC was further enhanced by the works of the OECD, as a successor to the OEEC. Since its first publication in 1963, Art. 26 of the OECD Model still represents the most relevant legal basis for international exchange of information. This norm has been subject to many changes over the years, notably in 1977, 2000 and 2005, broadening its scope and leading to successive implementations by the member states in their respective treaties.

In 2002, in particular, the OECD undertook a comprehensive review of Art. 26 to ensure that it corresponded to current practices and world developments.[39] The review took into account developments such as the Model Agreement on Exchange of Information on Tax Purposes (TIEA) in 2002, as well as the report Improving Access to Bank Information for Tax Purposes of 2000.[40] At that time, the OECD Model TIEA represented the standard for the effective exchange of information for the purpose of the OECD Initiative on harmful tax practice.[41] Following that review, several important changes were introduced to Art. 26 OECD Model. Since these developments are coordinated, we are of the opinion that the rules and commentary of the TIEA are also relevant to interpret the new version of Art. 26 of the OECD MC, as of 2005.[42]

Article 26 OECD, in its 2005 version, combined with the rules of the Model TIEA, represented the global standard for an effective exchange of information.

Later on, in particular as of 2009, we have seen that the global standard of Art. 26 of the OECD Model received a worldwide acceptance. New changes occurred in 2010 and 2014. With the path towards automatic exchange of information as the new global standard,[43] Art. 26 could further be modified in the near future.

---

[39]  OECD Commentary, n. 4 ad Art. 26.
[40]  Ibid.
[41]  Oberson, in: Danon/Gutman/Oberson/Pistone (2014), n. 13 ad Art. 26; Fort/Hondius/Neugebauer (2012), p. 92.
[42]  Oberson, in: Danon/Gutman/Oberson/Pistone (2014), n. 16 ad Art. 26.
[43]  See infra p. 184 ff.

## D. The UN Model DTC

Since 2011, Art. 26 of the UN Model corresponds to the version of the OECD Model, subject to two differences.[44] First, Art. 26 par. 1 of the UN Model provides in particular, that information shall be exchanged that would be helpful to a Contracting State in preventing avoidance or evasions of taxes. Second, under Art. 26 par. 6 of the UN Model, the competent authorities shall, through consultation, develop appropriate methods and techniques concerning the matters in respect of which exchanges of information shall be made.

## E. The US Model DTC

The United States also developed a model income tax treaty, which serves as a basis for negotiations and also includes an Art. 26 covering exchange of information. The structure and content of the US Model corresponds to the OECD Model. There are however some differences.[45]

First, the US standard provides for an exchange of information 'as may be relevant' for carrying out the provisions of the convention or of the domestic states concerning taxes of every kind and not 'as is foreseeably relevant', like the OECD Model (Art. 26 par. 1).

Second, Art. 26 US Model includes additional paragraphs. Article 26 par. 6 of the US Model provides, if specifically requested, for exchange of information 'in the form of depositions of witnesses and authenticated copies of unedited original documents (including books, paper, statements, records, accounts and writings)'. Article 26 par. 7 of the US Model covers assistance in the collection of taxes. According to Art. 26 par. 8 of the US Model, representatives of the requesting States are allowed to enter the requested State to interview individuals and examine books and records with the consent of the person subject to examination. Finally, competent authorities may develop an agreement upon the mode of application of this provision, including agreement to ensure comparable levels of assistance to each of the Contracting States (Art. 26 par. 9).

---

[44] Lang, Introduction, p. 157; for more details see Garcia Pratz (1999), p. 541.

[45] See in particular, for a broad description of the United States international tax policy in this context, United States Government Accountability Office (GAO), Report to the Permanent Subcommittee on Investigations, Committee on Homeland Security and Governmental Affairs, U.S. Senate, IRS's Information Exchanges with Other Countries Could Be Improved through Better Performance Information, September 2011.

## II.  THE SCOPE AND CONDITIONS OF EXCHANGE OF INFORMATION

### A.  Material Scope

### 1.  The standard of foreseeable relevance

The basic rule of exchange of information is Art. 26 par 1 of the OECD Model. It provides that the competent authorities of the Contracting States shall exchange such information as is *foreseeably relevant* for carrying out the provisions of this convention or for the administration or enforcement of the domestic laws concerning taxes of every kind and description imposed on behalf of the Contracting States, or of their political subdivisions or local authorities, insofar as the taxation thereunder is not contrary to the convention.[46]

In the past, some countries favoured a more restrictive approach in the field of exchange of information and adopted a so-called '*minor information clause*'. The minor information clause only grants an exchange of information that is necessary for carrying out the DTC. As a consequence, under such a clause, a Contracting State can only supply information that relates to a person who claims benefits from a treaty, typically in the form of a reduced tax at source. In addition, under a minor information clause, a request for information is not allowed for persons who are not covered by the treaty.[47]

The OECD standard calls however for a '*major information clause*', under which Contracting States exchange information foreseeably relevant for the application of domestic law. In this case, the scope of information is broad and may also be relevant only for the application of the domestic law in the requesting State. It follows that residence is not a condition for the admissibility of the request, because in this case Art. 26 par. 1 provides that the request is not restricted by Art. 1 of the OECD Model.[48]

At the implementation level, most states adopted a major exchange of information clause (according to Art. 26 par. 1), while some, such as Luxembourg or Switzerland, chose to include only a minor exchange of information clause, which includes only information necessary to carry

---

[46]  It should be noted, in passing, that in 1977, a minor change occurred in Art. 26 par 1 in the sense that the words 'taxation ... in accordance with' were replaced by 'taxation ... is not contrary'. This rather subtle change does not seem to have any significant impact in practice, see Gangemi (1990), p. 65.

[47]  Lang (2013), n. 525.

[48]  Ibid.

out the provision of the DTT. In such a case, should a taxpayer not claim the benefit of the DTT, no exchange of information could occur between the Contracting States.

The standard of 'foreseeable relevance' was introduced in 2005 in Art. 26 par. 1 (first sentence) and replaced the wording '*as is necessary*' in the old version. This new wording is not of huge importance but shows the willingness to implement a rather broad exchange of information. Indeed, according to the OECD, the standard of 'foreseeable relevance' is intended to provide for exchange of information in tax matters to the widest possible extent and, at the same time, to clarify that Contracting States are not at liberty to engage in 'fishing expeditions' or to request information that is unlikely to be relevant to the tax affairs of a given taxpayer.[49]

Exchange of information for criminal tax matters may also be based on bilateral (or multilateral treaties) on mutual legal assistance, to the extent they apply also to tax crimes.[50]

## 2. The prohibition of fishing expeditions

The standard of foreseeable relevance prohibits at the same time so-called fishing expeditions, i.e. requests for information that are merely searching for proof.[51] Even if not mentioned in the text of the Model DTC, the prohibition of fishing expeditions is implicit to Art. 26 par. 1 OECD Model. Commentators also tend to base the prohibition of fishing expedition on the principle of subsidiarity.[52] Fishing expeditions are characterized as 'speculative requests that have no apparent nexus to an open inquiry or investigation'.[53]

The purpose of this rule is indeed to avoid extensive and sometimes unnecessary investigations by the requested State, as long as the requesting State does not know what it is looking for. After all, in such a case the request cannot be characterized as foreseeably relevant for the requesting State. The content of this rule is however subject to criticism. McIntyre, in a powerful article, has compared the prohibition of fishing expeditions to a limitation similar to asking that a fisherman know the name of the fish before catching it.[54] This point of view goes too far.

---

[49]  OECD Commentary, n. 5 ad Art. 26.
[50]  Ibid.
[51]  OECD Model DTC Commentary, n. 5 ad Art. 26.
[52]  Pistone/Gruber (2011), p. 88.
[53]  See OECD Commentary, update of 2012, n. 5 ad Art. 26.
[54]  McIntyre (2009), p. 255.

Under the principle of subsidiarity, allowing fishing expeditions would just transfer all the investigation costs to the requested State.[55]

### 3. An alternative (intermediary) solution: exchange of information only in cases of 'tax fraud'

During an intermediary phase, Switzerland adopted an alternative approach between a major and a minor exchange of information clause. Following the United States/Swiss treaty of 1996, the approval of the OECD Report of 2000 on access to bank information, and the bilateral treaty with the EU on taxation of savings, Switzerland adopted a so-called 'new approach', crystallized, for instance in the Protocol of 2003 to the Germany-Switzerland Income and Capital Tax Treaty.

This change of policy led to a modification of Switzerland's reservation on Article 26 of the OECD Model, as of 2005. Under this new version

> Switzerland reserves its position towards paragraphs 1 and 5. It will suggest restricting the application of this article to information, which is necessary for the implementation of the dispositions of the convention. This reserve will not be applied to cases of tax fraud which is liable to a prison sentence in virtue of the laws of both Contracting States.

As a consequence, several tax treaties, notably those with European States, such as Spain, Finland, Norway and Austria, were amended in order to adapt the exchange of information clause, so that it would cover cases of tax fraud as defined under the law of the requested State.

This approach, however, had soon to be extended. In particular, under a Protocol of 29 June 2006 to the Spain/Switzerland double taxation treaty,[56] a most-favoured-nation clause (MFN) in favour of EU Member States was introduced. According to article IV (11)(a) of the Protocol, regarding the exchange of information, if Switzerland signs an agreement of any nature or a disposition in a tax treaty with an EU Member State relating to the taxes covered by this tax treaty, Switzerland should grant Spain the same level of assistance as that provided in such an agreement or disposition or a part thereof and Spain shall do the same.

In other words, in agreeing to this clause, Switzerland somehow played its last card before transitioning to exchange of information according to

---

[55]    See also Pistone/Gruber (2011), p. 89.

[56]    Convention between Spain and the Swiss Confederation for the Avoidance of Double Taxation with Respect to Taxes on Income and Capital [unofficial translation] (as amended through 2006), 26 April 1966, Treaties IBFD.

the OECD Model.[57] Indeed, a single agreement of this kind with any EU Member State would suffice in order to then apply it to Spain. A most-favoured-nation clause of this kind was also introduced, on 12 January 2009, in the France/Switzerland treaty. The protocol, which was never finally ratified by France, provided for a most-favoured-nation clause not only in favour of EU Member States following the Spanish model but also in favour of OECD Member countries (article 7(3)(b)). Nevertheless, the change of paradigm in favour of the OECD standard of Art. 26 Model DTC, adopted two months later by Switzerland, made the ratification of the Protocol with France unnecessary.

## 4. Identification of the taxpayer
As a matter of principle, in exchange of information upon request, the taxpayer involved has to be identified. The same is true for the information holder (bank, financial institution, etc.). In other words, this rule requires that the identity of the taxpayer may be sufficiently described in order to relate the person with the request. Otherwise, supply may be refused as a fishing expedition. According to the OECD standard, as far as the identification of the taxpayer is concerned, the request should give his or her identity. Further, the name of the information holder also has to be mentioned, but only, 'to the extent known'.[58] During the peer review process, it appeared for instance, that the Swiss norms were regarded as too restrictive in this respect. In most cases, Swiss treaties required that the name of the taxpayer has to be disclosed. Secondly, the rules regarding the identification of the information holder were regarded as too strict. As a consequence, on 13 February 2011, a change of practice took place in regard to these two aspects. The existing treaties, already ratified or signed, were adapted accordingly.

## 5. Group request
A group request is an assistance inquiry, which as such does not specify the names of the taxpayers involved, but describes a similar and systematic 'pattern of facts', which can be related to a specific tax evasion or avoidance schemes. As long as it can be related to a precise pattern of facts, linked with a bank or an institution, it is not characterized as a fishing expedition.

---

[57] Oberson (2013), p. 368 ff.
[58] See Art. 5 par. 5, lit. (e) of the OECD TIEA Model Agreement; Oberson, in: Danon/Gutman/Oberson/Pistone (2014), n. 43 ad Art. 26.

In 2012, the OECD Model Commentary was modified in order to allow a so called *'group request'* which still complies with the standard of foreseeable relevance of Art. 26 par. 1. According to the OECD, such a standard can be met both in cases dealing with one taxpayer (identified by name or otherwise) or several taxpayers. In the latter case, it will often be more difficult to establish that the request is not a fishing expedition, so it is required that the requesting State provide more information and description about the pattern of facts and its connection with the group.

In order to meet the foreseeably relevant standard, the request of the applicant State must in fact fulfill three requirements: (i) provide a 'detailed description' of the group, including the specific facts and circumstances that have led to the request; (ii) explain the applicable law and why there is reason to believe that the taxpayers in the group have been noncompliant; and (iii) show that the request would assist in determining compliance by the taxpayers of the group.[59] In practice, a third party, such as a bank or a financial intermediary, will usually assist the group in the non-compliance scheme. This was for instance the case in the 'UBS I' FAC Court judgment of 2009.[60] Under the United States/Switzerland Protocol of 2009, still not ratified by the US, the possibility of group requests was also introduced. However, by contrast, a request that simply describes the provision of financial services to non-residents, and mentions the possibility of non-compliance by non-resident taxpayers, will be too vague and be characterized as a fishing expedition.[61]

It is important to note that the modification of the Commentary about group requests did not lead to a change of the text of Art. 26 OECD Model DTC. Furthermore, the OECD Model DTC does not mention that international assistance should only be granted in a specific individual case. In other words, the adjunction to the OECD Model Commentary can only be viewed as a clarification of an existing rule.[62] Therefore, we are of the opinion that group requests are already allowed under the standard of foreseeable relevance, provided they are not fishing expeditions.

---

[59]  OECD Commentary, n. 5.2. ad Art. 26; see also Valdés Zauner (2013), p. 490.

[60]  FAC of 5 March 2009, A-7342/2008 and A-7426/2008.

[61]  OECD Model DTC, Commentary, n. 5.2 ad Art. 26; Valdés Zauner (2013), p. 491.

[62]  Oberson, in: Danon/Gutman/Oberson/Pistone (2014), n. 48 ad Art. 26.

An example of a group request can be found in the UBS case, which will be described in more depth later.[63] In this case, the first request of the IRS did not mention the identity of the relevant 250 US taxpayers but referred to a pattern of facts of similar behaviours, characterized as tax fraud and the like, under Art. 26 of the United States/Swiss DTC (1996). In its judgment ('so-called UBS I'), the Federal Administrative Court (FAC) admitted that the request was not a fishing expedition, since the pattern of facts was linked with a systematic behaviour, i.e. the inter-position of offshore entities (typically BVI or Liechtenstein Foundations), designed to circumvent the QI obligations under the agreement with the bank.[64]

## B. Personal Scope

Since 1977, the exchange of information under Art. 26 is not restricted by Art. 1 of the OECD MC. In other words, an exchange of information is possible, not only for residents of the Contracting States, but may also concern residents of third states or individuals or entities that are not subject to taxation according to Art. 4 OECD MC.[65] For instance, a requesting State may ask for information from a Contracting State where bank accounts, held in the premises of a local bank, as information holder, are opened by a resident in a third state.

## C. Taxes Covered

Since 2000, the scope of this provision is not limited by Art. 2 of the DTC. As a consequence, exchange of information may cover taxes of 'any kind and description', and not only taxes under the scope of the Model DTC, such as income (profit) or capital (wealth) taxes. It means, for instance, that information pertaining to VAT, excise taxes, gift or inheritance taxes may also be exchanged under Art. 26 par. 1 OECD Model. In principle, Art. 26 OECD Model could also cover custom duties since such duties are undoubtedly characterized as 'taxes'. In practice, however, the exchange of information rules have a legal basis in more specialized instruments that will generally prevail.[66]

---

[63] See supra p. 43.

[64] FAC of 5 March 2009, A-7342/2008 and A-7426/2008.

[65] Torres (2013), p. 77; Rust (2012), p. 185; Engelschalk in: Vogel/Lehner (2008), n. 57 ad Art. 26.

[66] OECD Commentary, n. 5.2. ad Art. 26.

## III.  COMPETENCE AND SECRECY RULE

Exchange of information occurs between competent authorities. In most cases, it will be the Ministry of Finance, which in turn delegates some of its powers to the tax administration.

The competent authorities must keep information received within the exchange of information process as *confidential*. The so-called secrecy clause of Art. 26 par. 2 OECD Model DTC – which was moved from par. 1 to par. 2 in 2005 – has a role to assure that both administrations 'will treat with proper confidence the information which it will receive in the course of their cooperation'.[67]

The obligation of secrecy provided by Art. 26 par. 2 has a double component.[68] First, the requesting State is obliged to keep the information received secret under the same conditions as information obtained under domestic law. Second, this provision will describe exactly to whom the information obtained may be transferred.

The exact content of the secrecy requirement has however evolved over the time. Under the 1963 OECD Model DTC secrecy rule, information 'shall be treated as secret and shall not be disclosed to any person or authorities other than those concerned with the assessment or collection of the taxes which are the subject of the Convention'. According to this rule, the secrecy standard was 'autonomous' and did not depend on the level of protection in the requesting State.[69] This rule was further transformed in 1977 into an 'equal treatment obligation', according to which the requesting State is obliged to apply the same secrecy rule to information that it receives, as information that it obtains under domestic law.[70] This new rule, which is in essence still applicable under the current OECD Model, tends to facilitate the use of information in the requesting State, but has the effect that the standard in the requested State is no more applicable.[71] It follows that while the OECD Model DTC of 1963 provided for an absolute secrecy protection (autonomous definition), a relative secrecy protection rule is applicable since the OECD Model DTC of 1977.[72]

---

[67]   OECD Commentary, n. 11 ad Art. 26.

[68]   Pistone/Gruber (2011), p. 92.

[69]   Rust (2012), p. 180; Engelschalk, in: Vogel/Lehner (2008), n. 78 ad Art. 26.

[70]   Ibid.

[71]   Rust (2012), p. 181.

[72]   Pistone/Gruber (2011) p. 93; Engelschalk, in: Vogel/Lehner (2008), n. 78 ad Art. 26.

Under Art. 26 par. 2 of the OECD MC,

> Any information received by a Contracting State shall be treated as secret in the same manner as information obtained under the domestic laws of that State and shall be disclosed only to persons or authorities (including courts and administrative bodies) concerned with the assessment or collection of, the enforcement or prosecution in respect of, the determination of appeals in relation to, the taxes referred to in paragraph 1, or the oversight of the above.

The possibility to disclose the information to oversight bodies (supervising authorities and enforcement authorities) was introduced in 2005.

The maintenance of secrecy in the receiving state, as well as the sanctions for violation of this rule, are a matter of domestic law.[73] The rules appear to be quite diverse among states in this respect. In a recent report,[74] the OECD suggested some basic principles that states should apply under the secrecy rule, in order to ensure a minimum common threshold of protection.[75] The absence of such minimum threshold could hamper an effective exchange of information. In principle, based on the equality of treatment rule of the requesting State, a lighter standard of protection in the state appears not to be a ground to refuse to supply information for the requested State.[76] However, under German law, the authorities can refuse to grant a response if an acceptable level of protection is not granted in the requesting State.[77]

The information may thus be disclosed only to the *persons or authorities* listed in this provision. The possibility to inform the courts was only added in 1977. But commentators tend to admit that even before that explicit change to the text, it was already possible to use the information in a tax court or a criminal court involved with the prosecution of the tax fraud.[78] In 2005, a further change of the text included the persons concerned with the oversight of the tax administration and the courts.

---

[73] OECD Commentary, n. 11 ad Art. 26.

[74] OECD, Keeping it Safe – the OECD Guide to the Protection of Confidentiality of Information Exchanged for Tax Purposes, July 2012.

[75] See also, in this respect, Kristofferson/Pistone (2014), p. 1 ff.

[76] Rust (2012), p. 181; Engelschalk, in: Vogel/Lehner (2008), n. 82 ad Art. 26.

[77] Drüen/Gabert (2009), p. 290; see also Court of Cologne judgment of 20 August 2008, 2V 1948/08, EFG 2008 1764 ff.

[78] Rust (2012), p. 182; Engelschalk, in: Vogel/Lehner 2008, n. 88 ad Art. 26.

The information may also be communicated to the taxpayer, his proxy or to the witnesses.[79] This interpretation is clear since the text of the MC refers to persons 'concerned with the assessment or collection' of the taxes, to which the taxpayers undoubtedly belong.[80] The secrecy rule refers to 'any information received under par. 1', which includes not only the information transferred but also the information received, i.e. information contained in the request. Therefore the request made may be passed on to the taxpayer.[81]

In addition, such persons or authorities shall use the information only *for the purposes* mentioned under paragraph 2. They may however disclose the information in public court proceedings or in judicial decisions (Art. 26 par 2 *in fine* OECD Model DTC).

In principle, information received by a Contracting State may not be disclosed to a third country, unless a specific provision of a DTC allows such disclosure.[82] On 17 July 2012, Art. 26 par. 2 OECD MC was however modified with an additional sentence, which provides that 'information received by a Contracting State may be used for other purposes when such information may be used for such other purposes under the laws of both States and the competent authority of the supplying State authorizes such use'. This sentence, which was previously mentioned as an option under the old MC version, is now in the text. The purpose of the rule is to allow the use of information for purposes which are of value to the receiving state, for instance to combat money laundering, corruption, and the financing of terrorism.[83]

In addition, the 2005 change provides for a new Art. 26 par. 4, under which the requested State cannot refuse to respond to an information request solely because it has no domestic interest in such information. The purpose of this clause, which appears as a clarification of an existing principle, is to prohibit the use of the so-called 'national interest clause', under which certain States, such as Singapore refused to exchange information.

If the requested State has knowledge or grounds to believe that the requesting State violates secrecy rules or transfers the information to non-legitimate persons or authorities, it may refuse to supply the information.[84]

---

[79]  OECD Commentary, n. 12 ad Art. 26.
[80]  Rust (2012), p. 184.
[81]  Ibid.
[82]  OECD Commentary, n. 12.2 ad Art. 26.
[83]  OECD Commentary, n. 12 ad Art. 26.
[84]  Pistone/Gruber (2011), p. 92.

The requirement for the state receiving the information to maintain the same level of secrecy, as under its domestic rules is a treaty obligation, which generates rights and obligations only for the Contracting States.[85] However, the domestic rules on secrecy are usually designed to safeguard also the rights of the individuals involved in the process; when this occurs such a guarantee results in an extension of protection in favour of the person in the other state who supplied the information.[86]

## IV.  FORMS OF EXCHANGE OF INFORMATION

In general, Art. 26 par. 1 allows information to be exchanged in three different ways (on request, spontaneously or automatically). These forms may be combined. In addition, this provision does not restrict the possibilities of exchanging information and other techniques, such as simultaneous examination or tax examination abroad.[87] The OECD further implemented a Manual on the Implementation of Exchange of Information for Tax Purposes in 2006. The Manual describes various forms of exchange of information, such as on request, spontaneous, automatic, or simultaneous tax examination or tax examination abroad.

### A.  Upon Request

Information upon request is the most frequent method applied so far. The requesting State requests from the other Contracting State information foreseeably relevant in a specific situation. Under the *subsidiarity* principle, the regular source of information available under the international taxation procedures should be applied in the first place before the request is made to the other state.[88]

### B.  Spontaneous

Spontaneous information exchange is the provision of information to another Contracting State that is foreseeably relevant to that party but has

---

[85]  Engelschalk, in: Vogel/Lehner (2008), n. 50 ad Art. 26.

[86]  Engelschalk, in: Vogel/Lehner (2008), n. 50 ad Art. 26.

[87]  OECD Commentary, n. 9 ad Art. 26; see also, OECD Tax Information Exchange between OECD Member Countries: A survey of Current Practices, Paris 1994.

[88]  OECD Commentary, n. 9(a) ad Art. 26; see also de Oliveira (2013), p. 447 ff.

not been previously requested.[89] This would apply for example if a state obtains certain information during investigations, which it supposes to be of interest to the other state.[90] By its nature, spontaneous exchange of information relies on the active participation of the local tax officials.[91] It can thus be more effective than automatic exchange because it concerns things detected and selected by tax officials during an investigation.[92] However, by contrast, the effectiveness and efficiency of this system very much depends on the initiative and motivation of the officials in the supplying country.[93]

## C.  Automatic

Automatic exchange of information means transmission of information, on a routine basis, at regular intervals, without any specific request from another state.[94] Under Art. 26 par. 1, this kind of transfer could occur for example when information about various categories of income having their source in one Contracting State (typically dividends, interest or royalties) is systematically transmitted to the receiving Contracting State.[95] This system of exchange typically covers recurring financial transactions, involving paying agents, such as interest, dividends, capital gains, or royalties.[96]

As of 2013, a global consensus has emerged in favour of the automatic exchange of information becoming the new standard.[97] On a bilateral level, treaties with a provision similar to Art. 26 of the OECD Model DTC could then already serve as a legal basis for an automatic exchange of information.

---

[89] OECD Manual on the Implementation of Exchange of Information Provisions for Tax Purposes, 2006, Module 2 on Spontaneous Exchange of Information, p. 3; Jeong (2013), p. 447 ff.

[90] OECD Commentary, n. 9 Art. 26.

[91] Jeong (2013), p. 447.

[92] OECD Manual on the Implementation of Exchange of Information Provisions for Tax Purposes, 2006, Module 2 on Spontaneous Exchange of Information, p. 3.

[93] Ibid. p. 3.

[94] OECD Manual on the Implementation of Exchange of Information Provisions for Tax Purposes, Module 3 on Automatic (or routine) Exchange of Information, 2012, p. 3; see also Parida (2013), p. 423 ff, 425.

[95] OECD Commentary, n. 9(b) ad Art. 26.

[96] See also Parida (2013), p. 424.

[97] See infra p. 184 ff.

## D. Tax Examination Abroad

This type of examination allows for the possibility to obtain information through the presence of a representative of the requesting State in the requested State.[98] For instance, to the extent allowed under the domestic law, a Contracting State may allow a representative of the other Contracting State to enter its territory and to interview individuals or examine books of records, or be present during interviews or examinations carried out by the authorities of the first mentioned state.[99] A similar form of assistance is also provided under the CoE/OECD multilateral conventions.[100]

This kind of assistance is possible provided (i) both Contracting States agree on the interpretation of the treaty and (ii) reciprocity requirements are fulfilled.[101]

## E. Simultaneous Examination

Under a simultaneous examination, two or more Contracting States examine simultaneously, each in its own territory, the tax affairs of a taxpayer in which they have a common interest or related interest, with a view of exchanging any relevant information which they so obtain.[102]

## F. Joint Audits

A joint audit is an arrangement between two or more states joining together to form a single audit team from tax auditors from each state to examine an issue or transaction of an individual or a legal person with cross-border tax activities.[103] Although neither Art. 26 OECD Model, nor

---

[98] OECD Commentary, n. 9.1. ad Art. 26.

[99] OECD Commentary, n. 9.1. ad Art. 26; OECD Manual on the Implementation of Exchange of Information Provisions for Tax Purposes, Module 6 on Conducting Tax Examinations Abroad, 2006; see also Roncarati (2013), p. 510 ff.

[100] See infra p. 71.

[101] OECD Commentary, n. 9.1. ad Art. 26; Roncarati (2013), p. 510.

[102] OECD Commentary, n. 9.1. ad Art. 26; OECD Manual on the Implementation of Exchange of Information Provisions for Tax Purposes, Module 5 on Conducting Simultaneous Exchange of Information, 2006; see also Roncarati (2013), p. 506 ff.

[103] OECD Manual on the Implementation of Exchange of Information Provisions for Tax Purposes, Module 9 on Joint Audits, 2010; see also Roncarati (2013), p. 511 ff.

its Commentary specifically mentions it, this provision can serve as the base for a joint audit since the list of forms of exchange described there is not exhaustive.[104]

## G.  Industry-wide Exchange of Information

An industry-wide exchange of information is an exchange concerning a whole economic sector (for instance oil, pharmaceutical industry, or banking sector) and not a taxpayer in particular.[105] The purpose of this kind of exchange is to secure comprehensive data on industry practices, enabling tax inspectors to conduct more knowledgeable and effective examinations.[106]

# V.  LIMITS TO THE EXCHANGE OF INFORMATION

## A.  In General

Art. 26 par. 1 OECD Model DTC, as a contract of international public law, entails an obligation to exchange information.[107] This obligation does not exist however, when the conditions of the exchange are not met or if the requested State refuses to supply the information based on a ground for refusal ('Verweigerungspflicht').[108] Such grounds for refusal are granted by Art. 26 par. 2 OECD Model DTC. They can be based on: (i) the domestic law of the requesting or requested State; (ii) the protection of a trade or business secret; (iii) the 'ordre public'. However, these limits are restricted by Art. 26 par. 5 of the OECD Model, which can be characterized as a derogation to paragraph 3.

When the grounds for refusal of Art. 26 par. 3 are met, the requested State is not obliged to supply information. However, according to the treaty, the requested State still has the *discretion* to grant information, even if some of the grounds for refusal are met.[109] The possibility to supply information, despite a ground for refusal under the treaty, may

---

[104]   OECD Commentary, n. 9.1. ad Art. 26.

[105]   OECD Commentary, n. 9(a) ad Art. 26.

[106]   OECD Manual on the Implementation of Exchange of Information Provisions for Tax Purposes, Module 4 on Industry-wide Exchange of Information (2006); see also Roncarati (2013), p. 517.

[107]   Engelschalk, in: Vogel/Lehner (2008), n. 2 ad Art. 26.

[108]   Pistone/Gruber (2011), p. 79.

[109]   Pistone/Gruber (2011), p. 80; Engelschalk, in: Vogel/Lehner (2008), n. 98 ad Art. 26.

however be restricted by domestic law.[110] According to the domestic law of many states, the granting of information, in the presence of a ground for refusal or when the conditions of exchange are not met, may have criminal law consequences.[111]

## B. Principle of Subsidiarity

This rule is applicable in the process of information upon request. Under this rule, the requesting State must first use a regular source of information available under its domestic law before sending a request to the other state.[112] In other words, a request of information may be treated as foreseeably relevant, only to the extent that the requesting State cannot obtain it under its own investigation.[113] The exchange of information under Art. 26 OED Model DTC is therefore secondary to the domestic information gathering process.[114]

## C. Domestic Limits and Principle of Reciprocity

A Contracting State cannot be obliged to carry out administrative measures that are at variance with the laws and administrative practice of that or the other Contracting State, or to supply information which is not obtainable under the laws or in the normal course of the administration of that or the other Contracting State (Art. 26 par. 3 lit. a and b OECD Model).

It follows that a state cannot be requested to adopt a measure that it cannot implement under its domestic law. Administrative measures are all actions that are requested by the requesting State.[115] These measures will be implemented under the domestic law of the requested State and are thus subject to the existing legal limits of that state, such as data protection rules, privacy rules or principles of legality.[116] In addition, existing domestic legal rules, such as a right of refusal of information for

---

[110]   Pistone/Gruber (2011), p. 80; Engelschalk, in: Vogel/Lehner (2008), n. 98 ad Art. 26. OECD Model DTC Commentary, n. 14 ad Art. 26.

[111]   Pistone/Gruber (2011), p. 81.

[112]   OECD Commentary, n. 9(a) ad Art. 26.

[113]   Pistone/Gruber (2011), p. 84; Engelschalk, in: Vogel/Lehner (2008), n. 35 ad Art. 26.

[114]   Pistone/Gruber (2011), p. 84.

[115]   Engelschalk, in: Vogel/Lehner (2008), n. 101 ad Art. 26.

[116]   Pistone/Gruber (2011), p. 96.

witnesses, information holders or taxpayers may prevent the supply of information.[117]

In some countries, the domestic law will include procedures for *notifying* the person concerned with the enquiry prior to the supply of information. According to the OECD standard, these procedures – which belong to procedural rights granted under domestic law of the requested State – should not be applied in a manner that, in the particular circumstances of the request, would frustrate the efforts of the requesting State.[118] It means that these notification rules should allow exceptions from prior notification, for instance 'in cases in which the information request is of a very urgent nature or the notification is likely to undermine the chance of success of the investigation conducted by the requesting State'.[119]

Under Art. 26 par. 3 lit. a and b OECD Model DTC, not only the domestic law of the requested State is relevant, but the domestic legislation and administrative practice of the *requesting State* also are to be taken into account. It follows that a state cannot be asked to implement a measure that the requesting State would not be in a position to obtain under its domestic rules. If the requesting State, based on its own domestic law or practice, would not be in a position to obtain information under its domestic rules, the requested State can refuse to supply it, based on the principle of reciprocity.[120]

It follows that a Contracting State cannot take advantage of the system of exchange of information of the other Contracting State if it is wider than its own.[121] In exchange of information, based on Art. 26 par. 3 OECD Model DTC, the *smallest common denominator* of the legal rules of both Contracting States is therefore applicable.[122]

For instance, many states recognize under domestic law that information cannot be obtained from a person if such a person can claim the privilege against *self-incrimination*. As a consequence, a requested State would be allowed to decline a request if a similar request would have been precluded under the rule against self-incrimination in the requesting State.[123] Similar

---

117    Ibid.
118    OECD Commentary, n. 14.1. ad Art. 26.
119    Ibid.
120    Pistone/Gruber (2011), p. 100.
121    OECD Commentary, n. 14.1. ad Art. 26.
122    Pistone/Gruber (2011), p. 100; Engelschalk, in: Vogel/Lehner (2008), n. 101 ad Art. 26.
123    OECD Commentary, n. 15.2. ad Art. 26.

rules are found in the TIEA Model.[124] The principle of reciprocity could even lead to a so-called '*de facto reciprocity*', which would occur when, in fact, the level of importance of information exchanged between the two states is too dissimilar, which could lead to a refusal of supply.[125] In order to ensure an effective exchange of information, it appears that only significant discrepancies between the two states, under the reciprocity principle, should be relevant.[126]

In some aspects the rules of sub-paragraph a) are included in that of subparagraph b), but the latter goes beyond in two cases.[127] Subparagraph b) also applies in cases where, even if obtaining the information would not go against domestic law, it is not possible of being *enforced*, or in cases where the information does not need to be obtained because it is *already available* to the authorities.[128] This could occur if the requesting authority, already in possession of the information, would be subject to a formal interdiction or a ban on using this potential evidence. The effect and content of such an interdiction would however depend on the domestic law of the requesting State.[129]

## D. Trade or Business Secret

A Contracting State is not obliged to supply information which would disclose any trade, business, industrial, commercial or professional secret or trade process (Art. 26 par. 3 lit. c OECD Model). According to the OECD, the secret mentioned in this provision should not be taken in a too wide sense; in particular, Contracting States should carefully weigh if the interests of the taxpayer really justify its application.[130] Indeed, if any information were characterized as 'secret', no effective exchange would occur. It follows that as a ground for refusal, Art. 26 par. 3 lit. c OECD Model DTC should only refer to information which needs special and relevant protection.[131] This should be the case only and to the extent that the protection of secrecy, granted by Art. 26 par. 2 OECD Model DTC,

---

[124]   See TIEA Commentary n. 73 ad 7.
[125]   Pistone/Gruber (2011), p. 101.
[126]   In the same vein, Pistone/Gruber (2011), p. 102; Engelschalk, in: Vogel/Lehner (2008), n. 102 ad Art. 26.
[127]   Engelschalk, in: Vogel/Lehner (2008), n. 103 ad Art. 26.
[128]   Ibid.
[129]   Ibid.
[130]   OECD Commentary, n. 19 ad Art. 26.
[131]   Pistone/Gruber (2011), p. 103.

appears not to be sufficient in view of the need of confidentiality of the information.[132]

A *trade or business secret* is generally understood 'to mean facts and circumstances that are of considerable economic importance and that can be exploited practically and the unauthorised use of which may lead to serious damage (e.g. may lead to severe financial hardship)'.[133]

The concept of 'trade or business secret' is not defined under Art. 26 par. 3 OECD Model. It would appear at first glance that this notion should be defined in accordance with domestic law (Art. 3 par. 2 OECD Model). This cannot correspond to the will of the drafter of the Model. Indeed, this notion is often not clearly defined under domestic law. In addition, it would lead to so many different definitions that it would result in an extent of secrecy protection being different in the country state, which would violate the principle of reciprocity.[134] Therefore the majority of commentators contend that the concept of trade or business secret requires an autonomous definition, which excludes a reference to the domestic law of the Contracting State.[135]

In this context, a state may decline information relating to confidential communications between attorney, solicitors or other admitted legal representatives in their role as such and their clients (*client-attorney privilege*).[136] According to the OECD the scope of protection under this rule should not be overly broad so as to hamper effective exchange of information. In particular, communications between clients and attorneys are only confidential if such representatives act in their capacity as attorney, solicitor or other admitted legal representatives and not in a different capacity, such as nominee shareholder, trustees, settlors, company directors or under a power of attorney to represent a company in its business affairs.[137] This rule is also found in the TIEA Model.[138]

---

[132]    Ibid.

[133]    OECD Commentary, n. 19.2 ad Art. 26; see also Engelschak, in: Vogel (1997), n. 110 ad Art. 26.

[134]    Engelschak, in: Vogel (1997), n. 108 ad Art. 26.

[135]    Pistone/Gruber (2011), p. 102; Engelschak, in: Vogel (1997), n. 108 ad Art. 26.

[136]    OECD Commentary, n. 19.3. ad Art. 26.

[137]    OECD Commentary, n. 19. 3 ad Art. 26.

[138]    TIEA Model, see infra p. 64.

## E. Public Policy

Finally, a state cannot be obliged to supply information, the disclosure of which would be contrary to public policy (ordre public) (Art. 26 par. 3 lit c OECD Model). It means that a requested State, in a specific situation, could refuse to exchange information, when the supply would infringe its 'fundamental evaluations' of its domestic law.[139] This rule should only apply in extreme cases.[140] An example of such a ground for refusal would be justified if a tax investigation from a requesting State were motivated by political, racial, or religious persecution.[141] This limitation could also apply in the case where the information constitutes a state secret, for example information held by secret service, the disclosure of which would be contrary to the vital interest of the requested State.[142]

An interesting issue in this context pertains to an exchange of information from a requesting State based on stolen data (CD, electronic tools, etc.). Some requests of this kind were issued, notably, towards Liechtenstein and Switzerland. Some countries tend to admit this kind of request, claiming that they fall under the exception of par. 5 to Art. 26 OECD Model DTC,[143] while others disregard them.[144] According to Steichen, the override of Art. 26 par. 3 lit. c (public policy) should not be possible in such a case. Indeed, the public policy doctrine is understood as the part of the body of principles that underpins the operation of legal systems in each state.[145] Following this opinion, public policy principles of the requested State could thus be a ground to deny a request of information, where for instance a Contracting State would have incited criminal action in the requested State by offering to pay for any relevant information provided to it.[146]

---

[139] Engelschak, in: Vogel (1997), n. 112 ad Art. 26.
[140] Pistone/Gruber (2011), p. 102; Engelschak, in: Vogel (1997), n. 112 ad Art. 26.
[141] OECD Commentary, n. 19. 5 ad Art. 26.
[142] Ibid.
[143] See infra p. 37.
[144] See Steichen (2012), p. 24 s.
[145] Steichen (2012), p. 25.
[146] Steichen (2012), p. 25.

## F.   The Derogation of Art. 26 par. 5 of the OECD Model

### 1.   Introduction

Following the changes of 2005, the limits clause of Art. 26 par. 3 OECD Model has been restricted by a new par. 5. It provides that:

> In no case shall the provisions of paragraph 3 be construed to permit a Contracting State to decline to supply information solely because the information is held by a bank, other financial institution, nominee or person acting in an agency or a fiduciary capacity or because it relates to ownership interests in a person.

This new paragraph is notably the result of the evolution of the international environment towards more global transparency, as reflected already in the publication, in 2002, of the TIEA Model.

For a while, this rule was difficult to implement for countries, such as Austria, Belgium, Luxembourg or Switzerland, which applied the domestic bank secrecy rule. As a consequence, these countries introduced a reservation to Art. 26 of the OECD Model DTC, according to which they reserve the right not to introduce par 5 of Art. 26 in their tax treaties.[147] This reservation was however lifted as of March 2009, after the 'big bang'.[148]

Art. 26 par. 5 OECD Model DTC makes a distinction between information which: (i) refers to the special status of the information holder (bank, financial institutions, etc.); (ii) concerns the legal capacity of the persons acting (agency, fiduciary, etc.) or (iii) relates to the ownership interest.

### 2.   Banks and financial institutions

Art. 26 par. 5 OECD Model DTC overrides par. 3, to the extent that some States would decline to supply information based on *bank secrecy* provisions under domestic law.[149] This rule should apply to banks and financial institutions.

It should be noted however that the refusal to provide information can still apply if the reasons, based on domestic law of the requested State, are unrelated to the person's status as a bank, financial institution, etc.[150] In our view, following the opinion of Steichen, the same should be true if

---

[147]   OECD Commentary, n. 23, 24 and 25 to Art. 26.
[148]   See supra p. 8.
[149]   OECD Commentary, n. 19.11 ad Art. 26.
[150]   OECD Commentary, n. 19.14. ad Art. 26.

the requested State were to claim reasons of public policy. In other words, information requests based on the purchase of stolen data could still be declined, according to Art. 26 par. 3 lit c OECD Model DTC, despite Art. 26 par. 5.[151] Indeed, in this case a fraudulent behaviour from the requested State, characterized as violation of public policy (ordre public), would not be protected by Art. 26 par. 5 simply by the fact that a bank holds the information.

### 3. Nominee, agent or fiduciary

In the same vein, a Contracting State cannot refuse information held by a person acting as a *fiduciary* or as an *agency* capacity, because it would be treated as a professional secret under domestic law.[152] A person

> is said to act in a fiduciary capacity when the business which the person transacts, or the money or property which the person handles, is not its own or for its own benefit, but for the benefit of another person as to whom the fiduciary stands in a relation implying and necessitating confidence and trust on the one part and good faith on the other part, such as a trustee.[153]

It follows that the concept of 'fiduciary' also includes persons acting as *nominee* or *trustee*. The word 'trustee', while not expressly mentioned in the OECD Model DTC, is however in the text of Art. 5 par. 4 lit. a of the TIEA Model.[154] The term *'agency'* is also broad and covers all forms of service providers (company formation agents, trust companies, etc.).[155]

By contrast, as mentioned above, lawyers, attorneys, solicitors or other admitted legal representatives may still be in a position to rely on *client-attorney privilege*, under domestic law, provided they act in such capacity.[156]

### 4. Ownership interest

Finally, Contracting States cannot decline to supply information because it relates to an *ownership interest* in a person, including companies and partnerships, foundations or similar organizational structures.[157] As a consequence, the requested State cannot refuse to supply information, on

---

[151] Steichen (2012), p. 25.
[152] OECD Commentary, n. 19.12 ad Art. 26.
[153] Ibid.
[154] Oberson, in: Danon/Gutman/Oberson/Pistone (2014), n. 140 ad Art. 26.
[155] OECD Commentary, n. 19.12 ad Art. 26.
[156] OECD Commentary, n. 19.3 ad Art. 26.
[157] OECD Commentary, n. 19.13 ad Art. 26.

the basis that such ownership information is characterized as a business secret according to domestic law.

As we will see later, the TIEA Model includes a more detailed corresponding provision. This Model confirms that the concept of ownership should not be interpreted restrictively. It can indeed happen that the legal and beneficial owner is not the same person. In such a case, a requested Contracting State should supply information on both.[158] In the case of a foundation or a trust, the Contracting State should be in a position to give information on the identity of the founder, the beneficiaries, and all persons who are in a position to control how the trust or the foundation assets should be managed.[159] In addition, the requested State should provide information about the persons in the ownership chain.[160]

Specific issues are however possible in case of requests pertaining to beneficiaries of a *trust*. For instance, in a case of 23 March 2011,[161] the Swiss Federal Administrative Court (FAC) had to consider whether beneficiaries of an irrevocable and discretionary trust should be regarded as beneficial owner, under the UBS settlement, whose name would then have to be disclosed to the IRS. Considering that in the present case, the beneficiaries only had expectations and no legal claims against the assets and income of the trust, the Court ruled that they could not be regarded as the beneficial owners of the assets. In the same line, the Commentary to the TIEA Model mentions that certain trusts or foundations may not have any identified group of persons as beneficiaries but support a general clause; in such a case, ownership information should be read to include only 'identifiable persons'.[162]

---

[158]    TIEA MC, n. 51.
[159]    TIEA MC, n. 52.
[160]    This rule, which is found in the TIEA Model Commentary, n. 51 ad Art. 5, can also be inferred from example a) in the Commentary ad Art. 26, n. 19.15.
[161]    FAC of 23 March 2011, A-6903/2010.
[162]    OECD Commentary, TIEA Model, n. 53 ad Art. 5.

# 4. A practical example: administrative assistance and exchange of information between the United States and Switzerland

## I. INTRODUCTION

The relationship between the United States and Swiss banks, as far as exchange of information in tax matters is concerned, has been tense for decades. Some Swiss banks, relying on bank secrecy rules, were suspected of helping US taxpayers to evade taxes. A series of scandals, notably the UBS case of 2008, led to various enforcement measures from the IRS and the United States Department of Justice (DoJ) in order to identify the US taxpayers who were hiding bank accounts in Switzerland in order to evade US taxes. Later on, the proceedings also targeted other Swiss banks and financial intermediaries, which had participated in tax evasion schemes.

In fact, the issue of exchange of information between the two countries may already be traced back to the 1950s, based on the existing double taxation convention of 1951 (DTC). But it really accelerated after the ratification of the new 1996 DTC. Finally, the UBS scandal of 2008 led to legal enforcement measures against the Swiss banks and US taxpayers involved, which are still going on today. In the meantime, the DTC was further revised in 2009, in accordance with the new OECD standard, but is still not ratified by the United States.

This legal saga will not only remain a delicate legal controversy, showing the limits of territorial secrecy rules, but has raised a number of delicate issues in the area of international exchange of information based on treaty provision. During the process, numerous court judgments were rendered, covering issues of international administrative assistance, such as the role of double taxation treaties, the scope of the exchange, its impact on human rights, or the rights of taxpayers involved, which were never analysed on such a scale before. In addition, in August 2013, the DoJ presented a programme, opening to the Swiss banks involved the possibility for a 'solution for the past', which could also serve as a model for future similar issues with other states.

We will therefore describe in more detail this legal adventure. Starting with the legal framework of exchange of information (hereafter II), namely the changing content of the applicable DTC, we will move on to analyse the UBS case and further investigations against other Swiss banks (hereafter III). Finally, we will briefly address the DoJ Program of 2013, still under way today, implemented with a view to settling the past (hereafter IV). The latter will however be developed further in Chapter 13 of the book.

## II. THE LEGAL FRAMEWORK

### A. The Switzerland-United States Income Tax Convention of 1951

There was already a specific rule regarding international assistance in article XVI (1) of the Switzerland-United States Income Tax Treaty of 1951, which was certainly not as wide as Art. 26 of the OECD Model DTC. However, it provided for an exchange of information that was necessary either for carrying out the provisions of the treaty or for the prevention of tax fraud and the like.

In two Supreme Court decisions, the scope of that particular clause was defined with more precision. First, the Supreme Court ruled that the term 'fraud' was to be interpreted according to Swiss law. It would cover tax evasion schemes, where false documents are used to deceive the tax authorities; in such a case, the Swiss bank secrecy is not an obstacle to the rendering of information under this provision.[163] Second, in a later case, the Supreme Court restricted the possibility to use the provision effectively, by considering that Art. XVI of the DTC did not compel the taxpayer to provide original documents to the IRS; the supply of a 'tax report' from the Swiss competent authority was regarded as sufficient.[164] This judgment put a (provisory) standstill on the administrative exchange of information for tax fraud cases under the treaty. But the situation would change with the new treaty of 1996.

---

163   Supreme Court (SC) of 23 December 1970, ATF 96 I 737.
164   SC of 16 May 1975, ATF 101 Ib 160.

## B. The Switzerland-United States Income Tax Convention (1996)

### 1. General principles

As in the past, the 1996 tax convention provides for an exchange of information necessary for carrying out the provisions of the convention or for the prevention of tax fraud and the like in relation to the taxes covered by the Convention (Art. 26 par. 1). However, the new tax treaty also provides some clarifications, especially (i) on the definition of the controversial notion of 'tax fraud and the like' and (ii) on the scope of information to be supplied.

Article 10 of the 1996 protocol to the treaty defines the concept of 'tax fraud and the like' in the following terms:

> The parties agree that the term 'tax fraud' means fraudulent conduct that causes or is intended to cause an illegal and substantial reduction in the amount of the tax paid to a Contracting State. Fraudulent conduct is assumed in situations where a taxpayer uses, or has the intention to use, a forged or falsified document such as a double set of books, a false invoice, an incorrect balance sheet or profit and loss statement, or a fictitious order or, in general, a false piece of documentary evidence, and in situations where the taxpayer uses, or has the intention to use a scheme of lies ('Lügengebäude') to deceive the tax authority. It is understood that the acts described in the preceding sentence are by way of illustration, not by way of limitation. The term 'tax fraud' may in addition include acts that, at the time of the request, constitute fraudulent conduct with respect to which the requested Contracting State may obtain information under its laws or practices.

It appears that the notion of 'tax fraud and the like' in Art. 26 of the 1996 DTC corresponds to the concept of 'tax fraud' ('escroquerie fiscale'; 'Abgabenbetrug'), which is used under the Swiss domestic law for international mutual assistance in criminal matters (IMAC).[165] In fact, the text of the Protocol to the 1996 DTC may be described as an English translation of the Swiss Supreme Court's case law analysis of the concept of tax fraud for IMAC matters. This opinion, first expressed in the Swiss Government's Message,[166] was later confirmed by the Swiss Supreme Court, as well as the Federal Administrative Court (FAC).[167] It can thus be concluded that the term 'tax fraud' implies the use of forged

---

[165] Oberson/Hull (2011), p. 282.

[166] Message of the Federal Council regarding the Switz.-U.S. Income Tax Treaty (1996), p. 992 (hereinafter Message).

[167] Supreme Court, 10 August 2006, 2A.608/2005, consid. 1; Federal Administrative Court, 5 Mar. 2009, A-7426/2008, consid. 5.3.

documents, as well as cunning behaviour (so-called 'scheme of lies').[168] Nevertheless, tax fraud requires specific manoeuvres from the taxpayer, stratagem or combination of lies, in order to deceive the tax administration;[169] the use of false documents is always regarded as a fraudulent behaviour for that purpose.

In order to make article 26 fully efficient, the authorities no longer exchange 'tax reports', as under the 1951 version of the convention, but 'authenticated copies of unedited original records or documents'.[170] In addition, the Contracting States reached a mutual agreement in 2003[171] with regard to the exchange of information based on article 26 of the Switzerland-United States Income Tax Treaty (1996). This text includes an explanatory memorandum and three examples, followed by a non-exhaustive list of 14 hypothetical cases of tax fraud. It is also interesting to note that as per paragraph 1 of this agreement, the parties agree that article 26 of the treaty will be interpreted 'to the greatest extent possible' in order to implement the exchange of information.

In a case of tax fraud, the exchange of information is not limited to the rules on the personal scope of application of the tax treaty (Art. 26 par. 1). In such a case, upon request of the competent authorities, the Swiss tax authorities are entitled to provide the US authorities with information on persons who are not covered by the Agreement, notably Swiss non-residents.[172]

If any difficulty or doubt arises as to the interpretation or application of the tax treaty, the case may, if both competent authorities and all affected taxpayers agree, be submitted for arbitration (Art. 25 par. 6).

The criminal procedure is also defined in detail under the Federal Ordinance of application.[173] Moreover, the procedure is regulated by

---

[168]    The Supreme Court has confirmed this opinion in various cases. See for instance, SC 27 January 2004, Revue de Droit Administratif et Fiscal (RDAF) 2004 II, p. 10; SC, 12 April 2002, RDAF 2002 II, p. 307.

[169]    SC, 12 April 2006, 2A.430/2005, consid. 4.4.; SC, 27 January 2004, RDAF 2004 II, p. 10.

[170]    See, Art. 8a of the Memorandum of Understanding (MOU) of the 1996 treaty.

[171]    Mutual Agreement of 23 January 2003, Regarding the Administration of Article 26 (Exchange of Information) of the Swiss-U.S. Income Tax Convention of 2 October 1996.

[172]    SC, 6 February 2002, 2A.250/2001, consid. 5a; SC, 12 April 2002, 2A.551/2001, consid. 3.

[173]    See Art. 20c to 20k of the Ordinance of the Federal Council regarding the application of the Switz.-U.S. Income Tax Treaty (1996).

article 184 of the Swiss Federal Direct Tax Law (DTL),[174] which is applied by analogy.[175]

## C. The Switzerland-United States Protocol of 2009

On 23 September 2009, a Protocol to the Switzerland-United States Income Tax Treaty of 1996 was signed and later approved by the Swiss Parliament, on 18 June 2010. This Protocol is however still not ratified by the United States. It adapts Art. 26 of the treaty to the OECD standard. The concept of tax fraud is no more relevant under this rule, since exchange of information will generally also be opened for information necessary for the carrying out of the domestic tax law of the Contracting States. Furthermore, group requests will also be possible under this new Protocol, following the approval of this new practice by the Swiss Federal Parliament on 6 March 2012.[176] To prevent fishing expeditions, in cases of group requests, the competent requesting authority has to: (1) establish the reasons why the information is needed; (2) provide a detailed description of the pattern of behaviour; (3) explain why it can be presumed that the persons concerned displaying that type of behaviour did not meet their legal obligations; and (4) make it plausible that the *information holder* or one of its collaborators engaged in behaviour that was both active and guilty.[177]

Once ratified by both Contracting States, the new Protocol should apply to exchange of information as of the date of signature, i.e. as of 23 September 2009. In the meantime, the old DTC of 1996, with the 'tax fraud and the like' requirement remains applicable.

## III. THE DEVELOPMENTS

### A. The UBS Saga

#### 1. The decision of the Federal Administrative Court (FAC) of 5 March 2009

The UBS affair will remain an emblematic example of issues that can arise within the framework of international administrative assistance in

---

[174] Swiss Federal Direct Tax Law, 'Loi fédérale sur l'impôt fédéral direct' (RS 642.11).
[175] SC, 27 Jan. 2004, RDAF 2004 II, 20.
[176] See Swiss Federal Gazette 2012, p. 3273.
[177] Swiss Federal Gazette 2011, p. 6144.

tax matters. The case unfolded in several stages, combined with several landmark Court decisions.

The first stage focused on the request made by the US Internal Revenue Service (IRS) to the Swiss federal tax authorities on 16 July 2008 to obtain approximately 300 names of taxpayers suspected of tax fraud, as defined under Art. 26 of the Swiss/US tax treaty of 1996. In a landmark case of 5 March 2009,[178] the FAC ruled on two controversial issues.

First, the request did not mention the names of the taxpayers but precisely described the 'pattern of facts' corresponding to the tax scheme used by them. In general, the US taxpayers concerned had tried to circumvent the US QI regime, by interposing offshore companies, which appeared as the holders of the unreported bank accounts. The FAC admitted that the request did not constitute a 'fishing expedition'. In fact, the 1996 treaty does not include any specific requirements that should be met for a request for information. However, according to the principle of proportionality, the related facts in the request should contain enough elements to allow for a presumption that a 'tax fraud' could have been committed.

Second, the FAC examined the material conditions of mutual assistance, the description of sufficient elements of a 'tax fraud or the like'. It confirmed that the notion of tax fraud requires either the use of false documents or the presence of a 'scheme of lies', within the meaning of the IMAC rules and jurisprudence. Thus, while a simple lie does not as such represent an astute behaviour, it might constitute a tax fraud and the like, should the taxpayer prevent the misled party from verifying certain information or assume that they will not verify such information based on a special *relationship of trust* between the two parties. In conclusion, the FAC conceded here the existence of a tax fraud, notably through an abusive use of *offshore* structures in violation of the special confidence relationship created through the legal relationship of QI. In particular, the Court saw fraudulent behaviour in using offshore companies, in the framework of this trust relationship, while interposing the legal independence of these structures in an abusive way, that is without the beneficial owner 'playing the rules of the company', and, in fact, not respecting its

---

[178]  FAC, 5 March 2009, A-7342/2008; see on this subject, among others, Behnisch (2008/2009); Waldburger (2009).

legal personality by acting directly with the bank as if the structure did not exist.[179]

However, the outcome of the case is rather surprising and paradoxical: the FAC nevertheless considered that the appeal was not founded, because the names of the taxpayers concerned had already been communicated to the United States, in the meantime, by the Swiss Financial Market Supervisory Authority (FINMA), based on the banking legislation rules.[180]

## 2. The UBS agreement

The communication of the 300 names requested by the United States did not suffice to put an end to this affair. The IRS then requested around 52,000 names of US taxpayers alleged to hold undeclared assets. On 19 August 2009, the Swiss Confederation and the United States came to an agreement targeting, specifically, exchange requests from the IRS concerning UBS.[181] The agreement, in particular, provides for a specific and detailed definition of the notion of 'tax fraud and the like', based on a range of various criteria, such as the use of forged or falsified documents, schemes of lies, and even unreported bank accounts of significant amounts.

At first, this agreement was challenged by the FAC, in a decision rendered on 21 January 2010. The Court ruled – rightly in the author's opinion – that the UBS agreement, as a mutual agreement, could not infringe the Switzerland-United States Income Tax Treaty of 1996.[182] The treaty terms of 'tax fraud or the like' require a fraudulent behaviour ('scheme of lies') and as such repeated failures to report significant

---

[179] For more details about this characterization, see Oberson (2012/13), p. 101.

[180] See in this respect, the first instance decision, FAC, 5 January 2010 (B-1092/2005) (considering the FINMA decision to forward name of tax evaders) and the second instance highly controversial judgment of the Supreme Court (SC) of 15 July 2011, ATF 137 II 431 (reversing the FAC decision and admitting the validity of supply of names under a so-called 'emergency and exceptional policy clause').

[181] Agreement between the Swiss Confederation and the United States of America regarding information requests from the Internal Revenue Services of the United States of America relating to the UBS, 19 August 2009, published (French translation) in: Archives de droit fiscal suisse 78 (2009/10), p. 413; see on this subject, Cottier, (2011), p. 97; Cottier/Matteotti, (2009/10).

[182] FAC, 21 January 2010, A-7789/2009; see on this subject, notably, Reich, (2010), p. 111.

amounts, as defined in the UBS Agreement's appendix, are not sufficient to be characterized as a tax fraud or the like, absent the subjective component of the behaviour.

To find a solution to this legal imbroglio, the Swiss Federal Council renegotiated a new Protocol with the United States of 31 March 2010 (Protocol 10), reflecting fundamentally the criteria agreed upon in the 2009 UBS Agreement, but raising up this Protocol to the level of a special international treaty, instead of a competent authority agreement. The Federal Parliament then ratified the 2010 Protocol on 17 June 2010. This time, in a case rendered on 15 July 2010,[183] the FAC upheld the validity of the Protocol, on the grounds that, as an international treaty, it is then able to derogate to the 1996 DTC by virtue of the *lex posterior* and *lex specialis* principles. In effect, the 2010 Protocol modifies retroactively the DTC of 1996 by opening exchange of information in the UBS case to procedures, opened between 2001 and 2008, of tax evasion with significant amounts. This Protocol covers periods that occurred before the signing of the new DTC of September 2009, which reflects the OECD standard and does not require any more a condition of 'tax fraud and the like'.

The UBS agreement, in its 2010 version, was then implemented. Switzerland turned over to the IRS the names of 4250 US taxpayers and had to pay a fine of 780 million dollars. There were still ongoing procedures and litigation, covering issues such as rights of the taxpayers involved, conditions for the exchange of information,[184] or the scope of information exchange in the case of a beneficial owner of a discretionary and irrevocable trust.[185] The basic elements of the UBS agreement were

---

[183]    FAC, 15 July 2010, A-4013/2010.

[184]    See for instance, FAC, 12 December 2011, A-2866/2011, concerning a US taxpayer, a shareholder in the BVI, with an undeclared account. In this case, not governed by the 2010 UBS Protocol, the FAC reiterated that 'tax fraud or the like' requires either a use of falsified documents or a 'scheme of lies' by the taxpayer such as cunning acts or special engineering in order to reduce his/her tax burden. In this particular case, however, the assistance request was rejected based on the fact that it did not contain enough elements showing fraudulent behaviour.

[185]    In this interesting case of 23 March 2011, (A-6903/2010) the FAC rejected a request for exchange of information, based on Art. 26 of the 1996 DTC, concerning beneficiaries of a discretionary and irrevocable trust, who did not have any firm right to claim the trust income or capital payment from the trust; beneficiaries of such a trust cannot be regarded as beneficial owners of a bank account.

however settled after the judgment of the FAC of 15 July 2010. On 15 November 2010, the IRS withdrew the John Doe Summons against UBS.

## B. Other On-going Procedures against Swiss Banks

Other procedures are still engaged against several Swiss banks or financial institutions in order to obtain the names of the US taxpayers involved.[186] In this context, two proceedings are of particular interest: the Credit Suisse and the Julius Baer cases.

First, the FAC rendered a decision, on 5 April 2012, related to a request addressed to the *Credit Suisse*.[187] Based on Art. 26 of the DTC of 1996, the IRS had requested information about US taxpayers, without mentioning their names, and offshore companies linked with them, that had decision-making authority over Credit Suisse accounts from 2002 to 2010. Those offshore companies, controlled by US beneficial owners, had owned assets in the form of US securities for which no 'W-9' form had been filed. In this decision, the FAC confirmed its 5 March 2009 judgment in the UBS case. In particular, the admissibility of 'group requests' was endorsed, provided that the 'pattern of facts' described in the request met the contours of a 'tax fraud or the like'. At this stage, the facts submitted were however not clear enough to support this demonstration, so that the request was rejected. In a second decision, however, based on a more precise request from the IRS, the exchange of information was accepted on the same case, both by the FAC[188] and the Supreme Court.[189] Later on, Credit Suisse accepted a settlement with the United States Department of Justice, under the DoJ Programme.[190]

Second, on 6 January 2014, the FAC also had to examine the validity of a request towards *Julius Baer* Group.[191] In this case, the request targeted US taxpayers (including related offshore companies) who were holding banks accounts in the bank, and in particular who, between 2002 and 2012, maintained a power of signature or other rights of disposal over those accounts. The 'group request' from the IRS, according to the Court, did not however meet the tests described in the UBS case. The

---

[186] It is important to note that, in January 2013, Wegelin bank reached an agreement with the Department of Justice of the United States in relation to approx. USD 75 million.

[187] FAC, 5 April 2012, A-737/2012.

[188] FAC, 13 March 2013, A-6011/2012.

[189] SC, 5 July 2013, 2C-269/2013.

[190] See infra p. 206.

[191] FAC 6 January 2014, A-5390/2013.

request appeared to be more of a 'fishing expedition' and serious grounds demonstrating tax fraud and the like were not sufficiently presented. The request was therefore dismissed. Discussions are however still under way between the DoJ and Julius Baer to find a solution for this issue.[192]

## C.   The DoJ Programme of 2013

In August 2013, the DoJ announced a programme, which offered to Swiss banks, suspecting of having participated in some tax fraud schemes of US taxpayers, to collaborate with the DoJ and implement a settlement on the issue.[193] The programme is described in more details further, in the chapter covering the 'solution for the past'.[194]

## D.   Conclusions

The Switzerland-United States Income Tax Treaty of 1996 led to a series of cases that attempted to provide a practical definition of the notion of 'tax fraud or the like'. This case law is now well settled. In a nutshell, group requests are allowed but the request must demonstrate, following the UBS case test, that sufficient elements of a tax fraud are present, i.e. a tax evasion scheme accompanied by false documents or an astute behaviour from the taxpayer, typically in the form of a 'scheme of lies'. In this context, the UBS settlement of 2010 is an exceptional regime, which also opens exchange of information provided systematic tax evasion of significant amounts is present. This exception is based on a *lex specialis* regime of a specific international Protocol 10, derogating to the 1996 DTC, covering the UBS situation.

As of 23 September 2009, once ratified by the United States, the new Protocol to the Switzerland-United States Income Tax Treaty should make information exchange much easier, in accordance with the OECD standard.

In the meantime, proceedings are still going on with various Swiss banks in order to settle the past, under the DoJ programme. For the future, it seems that the situation should definitely improve under the FATCA IGA, Model 2 agreement, which entered into force on 1 August 2014.[195]

---

[192]   See infra p. 206.

[193]   Joint Statement between the U.S. Department of Justice and the Swiss Federal Department of Finance, 29 August 2013.

[194]   See infra p. 206 ff.

[195]   See infra p. 159.

# 5. Assistance in the collection of taxes under DTC

## I. INTRODUCTION

The need to fight international tax avoidance also calls for an efficient system of collection of taxes. The increased mobility of taxpayers makes it indeed difficult for States to recover their taxes from persons who are constantly moving. Even if the focus of this book is more directed towards the development of transparency and exchange of information, we will also address the issue of collection and recovery of taxes because it is closely linked with the problem of international assistance and, at the same time, also requires exchange of information.

According to the OECD Manual on Assistance in the Collection of Taxes,

> Globalization not only makes it harder for tax authorities to accurately determine the correct tax liabilities of their taxpayers: it also makes the collection of tax more difficult. Taxpayers may have assets throughout the world but tax authorities generally cannot go beyond their borders to take action to collect taxes.[196]

According to the so-called '*Revenue rule*', it is generally admitted that the courts of one country will not enforce criminal and revenue laws of another country.[197] Indeed, enforcement or collection of tax claims is an attribute of sovereignty. It follows that international treaties are necessary in order to foster international assistance in this field.

International instruments in the area of collection of taxes were already drafted back in 1927 at the League of Nations, in a separate Draft Convention.[198] This draft was never implemented in this form. Later on, as of 1977, the OECD started to develop a model convention for the

---

[196] See the OECD Manual on Assistance in the Collection of Taxes.
[197] Schwarz (2013), p. 493.
[198] Carra Richter (2013), p. 136.

assistance in the recovery of taxes, which was published in 1981.[199] This Model was not successful among states. Assistance in the recovery of taxes is however provided for in the CoE/OECD Multilateral Convention on Mutual Assistance of 1988 (CMAAT), amended in 2011. Finally, such type of assistance was only introduced in the OECD Model DTC as of 2003, under a new Art. 27. This provision is largely inspired by the CMAAT. Assistance for the recovery of tax claims is also provided for in the US Model DTC, but integrated in the provision on exchange of information.[200] Finally tax recovery assistance is governed by a EU Directive, which was adopted on 16 March 2010.[201]

Despite this development, mutual assistance for the recovery of claims still remains difficult to implement in practice because of major differences at the international level.[202] The growing success of the CMAAT and the implementation of rules at the EU level should contribute to a larger use of provisions on collection of tax claims.

Article 27 OECD Model DTC still gives a lot of discretion to the Contracting States to limit the scope or, by mutual agreement, settle the mode of application of this provision (Art. 27 par. 1, *in fine*, OECD Model DTC). In fact, each State will need to decide whether and to what extent assistance should be given to the other State.[203]

## II.  SCOPE

Article 27 OECD Model is closely linked to Art. 26; the scope of application of these two provisions is in fact identical.[204] In a similar fashion, Art. 27 defines the scope in a broad way. Contracting States must provide assistance to each other in the *collection* of *revenue claims*, concerning *persons* who do not have to be residents of one or both of the contracting states. The provision only covers assistance in collection of taxes and not other types of assistance, such as tax examination abroad or

---

[199]  Tüchler (2011), p. 120.
[200]  See Art. 26 par. 7 US Model.
[201]  Directive 2010/24/EC concerning mutual assistance for the recovery of claims relating to taxes, duties and other measures, OJ L 84/1 of 31 March 2010; see infra p. 118 ff.
[202]  Pistone, in: Danon/Gutman/Oberson/Pistone (2014), n. 1 ad Art. 27.
[203]  OECD Commentary, n. 1 ad Art. 27.
[204]  Pistone, in: Danon/Gutman/Oberson/Pistone (2014), n. 5 ad Art. 27.

simultaneous examination.[205] A *revenue claim*, necessary for the assistance in the collection of taxes, means an amount owed in respect of taxes of every kind and description imposed on behalf of the contracting state, or of their political subdivisions or local authorities, insofar as the taxation thereunder is not contrary to this convention or any other instrument to which the Contracting States are parties, as well as interest, administrative penalties and costs of collection or conservancy related to such amount (Art. 27 par. 2 OECD Model DTC).

A request for assistance is not only possible against persons subject to tax, but may also target other persons, who are liable to tax jointly or for other legal reasons.[206] Such a request may also be directed towards each Contracting State, with assets that could be used for the collection of taxes; there is no priority in favour of the state of residence of the taxpayer.[207]

A request for assistance in a *triangular situation* raises an additional issue. Such a situation would occur where state A wishes to request collection of a claim in state C, with which it has no double taxation treaty with a clause similar to Art. 27 OECD Model, but such a treaty would exist between states A and B, and B and C.[208] According to the text of Art. 27 par. 2, state B, following the request by state A, cannot ask for collection from state C, of A's tax claims, because this provision does not allow for a state to ask for collection for taxes of another state.[209]

The exchange of information for the purposes of assistance in the collection of taxes is governed by Art. 26 OECD Model DTC. The confidentiality of information exchanged is therefore ensured.[210]

## III.  ASSISTANCE PROCESS

Art. 27 provides for two forms of assistance: assistance in collection (par. 3) and measures of conservancy (par. 4).

---

[205]  Engelschalk, in: Vogel/Lehner (2008), n. 15 ad Art. 27.

[206]  Engelschalk, in: Vogel/Lehner (2008), n. 21b ad Art. 27.

[207]  Ibid.

[208]  Tüchler (2011), p. 123.

[209]  Tüchler (2011), p. 124; Engelschalk, in: Vogel/Lehner (2008), n. 21 ad Art. 27.

[210]  OECD Commentary, n. 5 ad Art. 27.

## A.  Collection of Taxes

In order to start the assistance process, two conditions must be fulfilled in the requesting State.

First, in order to request assistance in the collection of a tax claim, the Contracting State should present a revenue claim. As described under Art. 27 par. 3 OECD Model DTC, that revenue claim, in order to be accepted, should meet the three following requirements:[211] (i) it is an amount in respect of a tax of any kind due to the government; (ii) the tax is not contrary to the tax treaty or any other agreement concluded between both states; and (iii) interest, penalties and cost of collection or conservancy can be included.

Second, the revenue claim of the requesting Contracting State has to be enforceable, under the law of that state and is owed by a person who, at that time, cannot under the law of the requesting State, prevent the collection (Art. 27 par. 2 OECD Model DTC). This means in principle that no appeal procedure (administrative or judicial) in the requesting State could prevent the collection.[212] It should be mentioned that the requested State may still be obliged to grant assistance, even if an appeal is pending in the requesting State, but subject to the condition that this enforcement is allowed by the domestic law of the requesting State and not contrary to the law of the requested State.[213]

Following these two conditions, that revenue claim shall, at the request of the Contracting State, be accepted for the purposes of collection by the competent authority of the requested State (Art. 27 par. 3 OECD DTC). The revenue claim will then be collected in accordance with the laws applicable to the enforcement and collection of its own tax, as if the revenue claim were its own (Art. 27 par. 3, *in fine*, OECD DTC; national treatment). This rule could sometimes restrict the assistance process if the domestic provisions of the requested State are stricter than the requesting State. For instance, in many state, a revenue claim can already be collected even though there is still a right to appeal; if the internal law of the requested State does not allow collection when an appeal is still pending, the collection, in that state is therefore not possible, and this is in accordance with the national treatment rule in the requested State.[214]

---

[211]  Carra Richter (2013), p. 140.
[212]  OECD Commentary, n. 15 ad Art. 27.
[213]  Pistone, in: Danon/Gutman/Oberson/Pistone (2014), n. 12 ad Art. 27; OECD Commentary n. 16 ad Art. 27.
[214]  OECD Commentary, n. 16 ad Art. 27.

## B. Measures of Conservancy

When a revenue claim may, under the law of the requesting State, be subject to measures of conservancy, that claim should also be accepted by the requested State, for the purposes of taking measures of conservancy (Art. 27 par. 4 OECD DTC). The requested State will implement such measures in accordance with its domestic law, as if the revenue claim were a claim of its own, even if, at the time when such measures are applied, the revenue claim is not enforceable in the requested State or is owed by a person who has a right to prevent its collection (Art. 27 par. 4, *in fine*, OECD DTC).

The measures of conservancy are here to guarantee the future collection of the taxes due. In other words, they are here to ensure that the process of collection of taxes, which has started or will follow, will be successful.[215] Their specific form will vary among states but will typically correspond to a seizure or freezing of assets, before final judgment.[216] The conditions required for taking conservancy measures will vary from one state to another, but in 'all cases the amount of the revenue claim should be determined beforehand, if only provisionally or partially'.[217]

## C. Disputes and Procedural Rules (Time Limits, Priority)

A request accepted by a Contracting State for collection of tax or for conservancy cannot be subject to *time limits* applicable to the revenue claim applicable under the law of the requested State by reason of its nature as such (Art. 27 par. 5 OECD Model DTC). It follows that the time limits rules of the requesting State only are applicable.[218] Contrary to the EU Directive on assistance in collection of claims, and to the CoE/OECD Mutual Administrative Assistance convention, Art. 27 of the OECD Model DTC includes no specific rule about interruption or suspension of time limits. It follows that the rule of the requesting State is applicable to that issue.[219]

Many states grant special *priority* position for tax claims in the collection process. These rules, which in fact serve the interest of

---

[215]  Carra Richter (2013), p. 150.
[216]  OECD Commentary, n. 20 ad Art. 27.
[217]  Engelschalk, in: Vogel/Lehner (2008), n. 70 ad Art. 27; OECD Commentary, n. 20 ad Art. 27.
[218]  OECD Commentary, n. 22 ad Art. 27.
[219]  Engelschalk, in: Vogel/Lehner (2008), n. 71b ad Art. 27.

domestic enforcement, are not applicable in the context of the collection of foreign tax claims.[220] According to Art. 27 par. 5 OECD Model DTC, the potential rules of priority of revenue claims of 'both the requested (first sentence) and requesting (second sentence) States giving their own revenue claims priority over the claims of other creditors shall not apply to a revenue claim in respect of which a request has been made'.[221]

Proceedings with respect to the existence, validity or the amount of a revenue claim of a Contracting State cannot be brought before the court of the other Contracting State (Art. 27 par. 7 OECD DTC). The purpose of this rule is to prevent administrative or judicial bodies of the requested State from having to judge whether an amount is owed under the internal law of the other Contracting State.[222]

If, after the request for assistance in the collection or for conservancy purposes has been made, the revenue claim loses its enforcement character or conservancy measures cease to be possible, the requesting State will promptly notify the requested State (Art. 27 par. 7b OECD DTC). As a consequence, the latter will have the option to ask the requesting State to either suspend or withdraw its request (Art. 27 par. 7 *in fine* OECD DTC).

## IV. LIMITS

According to Art. 27 par. 8, the requested State is not obliged to provide assistance in the following situations:

a)   The request is at variance with the laws and administrative practices of the requesting and requested States. This rule has the effect that a state cannot try to take advantage of the tax collection mechanism of the other Contracting State if it is wider that its own.[223]

b)   The requested State cannot carry out measures which would be contrary to public policy (ordre public). This rule corresponds to Art. 26 par. 3 OECD Model DTC.

c)   The requesting State has not pursued all reasonable measures of collection or conservancy, as the case may be, available under its law or administrative practices (principle of subsidiarity).

---

[220]   Engelschalk, in: Vogel/Lehner (2008), n. 72 ad Art. 27.

[221]   OECD Commentary, n. 25 ad Art. 27.

[222]   OECD Commentary, n. 28 ad Art. 27; Engelschalk, in: Vogel/Lehner (2008), n. 79 ad Art. 27.

[223]   Bal (2011), p. 600.

d)     The administrative burden for that state is clearly disproportionate to the benefit to be derived by the other Contracting State. In other terms, the requested State may refuse assistance 'if the cost that it would incur in the collection of a revenue claim of the requesting State would exceed the amount of the revenue claim'.[224]

---

[224]   OECD Commentary, n. 36 ad Art. 27.

# 6. Tax Information Exchange Agreements (TIEAs)

## I. INTRODUCTION

The development of Tax Information Exchange Agreements (TIEAs) started in the 1990s. The basic idea was to develop a tool for requesting information from countries that did not usually cooperate on tax matters, typically a tax haven. The main purpose of TIEAs was in fact to enable countries, mostly OECD members but not exclusively, to access information about their residents' offshore activities in tax havens.[225] The result was a model treaty focusing exclusively on exchange information for tax purposes (including criminal taxation).

Indeed, in the 1990s, international exchange of information in direct tax matters was essentially done within the framework of double taxation treaties. This system, however, started to show some *limits*. First, it only included countries with a treaty network. It could not encompass countries, notably tax havens, which had not ratified any DTC, in particular because they do not levy any significant tax. For these countries the issue of international double taxation does not occur. Second, even in the presence of a DTC, the requested Contracting State was in general not obliged to carry out administrative measures at variance with its laws and administrative practice or to supply information which is not obtainable under its laws or in the normal course of the administration of that state.[226] The requested state was therefore not bound to go beyond its own domestic law and administrative practice in putting information at the disposal of the other contracting state. Countries, such as Austria, Belgium, Luxembourg or Switzerland could thus refuse to supply information based on domestic secrecy legislation. Third, some countries only included minor exchange of information clauses and therefore made a reservation to Art. 26 of the OECD Model DTC and considered that this provision only obliged them to grant

---

[225] Stewart (2012), p. 161; Kofler/Tumpel (2011), p. 189.
[226] See Art. 26 par. 2 lit. a and b of the OECD Model Tax Convention.

information necessary for the correct application of the treaty, but not for the carrying out of domestic law.[227]

In 1998, in particular, the OECD launched its work to address harmful tax competition. The 1998 Report on Harmful Tax Competition clearly describes the lack of effective exchange of information as one important criterion in determining harmful tax practices. It should be noted that both Switzerland and Luxembourg abstained to approve the 1998 OECD report.[228] In 2000, the Global Forum on Transparency and Exchange of Information for Tax Purposes was established. The Forum included both OECD and non-OECD countries and seeks to promote the OECD standard for transparency and exchange of information, at meetings with tax officials and experts all over the world. In 2002, the OECD, as a result of the work of the Global Forum, published the Model Agreement on Exchange of Information on Tax Matters (TIEA Model). This Model represents the new standard for effective exchange of information for the harmful tax competition initiative.[229]

In this respect, the TIEA is a major development and even a *turning point* in the policy of exchange of information of tax matters. As a whole, it represents a shift of responsibility in favour of the requesting (applicant) State.[230] The TIEA opened the door to an exchange of information, upon request, which is foreseeably relevant for carrying out the taxation in the requesting State. The requested State, under the TIEA Model, is in particular no longer in a position to refuse to supply information held by banks or financial institutions or information about ownership.

This shift would later trigger some corresponding developments in other international instruments providing for exchange of information. Indeed, in 2005 Art. 26 of the OECD Model DTC was also modified to take into account the new rules developed under the TIEA Model. In 2006, the OECD went on to publish a Manual on the Implementation of Exchange of Information Provisions for Tax Purposes. The UN Model also followed in 2008. And, last but not least, the CoE/OECD CMAAT was further adapted in 2011.

At the beginning, only a few TIEAs were signed. After the publication of the Model TIEA, only a few countries entered into these types of agreements (six in 2002 and 44 between 2002 and 2008).[231] The situation

---

[227]  See OECD Model Tax Convention Commentary, n. 24 ad Art. 26 (2000).
[228]  Compare, however, OECD, Improving Access to Bank Information for Tax Purposes, Paris 2000, which Switzerland and Luxembourg approved.
[229]  Barnard (2003), p. 9.
[230]  Oberson (2003), p. 14.
[231]  Pankiv (2013), p. 158, Seer/Gabert (2001), p. 88.

changed drastically after the 'big bang' of March 2009. The main reason for this evolution can be seen in the increasing global world pressure against tax fraud and evasion, following the financial crisis in 2008.[232] On 2 April 2009, the G20 notably made a strong statement against tax fraud and agreed to take coercive action against 'non-cooperative' jurisdictions in tax matters.[233] In order to be placed in the 'white-list' of countries having endorsed the OECD standard (cooperative jurisdiction), the targeted jurisdictions had to sign a minimum of 12 agreements for exchange of information purposes, either in the form of a DTC, in accordance with Art. 26 OECD Model DTC, or of a TIEA.[234] As a result, between the G20 summit on 15 November 2008 and the G20 summit on 4 November 2011, 700 TIEAs have been signed.[235]

Since the TIEA Model aims at promoting exchange of information with countries with no double taxation agreements, it mainly focuses on *tax havens*, as defined under the 1998 initiative against harmful tax competition.[236] According to the OECD report on harmful tax competition of 1998, a tax haven is defined under a number of criteria: (i) no or insufficient nominal taxation; (ii) lack of effective exchange of information; (iii) lack of transparency and (iv) no requirement to carry on substantial activities. The first criterion is the necessary starting point, which should then be confirmed, in combination with the three other criteria, in order to characterize a country as a tax haven.[237] A list of so-called cooperative and non-cooperative tax havens was published and then constantly adapted.

At the Pittsburgh G20 Meeting of September 2009, a deadline of two years for major improvements towards global transparency was decided. As a consequence, the Global Forum started to implement a *peer-review* process with an action plan.[238] During its meeting in Mexico on 1 and 2 September 2009, the Global Forum initiated the peer review process, which ensures that member states of the Forum implement an effective exchange of information in tax matters in accordance with the OECD standard. The peer review process comprises two phases: (i) an examination of each jurisdiction's legal and regulatory framework (phase 1),

---

[232]   See also Kofler/Tumpel (2011), p. 184 ff, 187.
[233]   See G20, Global Plan for Recovery and Reform: the Communiqué from the London Summit, London 2 April 2009; Steward (2012) p. 161.
[234]   See OECD, Tax Co-operation 2009: Towards a Level Playing Field.
[235]   See Stewart (2012), p. 161.
[236]   Pankiv (2013), p. 156.
[237]   Malherbe/Beynsberger (2012), p. 123.
[238]   Kofler/Trumpel (2011), p. 187.

followed by (ii) an analysis of the effectiveness of the practical implementation of the standards (phase 2).[239] On 10 November 2010, the OECD stated that all countries in the Global Forum had committed to and 'substantially implemented' the internationally agreed tax standard for TIEAs.[240]

In the meantime, the number of TIEAs continues to grow. There are currently more than 1000 TIEAs around the world.[241] It is interesting to see that even countries like Austria or Switzerland, which had made a reservation to Art. 26 of the OECD Model DTC before 2009, are now signing TIEAs with tax havens or countries outside the OECD network.[242]

## II. THE OECD MODEL TIEA

### A. Introduction

In a nutshell, the TIEA Model provides for an exchange of information in tax matters upon request based on the conditions applicable under the law of the applicant (requesting) State. The Model includes both a bilateral and a multilateral version. The multilateral model, so far, has not been used in practice. We will therefore concentrate on the bilateral instrument.

In some aspects, the Model introduces major changes in the current system of exchange of information:

- The shift of the primary responsibility *to the applicant State* (and not the requested State) for determining whether the reasons to decline a request are applicable or not.
- The *abolition of the dual criminality principle*. The concept of criminal tax depends on the definition of the law of the applicant State (Art. 4 par. 1 lit. o).
- The *lifting of bank secrecy* (Art. 5 par. 4. lit. a), first for criminal tax matters and then, as of 1 January 2006, also for ordinary tax investigations.

---

[239] Malherbe/Beynsberger (2011), p. 126.
[240] Stewart (2012) p. 162; OECD Progress Report on The Jurisdiction Surveyed by the OECD Global Forum In Implementing The Internationally Agreed Tax Standard, 10 November 2010 (available at www.oecd.org/tax/transparency).
[241] See www.oecd.org/tax/transparency.
[242] For an analysis of Austrian TIEAs, see Kofler/Trumpel (2011), p. 193 ff.

- The introduction of *limited procedural rules* (client-attorney privilege, Art. 7 par. 3).

In some other respects, however, the Model TIEA remains within the limits of other international legal instuments.[243] First, the agreement only applies to taxes covered in the agreement (including estate, inheritance and gift taxes) and not necessarily to indirect taxes. Second, the agreement provides only for exchange of information upon request and not for automatic exchange of information. Fishing expeditions are not allowed.[244]

The Model TIEA entered into force as of 2004 for criminal tax matters, and as of 2006 for all other matters.

## B. Scope of Application

Under the general rule, the agreement provides for an exchange of information that is foreseeably relevant to the administration and enforcement of the domestic laws of the Contracting States. Such information includes information foreseeably relevant to the determination, assessment and collection of the taxes covered by the agreement, the recovery and enforcement of tax claims, or the investigation or prosecution of tax matters (Art. 1 TIEA Model).

Under Art. 3 TIEA Model, only information about *taxes* covered by this agreement can be exchanged. It includes, at minimum, income, profit, wealth, and estate and gift taxes, unless both parties agree to waive one of these taxes.[245]

The requested State is not obligated to provide information which is neither held by its authorities nor in the possession or control of persons who are within its territorial *jurisdiction* (Art. 2 TIEA Model). However, the scope of the agreement is not restricted by the residence or the nationality of the person to whom the information relates or the nationality or residence of the person in possession of the information.[246]

---

[243] See, for instance, the CoE/OECD Convention on Mutual Assistance in Tax Matters, 25 February 1998 (modified in 2011), and Art. 26 of the OECD Model DTC.

[244] See OECD Commentary to the TIEA, n. 57.

[245] OECD Commentary to the TIEA, n. 9.

[246] OECD Commentary TIEA, n. 7.

## C.  Forms of Assistance

### 1.  Exchange of information upon request

Under the general rule, the requested State must provide information upon request, for the purposes of Art. 1 (Art. 5 par. 1 TIEA). This information will be exchanged without regard to whether the conduct being investigated would constitute a crime under the laws of the requested State if such conduct occurred in that state (Art. 5 par. 1, *in fine*, TIEA). While the TIEA makes it clear that it covers only exchange of information *upon request*, contracting parties are free to consider expanding their cooperation by covering also *automatic* or *spontaneous exchange of information* or *simultaneous tax examinations*.[247]

If the information in the possession of the requested State is not sufficient to enable IT to comply with the request, the requested State will have to use 'all relevant information gathering measures' to provide the information, even if that state does not need such information for its own tax purposes (Art. 5 par. 2 TIEA). This rule clarifies two important points. First, it confirms that the requested State cannot rely solely on information 'in the possession of its competent authority' but may have to implement locally specific gathering measures in order to obtain the information from information holders.[248] Second, the requested State should act even if it does need the information for its own tax purposes. This rule makes sense because otherwise, absent a proper system of taxation in the requested State (tax haven), most if not all requests could be defeated on that ground.[249]

Each contracting party shall ensure that its competent authority has the authority to obtain and provide upon request:

a)  information held by banks, other financial institutions, and any person acting in an agency or fiduciary capacity including nominees and trustees;

b)  information regarding the owner of companies, partnership, trusts, foundations, and other persons (Art. 5 par. 4 TIEA).

It appears that any domestic bank secrecy rules in the requested State will therefore not be an obstacle for the exchange of information. However, the issue of bank secrecy provisions is also closely linked with so-called 'know your customer' provisions that do exist in various States. Such

---

[247]  OECD Commentary TIEA, n. 39.
[248]  In this sense, OECD Commentary TIEA, nn. 41, 42.
[249]  OECD Commentary TIEA, n. 43.

rules are essential for the efficient functioning of the system of exchange of information of the TIEA. Article 5 par. 4 lit. b of the Model seeks to promote such rules in the requested State by imposing that 'its competent authority has the authority to *obtain* and *provide* upon request' information on banks or about ownership. This implies the setting up of sophisticated 'know your customer rules', which all countries may not have yet introduced or enforced. As a consequence, a country with no bank secrecy rules but inefficient 'know your customer' provisions would not in the author's view offer an effective exchange of information, within the standard of the OECD TIEA.[250]

The applicant State will provide specific information to the requested State, in order to demonstrate the foreseeable relevance of the information request, namely:

a)  the identity of the person under investigation;
b)  a statement of the information sought, including its nature and form;
c)  the tax purpose for which the information is sought;
d)  grounds for believing that the information requested is held in the requested State or in possession or control of a person within the jurisdiction of the requested State;
e)  to the extent known, the name and address of any person believed to be in possession of the requested information (Art. 5 par. 5 TIEA).

Contrary to the OECD Model, the responsibility to ascertain the validity of the request is in the hands of the *requesting* (applicant) State. Indeed, the request for information will be admitted on the basis of a statement from the applicant State that the request is in conformity with its law and administrative practice and that, if the requested information were within the jurisdiction of the applicant State, then the competent authority of that State would be able to obtain the information (Art. 5. par. 5 lit. f TIEA). It implies that the requested State will thus be obliged to supply the requested information to an applicant State, even if it could not obtain such information under its applicable law. This is a real change and it could imply that a requested State would thus treat differently the taxpayers of a foreign applicant State than its own resident taxpayers.

This rule overrides the *principle of reciprocity*, which is explicitly granted for instance, under Art. 26 par. 2 lit. a and b of the OECD Model

---

[250]  Oberson (2003), p. 13.

DTC. Under this principle 'a requested State is under no obligation to carry out measures that are not permitted under its own laws and practice or to supply items of information that are not obtainable in the normal course of its own administration'.[251] In a report of 1994, the OECD underlined that this principle may, especially if the structure of the information systems of the two partners differs very much, lead to the result that little information is exchanged.[252] The exception to the reciprocity principle may be explained in the context of the TIEA, which is designed for countries with no DTC, such as tax havens.

## 2. Tax examinations abroad

Tax examinations abroad are allowed under the TIEA. A Contracting State may allow representatives of the other Contracting State to enter the territory to interview individuals and examine records with the written consent of the persons concerned (Art. 6 par. 1 TIEA).

However, contrary to the OECD Model, simultaneous tax audits are not included in the Model, although they may be agreed upon specifically by the Contracting States.[253]

## D. Secrecy Clause

Under Art. 8, information received by a contracting party shall be treated as confidential and may be disclosed only to the persons or authorities (including courts or administrative bodies) in the jurisdiction of the contracting party concerned with the assessment or collection of, the enforcement or prosecution in respect of, or the determination of appeals in relation to, the taxes covered by this agreement.

While this clause resembles the secrecy rule of Art. 26 of the OECD Model, it contains some differences. First, the concept of confidentiality is *autonomous* and does not refer to the law of the requesting State.[254] Second, the information exchanged may only be used for taxes covered by the agreement. Third, the TIEA Model does not include the super-vision authorities ('oversight') as persons to whom the information may be disclosed. However, information may be disclosed to any person not

---

[251] OECD, Tax Information exchange between OECD Member countries, Paris 1994, par. 47.

[252] OECD Tax Information exchange between OECD Member countries, Paris 1994, par. 49; see also as a comparison, the rules of Art. 26 par. 3 lit. a and b OECD Model DTC, supra p. 31.

[253] Pankiv (2012), p. 164; OECD Commentary TIEA, n. 39.

[254] Sota, in: Günther/Tüchler (2013), p. 99.

mentioned only with the express written consent of the competent authority of the requested party (Art. 8 *in fine* TIEA Model).

## E. Limits

### 1. Legislation of the applicant State

The requested party is not obliged to obtain information that the applicant State would not be able to obtain under its own laws for purposes of the administration or enforcement (Art. 7 par. 1 TIEA). We can see here again the consequence of the shift or responsibility because only the laws of the requesting State (applicant) are relevant.

### 2. Trade, business or professional secret (excluding bank secrecy)

In addition, in accordance with the OECD Model, a requested State cannot be obliged to supply information which would disclose any *trade, business, industrial, commercial* or *professional secret* or *trade process* (Art. 7 par. 2. TIEA). However, as mentioned above, bank secrecy or information about ownership – referred to in Art. 5, par. 4 – cannot be treated as a secret as such (Art. 7 par. 2, *in fine*, TIEA). Thus, a requested State is not allowed to decline a request on the grounds of domestic bank secrecy rules.

### 3. Client-attorney privilege

A contracting party will not be obliged to supply information which would reveal confidential communication between a client and an attorney, solicitor or other admitted legal representative where such communication is produced either for the purposes of providing legal advice or for use in existing or contemplated legal proceedings (Art. 7 par. 3 TIEA).

### 4. Public order

Similar to the OECD Model, the requested party may decline a request for information if it would be contrary to public policy (ordre public).

### 5. Enforcement of tax claim

A request for information cannot be refused on the grounds that the tax claim to which it relates is disputed.

### 6. Discrimination

The requested party may also decline a request for information if the information is requested to administer or enforce a provision of the tax law of the applicant party, or any requirement connected therewith, which discriminates against a national of the requested party as compared with a national of the applicant party in the same circumstances (Art. 7 par. 6 TIEA).

## F. Abolition of the Dual Criminality Principle

In the field of international assistance in criminal matters, many states follow the principle of *dual criminality*. Under this principle, assistance is only granted to the extent that the conduct involved is also regarded as a crime under the criminal law of the requested State. For instance, the dual criminality condition is applicable under Art. 2 lit. a of the European Convention on Mutual Assistance in Criminal Matters of 20 April 1999. Some states, such as Austria, Luxembourg or Switzerland, tended to also apply the dual criminality principle in the framework of international assistance in tax matters, at least before the shift of March 2009. The dual criminality principle remains however an important protection, which, according to commentators, may be justified on at least two grounds.[255]

First it is based on the so-called *cooperation principle*. A State should not be obliged to grant assistance and thus collaborate to repress conduct which is not regarded as criminal under its own law. This rule can be also regarded as a consequence of the 'revenue rule'.

Second, the dual criminality principle is also a means to protect the *constitutional rights* granted in the requested State. Indeed, in particular in the field of criminal assistance, the requested measures are often restrictions to constitutional rights (property, right to privacy, etc.). As a consequence, the principle of dual criminality is also a protection of the constitutional rights of the person resident in the requested State. It prevents such a State granting assistance measures – sometimes combined with coercive procedures such as seizures or freezing of assets – which are not based on any domestic legal provision. It is generally admitted that, under the constitutional principles of legality and of separation of powers, a State is only allowed to restrict human or constitutional rights of its citizen provided the measure is (i) based on a domestic legal provision (ii) is justified by objective public interest and (iii) is necessary to achieve that goal (principle of proportionality).

The agreement sees – at least in the first three years of its entry into force – assistance in criminal tax matters. Criminal tax matters are defined as matters involving intentional conduct, which is liable to prosecution

---

[255] See for instance, Popp (2001), p. 136 ff.

under the criminal law of the applicant Party (Art. 4 lit. b). This definition is very broad and rests entirely on the scope of the character-ization of the applicant State.[256] A compromise solution could be to define more precisely within the agreement itself the essential elements of a criminal tax offence.[257] As a consequence, under this solution, assistance would only be granted in the case of tax fraud as defined in detail within the TIEA itself. Thus, both Contracting States would be bound by the same notion of tax fraud. Under the dual criminality principle, both States would therefore only be obliged to grant infor-mation in the case of criminal tax conduct, which they would have mutually defined within an international agreement.

## G.  Protection of the Taxpayer

The TIEA as such does not provide for specific procedural rules. However, the rights and safeguards secured by the law of the requested State remain applicable, but only to the extent that they do not unduly prevent or delay effective exchange of information (Art. 1 *in fine*). In addition, the Model provides for the explicit protection of *attorney-privileged* information, which is however defined in a restrictive manner (Art. 7 par. 3 TIEA Model). The Model also permits, but does not require, notification of the taxpayer.[258]

In addition, if requested by the applicant State, the requested State shall provide information, 'to the extent allowable under its domestic law, in the form of depositions of witnesses and authenticated copies of original records' (Art. 5 par. 3 TIEA). This is one of the few references to the domestic law of the requested State. Otherwise, protection rules will rather be found in the domestic law of the requesting party. Indeed, according to Art. 7 par. 1 the requesting (applicant) State cannot request information that it would not be able to obtain in similar circumstances under its own law. This rule is intended to prevent the applicant State from trying to circumvent its domestic law limitations, by making use of greater power than it has.[259] For instance, if the domestic law of the applicant State prevents the obtaining of information from a person under the protection against self-incrimination, the requested State will be able to decline the request under the same rule.[260]

---

256  See Art. 4 of the agreement.
257  Oberson (2003), p. 15.
258  Pankiv (2013), p. 171.
259  Commentary TIEA, n. 73.
260  Commentary TIEA, n. 73.

# 7. The OECD Convention on Mutual Administrative Assistance in Tax Matters (CMAAT)

## I. INTRODUCTION

For many years, most of the exchange of information occurred through bilateral treaties, notably DTC. In 1972, however, the first Nordic Multilateral Treaty on Mutual Assistance in Tax Matters was signed by Denmark, Finland, Norway, Sweden and Iceland. It provided for an extended exchange of information, assistance in the collection of taxes and supply and service of documents, including tax returns.[261] This multilateral treaty then served as a model for the CoE/OECD Convention on Mutual Administrative Assistance in Tax Matters (CoE/OECD CMAAT).[262]

The Convention was opened for signature by the member states of the CoE and OECD in January 1988. Following ratification by five countries, the initial convention entered into force on 1 April 1995. The changes in the global environment, notably after March 2009, called for a more extensive exchange of information to fight against tax fraud and evasion, including within a multilateral instrument. The CoE and the OECD, therefore, introduced some amendments to the original convention. The amendments, adopted in 2010, entered into force in June 2011. In a nutshell, the purposes of the amendments are (i) to align the Convention to the global standard and (ii) to open it for signature also to non-CoE/OECD countries.[263]

The CMAAT is a 'powerful instrument' in the fight against offshore tax evasion and avoidance.[264] It is also a modern tool, which combines a multilateral approach with flexibility. Indeed, the parties may lodge

---

[261] Valkama (2013), p. 199 ff, 200.

[262] Valkama (2013), p. 199.

[263] See Wittman (2013), p. 178; Gabert/Seer (2011), p. 88; Daniels (1988), p. 101.

[264] Pross/Russo (2012), p. 361.

reservations on certain issues, for instance collection of taxes,[265] or have to implement specific additional mutual agreements for automatic exchange. In addition, a coordinating body monitors the implementation and development of the convention, under the aegis of the OECD;[266] this ensures a uniform application of the convention.[267] In comparison with the EU tax recovery assistance Directive 2010/24,[268] it is not as efficient within the EU, since it does not provide for a uniform instrument permitting collection in the requested State.[269]

## II. SCOPE

The convention provides for a mutual *administrative assistance* in tax matters, which covers various forms of exchange of information (including simultaneous tax examination and tax examination abroad), assistance in recovery of taxes and service of documents (Art. 1 par. 2).

The *personal* scope of the convention is not restricted to residents or nationals of the Contracting States (Art. 1 par. 3). According to commentators, the convention does not require a 'direct tax-relevant relationship' between the taxpayer under examination and any other third party involved.[270]

The convention applies to all types of taxes, in the broadest sense of the term, including social security contributions (Art. 2). Customs duties, however, are outside the scope of the convention (Art. 2 par. 1 lit. b, iii). Customs duties are governed by the International Convention on Mutual Administrative Assistance for the Prevention, Investigation and Repression of Customs Offences.[271] The existing taxes to which the convention applies are listed in Annex A. In addition, the convention also applies to any identical or substantially similar taxes, which are imposed by a Contracting State after the entry into force of the convention; in that event, the party concerned must notify the depositaries of the adoption of the tax in question (Art. 1 par. 4).

---

265  Pross/Russo (2012), p. 361.
266  See Art. 24 par. 3 CMAAT.
267  Pross/Russo (2012), p. 361.
268  See infra p. 118.
269  De Troyer (2014), p. 136.
270  Daniels (1988), p. 103; see also Wittman (2013), p. 181.
271  Convention of 9 June 1977 (amended in 1985) (so-called Nairobi Convention), see Wittman (2013), p. 181.

## III. SECRECY RULE

The secrecy rule, according to Art. 22, is quite restrictive and corresponds to a high standard of confidentiality.[272] Any information obtained by a contracting party must be treated as secret in the same manner as information obtained under the domestic law of the requested State, or under the conditions of the applicant State if such conditions are more restrictive (Art. 22 par. 2). This means that the higher standard of the domestic law between the requesting and requested State will then prevail. In addition, according to a new paragraph introduced by the 2010 Protocol, the party receiving the information must treat it with safeguards that may be required to ensure data protection and privacy under the domestic law of the supplying party.

Information received from a Contracting State may be disclosed only to persons or authorities (including courts or administrative bodies) involved in the assessment, collection or recovery of, the enforcement or prosecution in respect of, or the determination of appeals in relation to taxes of that contracting party, or the oversight of the above (Art. 22 par. 2).

This information may only be used by these persons and only for the purposes mentioned under this provision. They may however disclose it in public court proceedings or in judicial decisions relating to such taxes (Art. 22 par. 2). However, information may also be used for other purposes (for instance to combat money laundering, corruption or terrorist financing),[273] when the information may be used for such purposes under the laws of the requested State and the competent authority of that state authorizes such use (Art. 22 par. 4).

Because of its multilateral character, cooperation should open the possibility to extend the exchange of information between more than two States.[274] The passing on of the information received to a third State is only possible subject to a prior authorization by the competent authority of the supplying State (i.e., the State from where the information originates) (Art. 22 par 4 *in fine*).[275]

---

[272] Pross/Russo (2012), p. 363; Wittman (2013), p. 192.
[273] CoE/OECD Commentary, n. 225 ad Art. 22.
[274] Pross/Russo (2012), p. 364.
[275] Wittman (2013), p. 193.

## IV. FORMS OF ASSISTANCE

The Convention provides for different forms of administrative assistance in tax matters, which include the most significant measures that could be taken by tax administrations cooperating with each other.[276] This assistance includes the typical forms of exchange of information, such as information upon request, spontaneous and automatic, but also simultaneous tax examinations and tax examination abroad. It also provides for assistance in recovery and measures of conservancy. The service of documents is also included.

### A. Exchange of Information

In general, the contracting parties must exchange, upon request, information that is foreseeably relevant for the administration or enforcement of the domestic laws concerning taxes covered by the convention (Art. 4). The foreseeably relevant standard, added in 2010, corresponds to the rule of Art. 26 par. 1 OECD Model DTC.

The convention further provides for the *five* following main methods of exchange of information:[277]

(i)     Exchange on request: at the request of the applicant state, the requested State must provide information, which concerns particular persons or transactions (Art. 5). By referring not only to persons, but also to transactions, it implies that the requesting State must provide all relevant information not only on the taxpayer but also in the case of a 'group request' or, when relevant the intermediaries involved.[278] The OECD standard of foreseeable relevance, and the principle of proportionality remain however applicable (Art. 4 par. 1), which means that 'fishing expeditions' are not allowed.

(ii)    Automatic exchange: two or more parties must automatically exchange information in accordance with the procedures determined by mutual agreement (Art. 6).

---

[276]    Pross/Russo (2012) p. 362.
[277]    Commentary CoE/OECD Convention, n. 51 ad Art. 4 (2010).
[278]    Pross/Russo (2012), p. 362.

(iii)  Spontaneous exchange: without prior request, a party must forward to another party, information obtained during examination of a taxpayer's affairs, which might be of interest to the receiving state (Art. 7).

(iv)  Simultaneous tax examination: at the request of one of them, two or more parties agree to examine simultaneously, each in its own territory, on the basis of an arrangement between two or more competent authorities, the tax affairs of a person, or persons in which these states have a common or related interest, with a view to exchanging any relevant information obtained (Art. 8).

(v)  Tax examination abroad: at the request of the applicant State, the requested State may allow the presence of representatives of the tax administration of the requesting State at an examination of a tax matter in the requested State (Art. 9). The decision to allow the foreign representatives to be present lies exclusively with the competent authorities where the examination takes place.[279]

Article 4, however, does not restrict the possibilities of exchange of information. The classification under the relevant articles is determined more by the mechanism through which the information is exchanged than by the character of the information.[280]

*Automatic exchange of information* requires a preliminary mutual agreement between two or more Contracting States (Art. 6). Such an agreement will be concluded by the competent authorities, which may agree on the implementation of the convention (Art. 24).

## B.  Assistance in Recovery and Measures of Conservancy

The requested State must proceed with the recovery of tax receipts of the requesting State as if they were its own tax receipts (Art. 11 par. 1). In principle, the recovery applies only to tax claims which form the subject of an agreement permitting the enforcement in the applicant state and, unless otherwise agreed, which are not contested (Art. 11 par. 2). However, where the claim is against a nonresident of the applicant state, only par. 1 applies, unless otherwise agreed, in which case the claim may no longer be contested (Art. 11 par. 2).

Subject to these conditions, if some assets of a tax debtor are located in the requested State, the requesting State may ask the requested State to implement recovery measures, for taxes due in the requesting State. The

---

[279]  Pross/Russo (2012), p. 362.
[280]  Commentary CoE/OECD Convention, n. 51 ad Art. 4 (2010).

request can be targeted not only against the taxpayer but also against any person liable to the tax, under the terms of the domestic law of the requesting State.[281] The tax claim in which assistance is provided does not have in the requested State any priority specially accorded to the tax claim of that State (Art 15).

The request for administrative assistance must be accompanied by a declaration, as defined under Art. 13, which confirms that the tax claim pertains to a tax covered by the convention and, in the case of recovery, that, subject to par. 2 of Art. 11, the tax claim is not or may not be contested (Art. 13 par. 1 lit. a).

In addition, at the request of the applicant state, the requested State must take the appropriate measures of *conservancy*, even if the claim is contested or not yet subject to an instrument permitting enforcement (Art. 12).

The request for recovery is subject to time limits. Any questions concerning the period beyond which a claim cannot be enforced are governed solely by the law of the applicant State (Art. 14 par. 1). This rule is based on the premise that the claim has arisen under the law of the applicant State and it is therefore logical to apply its rule as far as the existence or extinction of such a claim is concerned.[282] In order for the requested State to apply such rules, the applicant State shall give appropriate information, especially concerning the time limits rule (Art. 14 par. 1). There is however an absolute time limit of 15 years from the date of the original instrument pertaining to enforcement (Art. 14 par. 3).

## C. Service of Documents

The convention provides assistance for the service of documents, including judicial decisions, which emanate from the applicant State and which relate to a tax covered in the convention (Art. 17). The requested State must serve upon the addressee the documents (including judicial decisions) which emanate from the requested State. The service occurs, either by a method prescribed by the domestic law of the requested State or, to the extent possible, by a particular method requested by the applicant state or the closest to such method available under its own law (Art. 17 par. 2).

---

[281]   Pross/Russo (2012), p. 362.
[282]   Wittman (2013), p. 189.

This assistance could occur in all phases of the tax proceedings, but in practice it will mostly pertain to the assessment phase.[283] The purpose is to ensure that documents reach the taxpayer before enforcement measures take place.[284]

## V.  LIMITS

### A.  Principle of Subsidiarity

The convention explicitly confirms the application of the principle of subsidiarity. According to Art. 19, a requested State shall not be obliged to accede to a request if the applicant State has not pursued all means available in its own territory, except where recourse to such means would give rise to disproportionate difficulty.

### B.  Other Limits

Article 21 lists a series of limits to the process of mutual assistance. This provision intends to achieve a 'proper balance' between the need to ensure an effective mutual administrative assistance in tax matters and the safeguards for the taxpayers and the requested State.[285]

In general, Art. 21 par. 1 'states explicitly what is implicit throughout the Convention: that the rights and safeguards of persons under national laws and administrative practices are not reduced in any way by the Convention'.[286] However, such domestic law rules or practices should not be applied in a manner that undermines the object and purpose of the convention.[287]

In particular, except in the case of Art. 14 (i.e. time limits for claims governed by the law of the requesting State), the requested State does not have the obligation to:

a)  Carry out measures at variance with its own laws or administrative practice or the laws or administrative practices of the applicant (requesting) State.

---

283   Wittman (2013), p. 189; Pross/Russo (2012), p. 362.
284   Pross/Russo (2012), p. 363.
285   Commentary CoE/OECD Convention, n. 178 ad Art. 21.
286   Commentary CoE/OECD Convention, n. 1 79 ad Art. 21.
287   Ibid.

b)  Carry out measures, which would be contrary to public policy (ordre public).

c)  Supply information, which is not obtainable under its own laws or its administrative practices or under the laws of the applicant state or its administrative practices.

d)  Supply information, which would disclose any trade, business, industrial, commercial or professional secret, or trade process, or information, the disclosure of which would be contrary to public policy (ordre public).

e)  Provide assistance if and insofar as it considers the taxation in the applicant to be contrary to generally accepted taxation principles or to the provisions of a DTC, or of any other convention, which the requested State has concluded with the applicant State.

f)  Provide assistance for the purpose of administering or enforcing a provision of the tax law of the applicant State, which discriminates against a national of the requested State as compared with a national of the applicant State in the same circumstances.

g)  To provide administrative assistance if the applicant State has not pursued all reasonable measures available under its laws or administrative practices, except where recourse to such measures would give rise to disproportionate difficulty.

h)  To provide assistance in recovery in those cases where the administrative burden is clearly disproportionate to the benefits to be derived by the applicant state.

Following the change of the OECD Model DTC of 2005, the 2010 Protocol also introduced *exceptions* to the limits. First, Art. 21 par. 1 confirms that the requested State cannot decline the request solely because it has no domestic interest in such information. Second, the provisions of the convention cannot be construed to permit a requested State to decline to supply information, solely because the information is held by a bank, other financial institution, nominee or person acting in an agency or a fiduciary capacity or because it relates to ownership by a person (Art. 21 par. 4). This provision, which corresponds to Art. 26 par. 5 of the OECD Model DTC, precludes in particular a requested State from refusing the supply of information based on domestic bank secrecy provisions.

## VI.  RIGHTS OF THE TAXPAYER

The preamble of the convention, under the fifth recital, states:

Considering that fundamental principles entitling every person to have his rights and obligations determined in accordance with a proper legal procedure should be recognized as applying to tax matters in all states and that states should endeavor to protect the legitimate interests of taxpayers, including appropriate protection against discrimination and double taxation.

The protection of rights of the taxpayer is therefore one of the founding principles of the convention.

However, despite this reference in the preamble, there is no detailed inclusion in the convention of specific rights of the taxpayer. Yet, according to Art. 21 par. 1, the rights and safeguards of the domestic law are not affected in any way, which implies that domestic procedural rights, such as *notification* rights, remain applicable.[288] They do however apply, to the extent that they do not unduly prevent or delay the effectiveness of the assistance.[289] In cases where domestic law provides that the authorities of the requested State may inform its resident or national before transmitting information concerning him or her, the concerned party may address such a declaration to one of the depositaries (Art. 4 par. 3).

## VII. IMPLEMENTATION OF THE CONVENTION: THE COORDINATING BODY

The implementation and development of the convention are monitored by a coordinating body composed of the representatives of the competent authorities of the parties, which work under the 'aegis' of the OECD (Art. 24 par. 3). States that have signed but not yet accepted, approved or ratified the convention are entitled to be represented at the meetings of the co-ordination body as observers (Art 24 par. 3).

This body shall recommend any action likely to further the general aims of the convention, in particular to act as a forum for the study of new methods and procedures to increase international cooperation in tax matters and, when appropriate, may recommend revisions or amendments to the convention (Art. 24 par. 3). It follows that the coordinating body may also recommend revision or modification to the convention.[290] The co-ordination body may have to furnish opinions on the interpretation of the convention (Art. 24 par. 4).

---

[288] Wittman (2013), p. 193.
[289] Commentary CoE/OECD Convention, n. 180 ad Art. 21.
[290] Commentary CoE/OECD Convention, n. 242 ad Art. 24.

Questions of application and interpretation of the convention should first be resolved by mutual agreement of the competent authorities of the states immediately affected by the problem (Art. 24 par. 5).[291] If they succeed they shall notify the competent authority.

## VIII. RELATIONS WITH OTHER INSTRUMENTS

Art. 27 favours the so-called 'pro-assistance principle'.[292] The possibilities offered by this convention do not limit or are not limited by those contained in existing or future international agreements or other agreements between the parties. In other words, the state may choose whichever instrument they consider most appropriate to a particular case.[293]

Parties to the convention that are also Member States of the EU can apply, in their mutual relations, the possibilities of assistance of the convention, in so far as they allow a wider co-operation than that provided under EU rules (Art. 27 par. 2). This new rule, added in 2010, confirms the 'pro-assistance principle', and modifies, for EU members, the previous rule, which provided that in mutual relations only community rules were applicable.[294]

## IX. SIGNATURE, ENTRY INTO FORCE AND RESERVATIONS

### A. Signature

As a multilateral instrument, the convention has introduced specific rules in order to enable, to the largest possible extent, countries to join the agreement. This is especially the case here, since the convention is now open to any country in the world, and not necessarily to CoE or OECD members. As far as the accession modalities are concerned, the countries are divided into three groups.[295] Countries which were parties to the original convention belong to the first group. They became party to the

---

[291] Commentary CoE/OECD Convention, n. 244 ad Art. 24.
[292] Wittman (2013), p. 194; Grau Ruiz (2006), pp. 196, 199.
[293] Commentary CoE/OECD Convention, n. 266 ad Art. 24; Wittman (2013), p. 194.
[294] See in this respect the analysis of Grau Ruiz (2006), p. 196 ff.
[295] Wittman (2013), p. 178.

2010 protocol by approving it. In the second group, there are member countries of the CoE or OECD that were not parties to the original convention. In order to become a party, they have to ratify the amended version. Parties not members to the CoE or OECD need to request to be invited to sign and ratify the convention (see Art. 28 par. 5).

## B. Entry into Force

The original convention entered into force on the first day of the month following the expiration of a period of three months after the date on which five states had expressed their consent to be bound by the convention (Art. 28 par. 1). As we have seen, the convention was opened for signature by the member states of the CoE and OECD in January 1988.

The amended convention of 2010 entered into force on the first day of the month following the expiration of a period of three months after the date of deposit of the instrument of ratification with one of the depositaries.

The date of effect of the convention varies according to the subject matter.[296] For civil tax matters, unless agreed otherwise, it has effect only in relation to future tax periods, or where there is no tax period, it has effect for administrative assistance related to charges to tax arising on or after 1 January of the year following that in which the convention entered into force in respect of a party (Art. 28 par. 6 2010). For criminal tax matters, however, it has effect as soon as it enters into force in relation to earlier taxable periods or charges of tax (Art. 28 par. 7 2010). In this case, the convention could then also apply in relation to past tax periods, unless a State makes a reservation that this rule does not apply in relation to tax periods beyond the fourth tax period.[297]

## C. Reservations

Each country party to the Convention has the opportunity to tailor the extent of its obligations, by virtue of declarations, notifications or by a detailed system of reservations expressly provided for in the text. In other words, each Contracting State may restrict its participation to certain types of mutual assistance or to assistance in connection with certain taxes. While the purpose of the convention is to facilitate mutual assistance in the field of taxes of any kind, it would be unfortunate to

---

[296] Pross/Russo (2012), p. 365.
[297] Ibid.

exclude States which could not, for practical, constitutional or political reasons, provide the full assistance envisaged by the convention.[298] Article 30 therefore opens the possibility for reservations and tries to fix a proper balance between a minimum standard for acceding to the convention and the declarations of specific reservations, defined under par. 1. Paragraph 1, in conjunction with par. 2 of Art. 30, sets out a 'system', under which states are able to negotiate reservations within limits, such as the type of tax to be covered and/or the type of assistance to be provided.[299]

The declarations, notifications and reservations can be formulated at the moment of the execution or of the deposit of the instrument of ratification by the Contracting State in order to be included in Annex A, B or C to the Convention.

A State that has declared a reservation cannot require from another Contracting State which did not make such a reservation, assistance for a matter for which the applicant State reserves its rights.[300]

In particular, according to Art. 30 par. 1, a State can still declare the following reservations, at the time of signature, or at the moment of deposing its instrument of ratification, acceptance or approval or at any, later date:

a)    Not to provide any form of assistance in relation to the taxes of other parties in any of the categories listed in sub-paragraph b of par. 1 of Art. 2 provided it has not included any domestic tax in that category under Annex A.

b)    Not to provide assistance in the recovery of tax claims or in the recovery of an administrative fine, for all taxes or only for taxes in one or more of the categories listed in par. 1 of Art. 2.

c)    Not to provide assistance in any tax claim, in existence at the date of entry into force of the convention, or, when a reservation has been made under subparagraph a or b above, at the date of withdrawal of such reservation in relation to taxes in the category in question. Since, in principle the convention applies to all enforceable tax claims, including those in existence before the convention

---

[298]   Commentary CoE/OECD convention, n. 281 ad Art. 30.
[299]   Commentary CoE/OECD convention, n. 282 ad Art. 30.
[300]   Wittman (2013), p. 180.

enters into force, this subparagraph is designed to make the accession easier for States which could have difficulty with this rule.[301]

d)    Not to provide assistance in the service of documents.

e)    Not to permit the service of documents through the post (see Art. 17 par. 3).

f)    To apply Art. 28 par. 7 (retroactive effect in criminal matters) exclusively for administrative assistance related to taxable periods beginning on or after 1 January of the third year preceding the one in which the convention, as amended under the 2010 protocol, entered into force with respect to a contracting party, or where there is no taxable period, for administrative assistance related to charges to tax arising on or after 1 January of the third year preceding the one in which the convention entered into force in respect of a party.

No other reservations can be formulated than the ones expressly provided by Art. 30 (Art. 30 par. 2).

---

[301]    Commentary CoE/OECD convention, n. 267 ad Art. 30.

# 8. The EU Directives

## I. GENERAL INTRODUCTION

Contrary to indirect taxation, where a legal basis provides for a legislative harmonization process at the EU level (Art. 113 TFEU; ex Art. 93 TEC), there is no legal provision in the TFEU pertaining to direct taxation. The tax rules adopted in this area are based on Art. 115 TFEU (ex Art. 94 TEC), which provides that

> the Council shall, acting unanimously in accordance with a special legislative procedure and after consulting the European Parliament and the Economic and Social Committee, issue directives for the approximation of such laws, regulations or administrative provisions of the Member States as directly affect the establishment or functioning of the internal market.

In other words, the unanimity principle is applicable here. In addition, the rules should be required for the proper functioning of the internal market. Some discretion is thus allowed at the Member States level and conflicting views in such a sensitive area as tax policy make the implementation process a difficult and slow task.[302]

## II. THE SAVINGS DIRECTIVE

### A. Introduction: Historical Developments

The EU Directive on the taxation of savings is one of the first instruments designed to provide for transparency among EU Member States in the taxation of cross-border interest. The effective taxation of cross-border interest became a crucial issue within the EU, notably after the liberalization of the movement of capital, guaranteed under Art. 69 TFEU, and implemented under the Directive 88/361/EEC of 24 June 1988.[303] This fact was compounded by the introduction of the euro, by

---

[302] Cosentino (2013), p. 287.
[303] Cosentino (2013), p. 283.

11 EU members in 1998, which created tax opportunities for taxpayers who could invest their savings in offshore jurisdictions where no (or low) withholding tax was applied.[304] Absent an effective exchange of information, or relying on banking secrecy rules in the source jurisdiction, these taxpayers could avoid taxation in their countries of residence.

The Directive represents a compromise between the need to ensure a minimum level of taxation on interest income within the EU, while taking into account the domestic bank secrecy rules existing in some EU States and the level playing field with third countries.[305]

Because of the unanimous decision requirement mentioned above, the adoption of the EU Savings Directive (EUSD) took various steps.

A first proposal, based on Art. 6 par. 5 of the Directive 88/361 for the implementation of Art. (then) 67 EC Treaty,[306] proposed a withholding tax at source of 15 per cent for taxation of savings. This project did not go through, notably because of the negative German experience of such a system.

Second, following an informal Economic and Financial Affairs Council (ECOFIN) meeting of 13 April 1996 in Verona, the Commission presented a communication to the Council, in the form of: 'A package to tackle harmful tax competition in the European Union', which comprised three components: (i) a code of conduct for business taxation; (ii) a directive on the taxation of savings; (iii) a directive on interest and royalties payments. As a consequence, a new proposal for a directive on the taxation of savings was published in 1988. It introduced the famous '*coexistence model*', according to which, Member States will either implement an exchange of information on interest from savings received by individual resident in another Member State or apply a 20 per cent withholding tax on such interest.[307]

The interesting aspect of this new approach was the combination of two alternative systems in the Savings Directive proposal (an exchange of information or a withholding tax mechanism), and a package of three different tax measures, with different effects within the Member States, which would open the door to potential compromises. In addition, in the draft Savings Directive, the new system departed from the so-called

---

[304] Cosentino (2013), p. 284.

[305] Schröder (2012), p. 60.

[306] Directive 88/361/EEC implementing Article 67 of the EC Treaty, OJ L 178 of 8 July 1988, p. 5, which was later withdrawn upon the liberalization of capital movement by the Treaty of Maastricht, which introduced Art. 63 TFEU; Terra/Wattel (2012), p. 401.

[307] Cosentino (2013), p. 288.

*debtor principle*, under which savings are subject to tax as long as the debtor of the investment (bond, deposit, etc.) is resident within the EU. The new proposal focuses instead on the *paying agent*, i.e., the last financial intermediary resident in the EU, which pays the interest to the individual resident in another Member State. As such, unanimity on the new proposal was still difficult to reach. In particular, it raised the issue of the proper tax treatment of the Eurobond market, notably in the London financial centre.

A compromise was reached at the meeting of the European Council of Santa Maria da Feira, on 19 and 20 June 2000.[308] They unanimously agreed on the following measures. As a main principle, exchange of information, on as wide a basis as possible should be the ultimate objective of the EU. However, under a transitional period, Austria, Belgium and Luxembourg were authorized to levy a withholding tax. In addition, in order to preserve the competitiveness of the European financial market, discussions were to be initiated with specific third countries (United States, Switzerland, Liechtenstein, Monaco, Andorra, San Marino) and Member States' dependent and associated territories (the Netherlands Antilles, Aruba, Jersey, Guernsey, Isle of Man, Anguilla, BVI, Cayman Islands, Montserrat and Turks and Caicos) in order to implement equivalent measures with those countries.

Following various discussions, the Commission issued a third proposal for the Savings Directive in July 2001.[309] It followed the principles agreed upon at the Santa Maria da Feira Council, with some further rules. In particular, the rate of the withholding tax during the transitory period for the three Member States concerned was fixed at 15 per cent for the first three years, and 20 per cent thereafter. In addition 75 per cent of the tax revenue of the withholding tax had to be transferred to the resident Member State of the individual receiving interest payments. A grandfather clause was introduced for bonds and debt securities issued before 1 March 2001. In addition, during the ECOFIN meeting of 21 January 2003, a third withholding tax rate of 35 per cent, as of January 2010, was introduced to increase the step up of the rate.[310]

---

[308] Cosentino (2013), p. 289.

[309] Proposal for a Council Directive to ensure a minimum effective taxation of savings income in the form of interest payments within the Community, COM (2001) 400 def. of July 2001.

[310] Cosentino (2013), p. 290.

The Council Directive on the taxation of savings was finally adopted on 3 June 2003.[311] It entered into force on 1 July 2005.[312]

It was based on necessary assurance[313] that five States, listed in Art. 17 par. 2 (i), had adopted equivalent measures to those contained in the Directive and all relevant dependent and associated territories, listed in Art. 17 par. 2 (ii), apply automatic exchange of information in the same manner as provided for in the directive (or during the transitional period, apply a withholding tax on the same terms). It is interesting to point out that, on 1 January 2003, the ECOFIN considered that equivalent measures were already in place in the United States. Therefore, the United States was dropped from the list of third states under Art. 17 par. 2 (i), contrary to the proposal of 2001, even though it appears that at this stage no significant equivalent measures had been adopted.

The ten new Member States that joined the EU in 2004 and the additional two Member States that joined in 2007 must apply the automatic exchange system and are not in the transitional withholding period.[314]

## B. Main Content and Functioning of the Directive

### 1. Essential features

The aim of the EUSD is to enable savings income in the form of interest payments made by one Member State to beneficial owners who are individuals resident in another Member State to be subject to effective taxation in accordance with their laws of residence (Art. 1 EUSD).

Under the terms of the Directive, Member States have to introduce an automatic exchange of information on interest payments paid by paying agents established within their territory to individuals (beneficial owners) resident in other Member States, who receive that payment.[315] During a transitory period, however, Austria, Belgium and Luxembourg are not required to apply the automatic exchange of information system, but may levy a withholding tax on interest paid by a paying agent resident in those three Member States to an individual resident in another Member State (Arts 10 and 11 EUSD). The withholding tax is levied at a rate of

---

[311] Council Directive 2003/48/EC on taxation of savings income in the form of interest payments, OJ L 157 of 26 June 2003, p. 38.

[312] Council Decision 2004/587/EC of 19 July 2004 on the date of application of Directive 2003/48/EC, OJ L 257, p. 7.

[313] Cosentino (2013), p. 290.

[314] Terra/Wattel (2012), p. 402.

[315] Schröder (2012), p. 62.

15 per cent for the first three years, 20 per cent for the subsequent three years, and 35 per cent thereafter. Twenty five per cent of the revenue from the tax is retained by the levying Member State and 75 per cent transferred to the Member State of residence of the beneficial owner of the income (Art. 12 EUSD). It should be noted that in March 2009, Belgium decided to introduce automatic exchange of information, as of 1 January 2010.[316]

## 2. Beneficial owner

As a rule, beneficial owner means any individual who receives an interest payment or any individual for whom an interest payment is secured, unless he provides evidence that it was not received or secured for his own benefit (Art. 2 par. 1 EUSD). Article 2 par. 1 (a, b and c) described three situations in which the presumption of being a beneficial owner can be reversed:[317] (a) the individual acts as a paying agent himself; (b) he represents either a legal person, subject to tax on profits, or an under-taking for collective investment in transferable securities (UCITS) (duly authorized in accordance with Directive 85/611/EEC), or an entity referred to in Art. 4 par. 2 (and the name and address of that entity are communicated) or (c) he acts on behalf of another individual who is the beneficial owner and discloses to the paying agent the identity of that individual.

If the paying agent has information suggesting that the individual who receives an interest payment is not the beneficial owner, or not a paying agent or a representative of a legal person, it shall take reasonable steps to establish the identity of the beneficial owner (Art. 3 par. 2 EUSD). If it is unable to identify the beneficial owner, it shall treat the individual who received the interest as the beneficial owner (Art. 3 par. 2 *in fine* EUSD).

In a nutshell, the definition of the beneficial owner is based on the presumption that the individual who receives an interest payment is the beneficial owner, unless he can prove that 'he is representing a legal person or identifies the ultimate beneficial owner'.[318]

The Member States shall adopt implementation rules, in order to allow the paying agent to identify the beneficial owners and their residence. The EUSD however lays down 'minimum standards' in Art. 3 paras 2 and 3 EUSD. In summary, these standards distinguish between the dates

---

[316] Ibid.
[317] Terra/Wattel (2012), p. 407.
[318] Terra/Wattel (2012), p. 408.

of the contractual relationship between the paying agent and the beneficial owner.[319]

## 3. Paying agent
Paying agent means:

> any economic operator who pays interest or secures the payment of interest
> for the immediate benefit of the beneficial owner, whether the operator is the
> debtor of the debt claim which produces the interest or the operator charged
> by the debtor or the beneficial owner with paying interest or securing the
> payment of interest (Art. 4 par. 1 EUSD)

An economic operator is any person or entity operating in the normal
course of his or her business.[320]

The purpose of this rule is to focus on the last intermediary (paying
agent) in the payment chain before the individual, beneficial owner.[321]
The location of the debtor of the investment is not relevant. The paying
agent approach has the advantage of avoiding the potential impact on the
issuers of Eurobonds or other debt instruments residing in the EU.
Placing the paying agent outside the EU however may easily circumvent
the rules of the EUSD. This is why the Commission tried to obtain at
least equivalent measures from significant competing financial centres
(under Art. 17 EUSD). In order to be effective, the paying agent system
should indeed be adopted globally.[322]

Article 4 par. 2 EUSD introduces an extension of the paying agent
definition to a non-individual entity to which interest is paid or for which
interest is secured for the benefit of the beneficial owner. These entities
'shall also be considered a paying agent upon such payment or securing
of such payment', unless the exception of Art. 4 par. lit a, b or c applies.
These entities are called 'paying agent upon receipt', as opposed to
'paying agent upon payment'.[323] The purpose of this rule was to try, for
anti-avoidance purposes, to include transparent entities, which would be
outside the scope of the directive, and could be interposed between the
paying agent and the final beneficial owner.[324] It appears that this
measure was not successful in respect of specific entities, such as trusts,

---

[319] See Art. 3 paras 2 and 3 EUSD.
[320] Terra/Wattel (2012), p. 407; Explanatory Memorandum to Art. 4, par. 1.
[321] Terra/Wattel (2012), p. 407.
[322] In the same vein, Terra/Wattel (2012), p. 411.
[323] Cosentino (2013), p. 293.
[324] Ibid.

foundations, partnerships, or associations, whose classification as legal entity is unclear.[325]

## 4. Interest payment

Interest is defined under Art. 6 par. 1 as: a) interest paid or credited to an account, relating to debt claims of every kind; b) interest accrued or capitalized on the sale, refund or redemption of the debt claims; c) income deriving from interest payments either directly or through an entity referred to in Art. 4 par. 2, distributed by certain collective investment (UCITS); d) income realized from the sale, refund or redemption of shares or units in entities, if they invest directly or indirectly, via other undertakings for collective investment or entities described under Art. 6 par. 1 lit. d, more than 40 per cent of their assets in debt claims. As of January 2011, the percentage is 25 per cent (Art. 6 par. 7 EUSD).

While the general definition of interest, under Art. 6 par. 1 EUSD, seems to correspond to Art. 11 par. 3 of the OECD Model DTC, the concept is broader. Indeed, the EUSD covers not only payment or crediting of interest, but also income stemming from the increase in value of zero bonds and deep discount bonds, and income from interest or distribution of collective investment units investing in debt-claims, and income from gain or redemption of shares or units in debt-claim investment vehicles.[326]

Detailed implementation rules can be found in paras 2 to 6 of Art. 6. They also introduced an option for Member States to require paying agents to annualize the interest over a period of time, which may not exceed one year, and treat such annualized interest as yearly payments (par. 5).

## C. Automatic Exchange of Information

The EUSD introduced a system of automatic exchange of information on interest payments made by a paying agent to an individual resident in another Member State. This system, following the transitory period, should be the ultimate mechanism in place.[327]

Under the automatic exchange of information system, the competent authority of the Member State of the paying agent shall communicate the information listed in Art. 8 to the competent authority of the Member State of residence of the beneficial owner (Art. 9 par. 1 EUSD). The communication is automatic and shall take place at least once a year,

---

[325]   Cosentino (2013), p. 293; Vanistendael (2009), p. 155.
[326]   Terra/Wattel (2012), p. 408.
[327]   Cosentino (2013), p. 295.

within six months following the end of the tax year of the Member State of the paying agent for all interest paid during that year (Art. 9 par. 2 EUSD).

According to Art. 8, the minimum information which the paying agent must report to the tax authorities of its Member State shall consist of:

a)  the identity and residence of the beneficial owner established in accordance with Art. 3;
b)  the name and address of the paying agent;
c)  the account number of the beneficial owner or, where there is none, identification of the debt claim giving rise to the interest;
d)  information concerning the interest payment, notably the amount of interest paid, credited, distributed or computed in accordance with Art. 8 par. 2.

A Member State may however restrict the minimum amount of information concerning interest payments to be reported by the paying agent to the total amount of interest or income and to the total amount of the proceeds from sale, redemption or refund (Art. 8 par. 2 *in fine* EUSD).

The date of the payment of interest is not on the list of the minimum information that has to be reported.[328]

## D.  The Transitional Withholding Tax Mechanism

### 1.  The system
As already mentioned, Austria, Belgium and Luxembourg were allowed, during a transitory period, to apply, instead of automatic exchange of information, a withholding tax on interest paid by a paying agent in their territory to an individual resident in another Member State.

The rate was 15 per cent until 1 July 2008, 20 per cent thereafter for three years, and 35 per cent after 1 July 2011. The countries in the transitional provisions must however receive information from the other Member States who apply the automatic exchange (Art. 10 par. 1 EUSD). Seventy five per cent of the revenue from the tax will be transferred to the Member State of residence of the beneficial owner of the interest, and the transferring Member State retains 25 per cent (Art. 12).

Member States applying the withholding tax must provide for one or both of the following procedures in order to ensure that the beneficial owner may request that no tax be withheld: a) a procedure which allows

---

[328]  Terra/Wattel (2012), p. 410.

the beneficial owner to authorize the paying agent to report information on interest paid; b) a procedure where the beneficial owner presents to his paying agent a certificate, which indicates his name and address and will ensure that the tax will not be levied (Art. 13 EUSD).

The State of residence of the individual beneficial owner has to ensure the elimination of any double taxation, which might result from the imposition of the withholding tax (Art. 14 par. 1 EUSD). This is done by a credit of the withholding tax against the income tax (Art. 14 par. 2 EUSD). Where this amount (the withholding tax) exceeds the amount of tax due in national law, the Member State of residence will repay the excess amount withheld (Art. 14 par. 2). This rule, which can be viewed as derogation from international tax rules, can be explained by the fact that the State of residence gets 75 per cent of the withholding tax.[329]

## 2. End of the transitional period

The transitional period will be terminated at the end of the first full fiscal year following the later of the following dates (Art. 10 par. 2 EUSD):

- the entry into force of an agreement between the EU and Switzerland, Monaco, San Marino, Liechtenstein and Andorra, following a unanimous decision of the Council, providing for (i) exchange of information upon request as defined under the OECD TIEA Model of 2002 with respect to interest payments to individuals resident in EU and (ii) the simultaneous application of a withholding tax on such payments (at a rate of 35 per cent);
- a unanimous agreement from the Council that the United States is committed to exchange information upon request as defined in the OECD TIEA Model of 2002 with respect to interest payments.

Belgium in the meantime has already left the transitional regime and introduced the automatic exchange of information as of January 2010.

## E.  Agreements with Third Countries

### 1.  In general

On the same date as the entry into force of the EUSD, similar measures were introduced in ten dependent or associated territories of EU Member States through bilateral agreements signed by each of the EU Member

---

[329]   Terra/Wattel (2012), p. 406.

States, and equivalent measures were applied in five third-party countries (Switzerland, Liechtenstein, San Marino, Monaco and Andorra).[330]

The essential features of the agreements with the five third-party countries correspond to the conditions set forth at the ECOFIN Council of 23 January 2003, which represent 'equivalent measures' to the EUSD. The four conditions are the following:[331]

- a retention of a withholding tax with revenue sharing (25/75) under similar terms to the tax applied by Austria, Belgium and Luxembourg under the transitory period;
- an option for the individual beneficial owner to allow the disclosure of the payment in order to avoid the retention;
- an exchange of information upon request in case of tax fraud or the like;
- a review clause to allow the parties to reexamine the arrangements.

In addition, parallel arrangements or agreements were concluded between each of the Member States and each of the dependent or associated territories identified in the Feira meetings.[332] Aruba, Anguilla, the Cayman Islands and Montserrat introduced exchange of information, joined subsequently by Guernsey and the Isle of Man and later by BVI and Turks and Caicos. A withholding tax is applied by the other territories.

The Commission also held exploratory talks with Hong Kong, Macao and Singapore for the introduction of equivalent measures to the EUSD but no formal negotiations have been started.[333]

### F. A Concrete Example: The EU-Swiss Agreement on the Taxation of Savings

#### 1. Background

In January 2001, Switzerland initiated a second round of bilateral negotiations with the EU, the so-called Bilateral II. They initially extended to ten subjects, notably, as far as taxes are concerned, the taxation of savings, the fight against fraud, the application of the Schengen/Dublin 'acquis' and services. Later however, the services dossier was withdrawn from the negotiations.

---

[330] Schröder (2012), p. 62 f.
[331] Terra/Wattel (2012), p. 402; Cosentino (2013), p. 290, note 39.
[332] Schröder (2012), p. 63 f.
[333] Schröder (2012), p. 65.

On 17 May 2004, the EU Council of Ministers and the Swiss Federal Council approved the results of the bilateral negotiations. A political agreement was reached at the Brussels Presidents' Summit, on 19 May 2004. The bilateral agreements were signed in Luxembourg on 26 October 2005. No referendum was asked against the agreement, which entered into force on 1 July 2005, in parallel with the EUSD.

The bilateral agreement on the taxation of savings (hereafter Savings Agreement) represented an important step both for the EU and Switzerland.[334] For the former, it corresponds to the implementation of 'equivalent measures' in the sense of Art 17 par. 2 EUSD. For Switzerland, it is the result of a balanced compromise between the introduction of unilateral measures to secure the taxation of interest within the EU, while, at the same time, still preserving bank secrecy. In addition, as a counterpart, Switzerland has obtained in such agreement the abolition of taxation at source on dividends, interest and royalties paid between associated companies, under specific conditions.

## 2. Main features of the Savings Agreement

The agreement with Switzerland on the taxation of savings income is an international agreement, based on Art. 54 of the Swiss Constitution. In this agreement, Switzerland unilaterally accepts to implement a retention in order to secure the taxation of interest within the EU. There is no reciprocity in this context. For instance, a Luxembourg paying agent is not obliged to levy the retention on interest paid by a Luxembourg paying agent to a Swiss resident.

It should be stressed here that the Savings Agreement is not as such a mere replication of the EUSD. It is an international agreement subject to interpretation according to the rules of the Vienna Convention. In addition, even if it is widely inspired by the Directive, the rules, definitions and concepts of the Savings Agreement are to be defined within the framework of such agreement. As a matter of fact, the Savings Agreement is not identical to the Directive. Some definitions are different, some rules are specific and the scope of this agreement is not the same.

The Savings Agreement is fundamentally made of three pillars:

(i)     The implementation of retention (withholding tax) on interest from Swiss paying agents. The retention may be avoided by a voluntary disclosure of the beneficial owner of the interest payment.

---

[334]     Oberson (2005), p. 108.

(ii)   The introduction of an exchange of information in case of 'tax fraud and the like' on elements covered by the agreement. In addition, Switzerland accepts having to negotiate in its double taxation treaties with EU Member States an exchange of information on income covered by those treaties in the case of 'tax fraud and the like'.

(iii)   The extension to Switzerland of rules comparable to the EU Parent–Subsidiary[335] and EU Interest and Royalty Directives.[336]

In a Memorandum of Understanding (MoU), the signatories have accepted a declaration of intent in which they consider the Agreement 'to provide an acceptable and balanced arrangement that can be considered as safeguarding the interests of the parties. They will therefore implement the agreed measures in good faith and will not act unilaterally to undermine this arrangement without due cause'.[337]

In order to implement the Savings Agreement, a Federal Law on the Taxation of Saving has been adopted by the Federal Parliament on 17 December 2004. This legislation mainly refers to the agreement on all important concepts (interest, paying agent, beneficial owner) and provides for procedural and implementation measures. It entered into force on the same date as the Agreement, namely on 1 July 2005.

## 3.   The retention of interest

The main aspect of the Savings Agreement is the implementation of a *retention* (withholding tax)[338] on interest payments which are made to an individual resident of an EU Member State by a paying agent established in Switzerland, of 15 per cent during the first three years from the date of

---

[335]   Council Directive 90/435/EEC of 23 July 1990, on the common system of taxation applicable in the case of parent companies and subsidiaries of different Member States.

[336]   Council Directive 2003/49/EC of 3 June 2003, on a common system of taxation applicable to interest and royalty payments made between associated companies of different Member States.

[337]   See MoU, signed on 26 October 2004.

[338]   It is interesting to note that the Savings Agreement uses the word 'retention' instead of 'withholding tax'. In my view, this confirms that from the perspective of Switzerland the retention is not really a tax at source but merely a mechanism levied in the interest of the EU. A parallel may be draw here, for instance, with the so-called additional retention which used to be levied by Switzerland in the context of the double taxation treaty with the US and was drastically modified in 2001, after the implementation by the United States of the famous 'QI Regulations'.

application of the Agreement, 20 per cent for the subsequent three years, and 35 per cent thereafter (Art. 1 par. 1).

The beneficial owner may avoid the retention by expressly authorising his paying agent in Switzerland *to report* the interest payments to the competent authority of that country. Such communication is automatic and will take place at least once a year within six months following the end of the tax year. The competent authority of Switzerland must communicate the information to the competent authority of the Member State of residence of the beneficial owner (Art. 2 par. 3).

The Savings Agreement provides for a non-discrimination clause, in the sense that, in case of voluntary disclosure, the interest income concerned shall be subject to tax in that Member State at the same rates as those applied to similar income arising in that State (Art. 2 par. 4).

For the retention to apply, the following *4 conditions* have to be met:

(i)    there should be an interest payment
(ii)   the interest payment is made by a Swiss paying agent
(iii)  the Interest is paid to an individual resident in an EU Member State
(iv)   the resident individual is the beneficial owner

*i) Interest*    Interest payment means interest paid or credited to an account, relating to a debt-claim of every kind including interest paid on fiduciary deposits by Swiss paying agents for the benefit of beneficial owners, whether or not secured by mortgage and whether or not carrying a right to participate in the debtor's profits and, in particular, income from government securities and income from bonds and debentures, including premiums and prizes attached to such debt (Art. 7 par. 1 lit. a). It also covers interest capitalized on the sale, refund or redemption of the debt (zero coupon, for instance) (Art. 7 par. 1 lit. b).

In this context, a delicate issue is the application of the retention to interest from *undertakings for collective investment* (UCI). As a general rule, interest *paid* by UCI is subject to tax, provided they have invested more than 15 per cent of their assets in debt claims (according to subparagraph 1.a). In addition, income realized upon the *sale, refund or redemption* of shares or units in such undertakings is also subject to tax, provided they invest directly or indirectly more than 40 per cent of their assets in debt-claims as referred to in (a) (Art. 7 par. 1 lit. d).[339]

The application of this rule to UCI raises however a few questions. In particular, the wording of the agreement here is a little different from the

---

[339]    Such percentage will be 25 per cent as of January 2011 (Art. 7 par. 5).

Directive, which raises additional controversial issues. In particular, the EUSD seems to cover interest paid by UCI 'authorized according to Directive 85/611/EEC' as subject to the retention.[340] By contrast, the Savings Agreement simply mentions 'undertakings for collective investments domiciled in a Member State'.[341] Thus, a strict application of that rule could imply that a UCI in the EU, non-authorized, would not be subject to the Directive, but still covered by the Savings Agreement. To our knowledge, the Swiss Federal Tax Administration (FTA) tends not to follow this interpretation and to apply a rule similar to the EUSD.

It is important to note that Swiss investment funds, which are exempt from the Swiss anticipatory tax on payments to individuals, resident in the EU, are also subject to the retention (Art. 1. par. 4; Art. 7 par. 1 lit. c(iv) and lit. d(iv)). It appears that this rule refers to so-called 'affidavit funds' which, provided 80 per cent of their income is from foreign sources, are exempt from the Swiss anticipatory tax. However, should Switzerland extend the scope of the affidavit exemption in the future, such funds would be subject to the retention for individual EU customers. In our view, this rule does however not apply to specific types of income from such funds, which are exempt, such as capital gains. Indeed, capital gains on private movable assets are in any event exempt under Swiss law.[342] It should also not apply to income from investment funds, which are capitalized and retained in a so-called 'retained income' account.[343]

The retention is not applicable to the following types of income:

- dividends and income from participations;
- derivative products;
- insurance products (life insurance);
- benefits of pension plans;
- rents.

In addition, certain types of interest are also not covered, such as:

- Interest on debt claims issued by Swiss resident *debtors* or a Swiss permanent establishment of non-residents is excluded from the retention (Art. 1 par. 2). This rule is justified by the fact that, under

---

[340] See in particular Art. 6 par. 1 lit. c and d of the EC Directive (2003/48).

[341] See in particular Art. 7 par. 1 lit. c (i) and d (i) of the Savings Agreement.

[342] See Art. 16 par. 3 of the Federal Direct Tax Law, see also Oberson/Hull (2011), p. 49 ff.

[343] See FTA, Directives 'Instruments de placement collectif, Impôt anticipé et impôts étrangers à la source'.

the conditions set forth in Art. 4 of the Swiss Federal Withholding Tax Law (WTL), Switzerland levies an anticipatory tax of 35 per cent on specific interest from Swiss sources.[344] However, if Switzerland reduces the anticipatory tax of 35 per cent on Swiss source interest payments to individuals resident in the EU, it shall levy a retention at a rate which corresponds to the difference between the retention and the new anticipatory tax (Art. 1 par. 3).[345] The same would be true, as we have seen, for Swiss investment funds, which would become exonerated.

- Interest on loans between private individuals not acting in the course of their business are also excluded (Art. 7 par. 1 letter a).
- Penalty charges for late payment (Art. 7 par. 1 letter a).
- Structured products with an interest component (reverse convertible, capital protected units).
- Domestic and international bonds and other negotiable debt securities which have been issued before 1 March 2001, or for which the original issuing prospectuses have been approved before that date, provided no further issues of such negotiable debt securities are made on or after 1 March 2002 (Art. 16) ('grandfather' rule). Such rules apply until 31 December 2010.

*ii) Paying agent*    The retention only applies to interest paid by a paying agent established in Switzerland. A paying agent

> shall mean banks … securities dealers … natural and legal persons resident or established in Switzerland, partnership and permanent establishments of foreign companies, which even occasionally, accept, hold, invest, or transfer assets of third parties or merely pay or secure interest in the course of their business (Art. 6).

It should be noted that the agreement does not contain a provision similar to Art. 4 par. 2 of the EUSD ('entity system'). This will make the life of Swiss paying agents easier, who should only check whether the beneficial owner is a legal entity or an individual.[346]

---

[344]   In particular, the anticipatory tax applies on interest from Swiss bonds and similar instruments and interest on deposits with Swiss banks, see Art. 4 par. 1 lit. a and d WTL.

[345]   It should be noted that interest from savings accounts which is less than 50 Sfr. per year and currently exempt from the anticipatory tax will still not be subject to the retention.

[346]   See in this context Directive of the Swiss Banking Association (SBA) of 17 December 2003 n. 4.

*iii) Interest paid to a resident of an EU Member State*   Interest must be paid to an individual resident of an EU Member State. Interest paid within Switzerland is not subject to the retention. The same is true for interest paid to non-EU States. In particular, interest paid to individuals resident in the specific third States mentioned in Art. 17 par. 2 (i) EUSD, namely Liechtenstein, Monaco, San Marino and Andorra, are not covered.[347] Accordingly, interest paid to residents of dependent or associated territories of some EU Member States, within the meaning of Art. 17 par. 2(ii) EUSD, is also not subject to the retention.[348]

However, foreign source interest, even from non-EU sources, is also subject to the retention, provided it is paid by a Swiss paying agent to an individual beneficial owner resident in a Member State.

*iv) The individual is the beneficial owner*   This condition reduces the scope of application of the retention since it only applies to interest paid to an individual acting as the beneficial owner. It implies that payments to a legal entity are not covered by the agreement.

The beneficial owner is an individual who receives an interest payment or any individual for whom interest payment is secured, unless such individual can provide evidence that the interest payment was not received or secured for his or her own benefit (Art. 4). Under Art. 4 par. 1, second sentence, of the Agreement, the individual is not deemed to be the beneficial owner when he or she: a) acts as a paying agent within the meaning of Art. 6 or b) acts on behalf of a legal person, an investment fund or a comparable or equivalent body for common investments in securities or c) acts on behalf of another individual who is the beneficial owner and who discloses to the paying agent his or her identity and State of residence (Art. 4 par. 1).

It should be stressed that this definition is specific to the agreement. In particular, it does not necessarily correspond to the definition of the beneficial owner used in double taxation treaties.[349]

The paying agent must establish the identity and the State of residence of the beneficial owner. In practice, he/she shall keep a record of the

---

[347]   Swiss Federal Tax Administration (FTA) Directives on the taxation of savings (as at 1 July 2013) (hereafter FTA Directive), n. 34.

[348]   According to the FTA Directive, this list includes Jersey, Guernsey, Isle of Man, Anguilla, Cayman Islands, Montserrat, Turks and Caicos, BVI, Netherlands Antilles and Aruba.

[349]   See Art. 10 par. 2, Art. 11 par. 2 and Art. 12 par. 1 of the OECD Model Double Taxation Convention on Income and Capital.

name, first name, address and residence details in accordance with the Swiss legal provisions against money laundering (Art. 5).[350]

The State of residence of the beneficial owner is defined in accordance with the explanations of the contracting party. As a rule, the agreement does not set additional requirements and documents about the identification of the customer, which would go beyond the current practice, set forth under the domestic legal provision.[351] However, in the case of contractual relationships concluded after 1 January 2004, for individuals presenting a passport or official identity card issued by an EU Member State who declares themselves as residing outside the EU or Switzerland, a tax residence certificate issued by the competent authority of the country in which the individual claims to be a resident is necessary. Failing such a certificate, the EU Member State which issued the passport will be considered the country of residence (Art. 5).

In addition, where a paying agent has some information suggesting that the individual who receives the interest may not be the beneficial owner, the paying agent 'shall take reasonable steps to establish the identity of the beneficial owner' (Art. 4 par. 2). This clarification requirement is notably applicable in the case where the contracting party is an *individual*, while the banking documentation (Form A in particular) mentions another person as beneficial owner.[352] In such a case, the retention is applicable only to the extent that the beneficial owner appears to be an individual resident in the EU.

If, however, the contracting party is a *legal entity*, the retention will in principle not apply since legal entities are outside the scope of the agreement. In particular, the owners (shareholders) of such entity are not relevant.[353] Under the current regulations, additional verifications are only necessary in the case where the paying agent has written information suggesting that the legal entity acts as a nominee or as a usufructuary.[354]

The most delicate situation in this context is certainly the situation where the contracting party is a trustee. As such, the *trust* is not a legal entity and thus cannot be party to the contract. The Directive provides that in the case of a trust relationship, either the trustee is treated as the

---

[350]    These rules are detailed in the Federal law on money laundering of October 10, 1997 and on the numerous implementation regulations.

[351]    For instance, in the case of banks, the standards of the Banking Diligence Convention are applicable.

[352]    FTA Directive, n. 62.

[353]    FTA Directive, n. 76.

[354]    FTA Directive, n. 77.

beneficial owner, or it is a paying agent.[355] The trustee is a paying agent if it is obliged to transfer directly income from the trust assets to the beneficiary (such as in a 'life interest trust' or 'fixed interest trust').[356] In other cases, the trustee will be regarded as the beneficial owner.

### 4. Basis of retention

When the conditions are met, the paying agent shall withhold the retention, typically on the gross amount of interest credited (Art. 3 par. 1). However, contrary to the EC Directive, taxes and retentions other than the retention provided for in the agreement on the same payment of interest will be credited against the amount of the retention (Art. 3 par. 3).

### 5. Elimination of double taxation and revenue sharing

Double taxation conventions between Switzerland and the EU Member States do not prevent the levying of the retention (Art. 14, Savings Agreement). Double taxation may occur and is eliminated according to the rules of Art. 9 of the Savings Agreement. In particular, if the interest received by a beneficial owner has been subject to retention by a Swiss paying agent, the EU Member State of residence of the beneficial owner shall grant him a tax credit equal to the amount of the retention. Where this amount (i.e. the retention) exceeds the amount of tax due on the interest subject to retention in accordance with its national law, the Member State of residence shall repay the excess amount of tax withheld to the beneficial owner. A similar credit system also applies in the case of taxes and retentions other than the retention of the Agreement.

Switzerland will keep 25 per cent of the revenue generated by the retention and transfer 75 per cent of the revenue to the EU Member State of residence of the beneficial owner (Art. 8).

### 6. Exchange of information

*i) Overview*   The agreement provides for an exchange of information in case of tax fraud under the laws of the requested State or the like for income covered by the Agreement (Art. 10 par. 1). The exchange of information will occur between the competent authorities of Switzerland and any EU Member States in accordance with the procedures laid down in double taxation conventions. In Switzerland, the competent authority is the FTA.

---

[355] FTA Directive, n. 79.
[356] FTA Directive, n. 80.

In accordance with the principle of double incrimination, tax fraud or the like is defined by the laws of the requested States. However, the requested State will apply the statute of limitation under the laws of the requesting State. The procedural rules are defined in Art. 16 ff of the Federal Law on the Taxation of Savings. In particular, the person involved in the request will receive notification of the request and has the right to participate in the procedure and to consult the file. At the end of the procedure, the FTA will render a motivated formal decision granting or refusing the exchange of information. An appeal to the Federal Supreme Court with a suspensive effect is available against the final decision of the FTA.

In addition, in the Memorandum of Understanding, it was agreed that, as soon as the agreement was signed, Switzerland and each Member State would enter into bilateral negotiations with a view to:

- including in their double taxation convention on income and capital, provisions on administrative assistance in the form of exchange of information on request for all administrative, civil or criminal cases of tax fraud under the laws of the requested State, or the like, with respect to income not subject to the Agreement but covered by their respective conventions.
- defining individual categories of cases falling under 'the like' in accordance with the procedures of taxation applied by those States.

In a nutshell, Switzerland has accepted to introduce an exchange of information with the EU Member States in the case of tax fraud and the like, as defined under the laws of the requested State (i) on income covered by the agreement and (ii) on income not covered by the agreement but covered by their respective double taxation conventions. The like 'includes only offences with the same level of wrongfulness as is the case of tax fraud under the laws of the requested State' (Art. 10 par. 1 Savings Agreement).

*ii) Tax fraud and the like*    At the time of signing the Savings Agreement, international exchange of information in tax matters with Switzerland was only possible in the case of tax fraud ('escroquerie fiscale', 'Abgabebetrug'), as defined under Swiss Law. In particular, international judicial assistance was possible in cases of tax fraud, based on the Federal Law on International Mutual Assistance in Criminal Matters (IMAC).[357] In this context, tax fraud is defined under Art. 14 par. 2 of the

---

[357]    Federal Law of 20 March 1981, which entered into force on 1 January 1983.

Swiss Criminal Administrative Law.[358] According to a long series of Supreme Court cases, the concept of tax fraud in this context means tax avoidance of significant amounts when the taxpayer either uses forged or falsified documents or adopts a fraudulent conduct to deceive the tax administration.[359] A fraudulent behaviour of the taxpayer is often described as a so-called 'scheme of lies' ('Lügengebäude').

Article 26 of DTC with the United States of 1996 also provides for an exchange of information in the case of tax fraud and the like. As we have seen above, the concept of 'tax fraud' in this context is basically the same as the definition applied under IMAC.[360]

At the time of signing the Savings Agreement, the introduction of exchange of information rules in cases of tax fraud or the like could have been seen as an important development in favour of more global transparency. In the meantime, especially after the shift of March 2009, with the adoption of the global OECD standard, the rules of the Savings Agreement in this area have been superseded. As a matter of fact, since then, the DTC concluded by Switzerland have now introduced an exchange of information upon request which corresponds to the standard of foreseeable relevance and, contrary to the Savings Agreement, does not require a 'tax fraud or the like'. In addition, the political commitment of 6 May 2014 in favour of the OECD standard for automatic exchange of information will further modify the existing framework.[361] As soon as automatic exchange becomes the norm in the relationship between Switzerland and the EU, the rules of the Savings Agreement will simply become obsolete.

## 7. Extension of rules comparable to the EU Parent-Subsidiary and EU Interest and Royalty Directives

As we have seen, the Savings Agreement also encompasses rules comparable to the EU Parent-Subsidiary and the Interest and Royalty Directives. These rules form what we may call a sort of counterpart to the new unilateral obligations that Switzerland has accepted in the field of retention and exchange of information.

---

[358] Federal Law of 22 March 1974, on Criminal Administrative Law (CAL). Indeed, Art. 24 par. 1 of the IMAC Ordinance refers directly to Art. 14 par. 2 of the CAL.

[359] See for instance, Supreme Court judgment of 4 April 1989, ATF 125 II 250; 22 June 1984, ATF 110 Ib 246.

[360] See supra p. 41.

[361] See infra p. 184.

Without prejudice to the application of domestic or agreement-based provisions for the prevention of fraud or abuse in Switzerland and in Member States, *dividends* paid by subsidiary companies to parent companies shall not be subject to taxation in the source States where:

(i)     the parent has a direct minimum holding of 25 per cent of the capital of such a subsidiary for at least two years;
(ii)    one company is resident in an EU Member State and the other company is a resident of Switzerland;
(iii)   under any double taxation treaty with any third State, neither company is resident in that third State;
(iv)    both companies are subject to corporation tax without being exempted and both adopt the form of a limited company[362] (Art. 15 par. 1 Savings Agreement).

It should be noted that there are differences between Art. 15 par 1 of the Savings Agreement and the rules of the EU Parent-Subsidiary Directive, notably after the modification of the latter, which was adopted in December 2003[363] and entered into force on 1 January 2005. First, the Savings Agreement provides for a direct threshold of 25 per cent, while the new version of the EU Directive has reduced such threshold to 10 per cent. Second, the permanent establishment is not included in the Savings Agreement, contrary to the new version of the Directive. Third, by contrast to Art. 3 paras 1 and 2 of the EU Directive, there is no possibility of replacing the participation criteria by a voting right condition.

Under the Savings Agreement, both companies should adopt the form of a limited company. In footnote 10, the Swiss 'limited companies' include 'société anonyme, société à reponsabilité limitée et société en commandite par actions', but surprisingly not the 'société cooperative', which clearly qualifies in our view as a limited company. The list of companies in the EU Member States covered by the agreement is missing. At first glance, the list provided for in the Parent Subsidiary Directive (prior to modification) seems appropriate. In an interesting case of 18 October 2012, the Swiss Supreme Court confirmed that the cooperative limited liability company of Italian law should be included in

---

[362]   The term 'limited company' covers, as far as Switzerland is concerned, 'société anonyme, société à responsabilité limitée' and 'société en commandite par actions'.

[363]   See Council Directive 2003/123/EC of 23 December 2003 modifying Directive 90/435/CEE.

the list.[364] The reasoning of the SC is precisely based on the list of companies in the Annex to the EU Parent Subsidiary Directive.

Finally, the Savings Agreement does not provide for rules similar to Arts 6 and 7 of the EU Parent Subsidiary Directive.

When the conditions of Art. 15 par. 1 of the Savings Agreement are met, the source State shall not 'subject to taxation' the dividends paid by the subsidiary.[365] Should the subsidiary be a Swiss company, it implies that Switzerland may not levy its 35 per cent anticipatory tax (withholding tax) on the dividends paid. In addition, it implies, in our view that the current Swiss refund system is no longer possible. Provided the conditions are met, a direct application of the agreement would simply require for the Swiss withholding tax to be no longer levied.

Without prejudice to the application of domestic or agreement-based provisions for the prevention of fraud or abuse in Switzerland and in Member States, *interest and royalty* payments made between associated companies or their permanent establishment shall not be subject to taxation in the source States where:

(i) such companies are affiliated by a direct minimum holding of 25 per cent for at least two years or both are held with a third company which has directly a minimum holding of 25 per cent in the capital of the first company, and in the capital of the second company for at least two years;

(ii) where a company is resident or a permanent establishment is located in a Member State and the other company is resident or a permanent establishment is located in Switzerland;

(iii) under any double taxation treaty with any third State neither company is resident in that third State;

(iv) all companies are subject to corporation tax without being exempted in particular on interest and royalty payments and each adopts the form of a limited company[366] (Art. 15 par. 2 Savings Agreement).

---

[364] ATF 138 II 356.

[365] Estonia may however still, until 31 December 2008, tax dividends of subsidiary companies to Swiss parent companies, See Message of the Federal Council on the Bilateral Agreements II, October 1st, 2004, Federal Gazette ('Bundesblatt') 2004, p. 5593 ff, 5836.

[366] The term limited company covers, as far as Switzerland is concerned, 'société anonyme, société à responsabilité limité' and 'société en commandite par actions' (the société coopérative is not mentioned).

There also are differences between Art. 15 par 2 of the Savings Agreement and the rules of the Interest and Royalty Directive,[367] notably according to the proposed modification of 30 December 2003.[368] The threshold of 25 per cent is however the same. The main differences are: (i) the fact that, contrary to Art. 5 par. 1 of the Directive, there is no possibility to replace the participation criteria by a voting right criteria, and (ii) the restricted scope of the Savings Agreement, at least on the Swiss side, to specific companies in the form of a limited company.

When the conditions of Art. 15 par. 2 of the Savings Agreement are met, the source State cannot 'subject to taxation' the interest and royalty payments between associated companies and their permanent establishments.[369] Again, this implies that Switzerland may not levy any withholding tax on the interest and royalties paid by a Swiss limited liability company to an associated company (or permanent establishment) in a EU Member State.

## G. Assessment and Proposal for Changes

Based on Art. 18 EUSD, the Commission prepared a report to the Council, which was delivered on 9 September 2008.[370] It showed that the major part of revenue from the withholding tax in 2005 and 2006 came from Switzerland and Luxembourg, which accounted, respectively, for more than 45 per cent and 22 per cent of the total revenue. By contrast, the largest beneficiaries of the tax were Germany and Italy. The report emphasized that the EUSD has proven effective but recognized that the current coverage is not as wide as the ambitions expressed in the Council conclusions of 26 and 27 November 2000. In particular, it identified four issues. First, since the Directive only covers interest payments made for the immediate benefit of an individual, it could provide opportunities to circumvent the directive by interposing legal person or arrangement. Second, the definition of paying agent raised questions, in particular as far as the 'paying agent upon receipt' is concerned. Third, the definition

---

[367] Directive 2003/49 of 3 June 2003, which entered into force on 1 January 2004.

[368] The proposal of 30 December 2003 (COM [2003] 841 final) has not yet been adopted.

[369] Some States have a transitory period, see Message of the Federal Council p. 5837.

[370] Report from the Commission to the Council in accordance with Article 18 of Council Directive 2003/48/EC on taxation of savings income in the form of interest payments, 15 September 2008, COM (2008) 552 final.

of interest could be broadened so as to include innovative financial products or securities which are equivalent to debt claims. Other refinements could also be considered in relation to investment funds, i.e. undertakings for collective investment. Fourth, improvements are also desirable on procedural aspects.

This report was followed by a proposal for a new directive,[371] issued on 13 November 2008, which would aim at closing the loopholes identified in the report.[372] The proposal seeks to ensure the taxation of interest payments channeled through intermediate tax-exempted structures (such as trusts, foundations, offshore entities) by better identifying the effective beneficial owner of the interest.[373] Indeed, the EUSD does not cover payments made to legal entities and arrangements held by individuals, which can create opportunities to circumvent the Directive by interposing a legal person. The solution of the proposal would be to ask paying agents subject to money laundering obligations to use the information already available to them in order to identify the actual beneficial owner of a payment made to some legal persons or arrangements ('look-through' approach). This rule should apply to payments channeled through untaxed structures (also listed in Annex I) managed outside the EU.[374] For payments channeled through untaxed structures established in the EU (also listed in Annex III of the proposal), however, such intermediate structures will have to apply the provision of the EUSD upon receipt of the interest payment from any economic operator wherever established.[375] This would mean that the Directive would be applied by

> these structures – including legal arrangements such as certain kinds of trusts and partnerships – upon receipt of interest payments from any upstream economic operator, regardless of where this operator is established (inside or outside the EU), as long as the beneficial owner is an individual resident in another EU [Member State].[376]

In addition, the Commission proposes to broaden the scope of the Directive to innovative financial products and life insurance products,

---

[371] Proposal for a Council Directive amending Directive 2003/48/EC on taxation of service income in the form of interest payments, 13 November 2008, COM (2008) 727 final.
[372] Cosentino (2013), p. 300.
[373] Schröder (2012), p. 68 f.
[374] Schröder (2012), p. 68.
[375] Schröder (2012), p. 69.
[376] Directive Proposal, COM (2008) 727 final, p. 5.

which are comparable to debt claims. In the same vein, the Commission suggests applying the Directive to interest obtained through any kind of investment fund, regardless of its legal form or of an authorization under the UCITS Directive.

A second review of the EUSD and a report were published on 2 March 2012.[377] This report was more focused on the functioning and economic valuation of the EUSD.[378] It showed the use of offshore jurisdictions in order to circumvent the Directive by interposing intermediary entities. In addition, the necessity to broaden the scope of the Directive to sophisticated financial instruments comparable to debt-claims was again emphasized.

The international development toward global automatic exchange of information will however further continue to modify the scope and implementation of this directive. In fact, it appears that the recent global acceptance of automatic exchange of information as the new global standard requires a completely new analysis of the situation. As a consequence, the trend now is more to expand the scope of the EU Directive on administrative assistance (EUDAC) in line with the new OECD global standard on automatic exchange of information AEOI.[379] This could imply a potential repeal of the EUSD. As a consequence, the EU Commission would be concluding negotiations on new tax agreements with Switzerland, Andorra, Monaco, Lichtenstein and San Marino.

## III. THE DIRECTIVE ON ADMINISTRATIVE COOPERATION IN THE FIELD OF TAXATION

### A. Introduction

The Directive on administrative cooperation in the field of taxation (DAC) was adopted on 15 February 2011.[380] It is the result of a lengthy process, due in particular to political reservations of some Member States

---

[377] Report from the Commission to the Council in accordance with Article 18 of Council Directive 2003/48/EC on taxation of savings income in the form of interest payments, 2 March 2012, COM (2012) 65 final.

[378] Cosantino (2013), p. 301.

[379] See infra p. 118.

[380] Council Directive 2011/16/EU of 15 February 2011 on administrative cooperation in the field of taxation and repealing Directive 77/799/EEC, OJ L 64 of 11 March 2011, p. 1.

pertaining to the automatic exchange of information.[381] The Proposal for a DAC was in fact already published in 2009.[382]

The DAC repealed at the same time the old exchange of information Directive of 1977, concerning mutual assistance by the competent authorities in the field of direct taxation and taxation of insurance premiums (hereafter EID).[383] The EID was modified several times.[384] In particular, its scope was extended to cover VAT in 1979,[385] excise duties in 1992[386] and taxes on insurance premiums in 2003.[387] Since that time, the EID has focused only on mutual assistance in the field of direct taxes and insurance premiums, because VAT and excise taxes have been covered by separate legal instruments.[388] Despite further changes, the Directive 77/799, designed in a different world environment, did not match the new developments and needs in the field of administrative cooperation. Instead of a simple modification of this Directive, a new approach was necessary and the EID was repealed and replaced by a new instrument.

It is interesting to mention that the development of the exchange of information rules within the EU is also influenced by the various judgments of the ECJ, notably concerning the impact of the fundamental freedoms and the tax systems of the Member State.[389] In essence, by stating in a series of cases that a Member State cannot justify a discriminatory rule by the need to ensure the effectiveness of fiscal controls in cross border cases, the ECJ has pushed the Member State to make use of the existing instruments for exchange of information.[390]

---

[381]   Gabert (2011), p. 342.

[382]   COM (2009) 29.

[383]   Council Directive 77/799/EEC of 19 December 1977 concerning mutual assistance by the competent authorities of the Member States in the field of direct taxation and taxation of insurance premiums, OJ L 336 of 27 December 1977, p. 15.

[384]   See in this respect Muñoz Forner (2013), p. 263 f.

[385]   Council Directive 79/1070/EEC of 6 December 1979.

[386]   Council Directive 92/12/EEC of 25 February 1992.

[387]   Council Directive 2003/93/EC of 7 October 2003.

[388]   Schilcher/Spies (2013) p. 210.

[389]   Schilcher/Spies (2013) p. 323.

[390]   Terra/Wattel (2012) p. 418; in the same vein, Schilcher/Spies (2012), p. 323, who also refer to the tendency of the ECJ to require in cross-border cases that the taxpayers concerned provide sufficient information, before the Member State uses the Directive on exchange of information; see for example ECJ, 27 January 2009, C-318/07, *Persche*, ECR I-359; ECJ 10 February 2011, C-436/08 and C-437/08, *Haribo and Österreichische Salinen*, ECR I-305, par. 102.

In essence, the DAC has a broader scope and tends to implement, gradually, automatic exchange of information as of 1 January 2015. It also corresponds to the global standard on exchange of information and takes into account, notably, the recent changes of the OECD Model DTC (2005) and TIEA Model (2002). Contrary to the old EID, the DAC is not limited to assistance as regards 'assessment' but includes cooperation for the administration and enforcement concerning taxes covered by this instrument.[391] This however does not affect the rules on mutual assistance in criminal matters (Art. 1 par. 3 DAC). The new DAC also introduces time limits for the various types of exchanges of information. It appears that the lack of time limits under the old EID was one of the main weaknesses of the exchange of information process.[392]

The Member States have to implement the rules of the new Directive by 1 January 2013, except for automatic exchange of information, which will be implemented gradually, as of 1 January 2015.

## B. Scope

Under the general rule, the Member States must cooperate with each other with a view to exchanging information that is *foreseeably relevant* to the administration and enforcement of the domestic laws of the Member States (Art. 1 par. 1 DAC). This rule is also found in Article 26 par. 1 OECD Model DTC. Therefore, the standard of foreseeable relevance is intended to provide for exchange of information in tax matters to the widest possible extent, but at the same time to clarify that Member States are not allowed to engage in 'fishing expeditions.[393]

The DAC applies to all taxes of any kind levied by, or on behalf of, a Member State or the Member State's territorial or administrative subdivisions, including local authorities (Art. 2 par. 1 DAC). However, according to an *exhaustive* list,[394] the Directive does not apply to VAT, customs duties and excises taxes covered by other EU legislation on administrative cooperation between Member States, as well as social security contributions (Art. 2 par. 2 DAC). The DAC does not include fees for certificates and other public documents and dues of a contractual nature (Art. 2 par. 3 DAC). In any event, the scope of application is broader than the old EID. In addition to income and capital taxes, the

---

[391]    Terra/Wattel (2012), p. 420.
[392]    Muñoz Forner (2013), p. 277.
[393]    DAC recital par. 9.
[394]    Schilcher/Spies (2013), p. 211.

DAC covers, notably inheritance taxes, real estate transfer taxes, car taxes and environmental taxes.[395]

The personal scope is also very broad. Indeed, according to Art. 3 par. 11 DAC, the term person means a natural or a legal person, including, where the legislation in force so provides, an association of persons, or any other legal arrangements regardless of whether it has legal personality, which are subject to taxes covered by the Directive. It can therefore be admitted that information pertaining to non-residents of the EU, regardless of their nationality, may be exchanged as long as the information is foreseeably relevant to taxes in the scope of the DAC.[396] However, automatic exchange of information, as regulated by Art. 8 DAC, only applies to information concerning residents of a Member State.[397]

The Member States have to implement the Directive with effect from 1 January 2013 (Art. 29). The DAC will apply immediately to all pending cases. However, according to Art. 18 par. 3, Member States may refuse the transmission of requested information where such information concerns taxable periods prior to 1 January 2011 and where the transmission of such information could have been refused on the basis of Art. 8 par. 1 DAC if it had been requested before 11 March 2011. In other words, countries which applied domestic bank secrecy rules preventing the disclosure of information may deny requests concerning bank information prior to 1 January 2011.[398] Otherwise, for cases not specifically regulated, requests may relate to a taxable period, which predates the entry into force of the Directive, as long as there are no rules in the DAC on the taxable period to which the request of information has to be related.[399]

## C. Organization

The Member States have to name a 'competent authority' for the purpose of the Directive (DAC). This competent authority has then to designate a single central liaison office, which will be responsible for cooperation under the DAC and notably contact with other Member States (Art. 4 par. 2 DAC). The same organization system exists for VAT and for the

---

[395]  Schilcher/Spies (2013), p. 212.
[396]  Muñoz Forner (2013), p. 265.
[397]  Schilcher/Spies (2013), p. 210.
[398]  Muñoz Forner (2013), p. 266.
[399]  Schilcher/Spies (2013), p. 213.

Directive for the assistance in recovery of claims.[400] In addition, the Member State may also designate a liaison department and competent officials (Art. 4 par. 3 DAC). The DAC, as a consequence, provides for a direct communication between two different offices of different Member States.[401] If the liaison office or competent officials are in direct contact with authorities of different Member States, they have to inform the central liaison office (Art. 4 par. 6 DAC).[402]

## D.   Forms of Administrative Assistance

### 1.   In general

The Directive provides for three methods of exchange of information, upon request, spontaneous or automatic. There is no hierarchy among these methods and each of them corresponds to a different need. While information upon request and spontaneous exchange concern a specific situation, automatic exchange is more abstract.[403]

For the exchange of information process, the use of standard forms and computerized formats is required (Art. 20 DAC). In particular, requests for information, pursuant to Art. 5, and their replies, or refusal, pursuant to Art. 7, will as far as possible be sent using standard forms (Art. 20 par. 1 DAC). The same is true for spontaneous information (Art. 20 par. 3 DAC). Automatic exchange of information will be done using a computerized format (Art. 20 par. 4 DAC). The information communicated pursuant to this Directive will be provided, as far as possible, by electronic means using the CCN Network (Art. 21 DAC).

### 2.   Exchange of information upon request

Under Art. 5 DAC, the requested authority must communicate to the requesting authority any information, referred to in Art. 1 par. 1, that it has in its possession or that it obtains as a result of administrative enquiries. Based on the requirements of Art. 1 par. 1 DAC, the request must meet the standard of foreseeable relevance, which forbids in particular 'fishing expeditions'.

To that end, according to Art. 20 par. 2 DAC, the standard form of the request must contain sufficient information, i.e.: a) the identity of the person under examination, and b) the tax purpose for which the information is sought. To the extent known, and in line with international

---

[400]   Gabert (2011), p. 342.
[401]   Schilcher/Spies (2013), p. 213; Gabert (2011), p. 343.
[402]   Schilcher/Spies (2013), p. 214.
[403]   Gabert (2011), p. 343.

developments, the requesting authority may provide the name and address of any person believed to be in possession of the requested information as well as any element that may facilitate the collection of information by the requested authority (Art. 20 par. 2 DAC). This rule corresponds to the OECD standard under Art. 26 OECD MTC for exchange of information upon request.

If these conditions are met, the requested State is obliged to answer, unless it can rely on a ground for refusal.[404] The requested authority, in order to obtain the requested information, must follow the same procedures as it would when acting on its own initiative or at the request of another authority in its own State (Art. 6 par. 3 DAC). The requested State must carry out its enquiries even if it may not need such information for its tax purposes (Art. 18 par. 1 DAC). It must also communicate original documents provided that this rule is not contrary to its domestic provisions (Art. 6 par. 3 DAC).

The requested authority shall provide the information as quickly as possible, but at least no later than six months from the date of receipt of the request (Art. 7 par. 1 DAC). However, when the information is already in the possession of the requested authority, the *time limit* is reduced to two months.

### 3. Spontaneous exchange of information

Spontaneous exchange of information takes place without a request of another State. It is a form of mutual administrative collaboration between states, under which they help one another to combat tax fraud or evasion without the need for a formal request.[405] Spontaneous information exchange can be either mandatory or voluntary.[406]

According to Art. 9 par. 1 DAC, a Member State *must* communicate the information, without prior request, in five circumstances. It should be noted that this provision corresponds in essence to the rules of the old EID, for which the ECJ has already clarified some aspects, and notably the fact that Art. 9 par. 1 entails an obligation to communicate when the conditions are met.[407] The five circumstances are the following:

a) There may be grounds for supposing that there may be 'a loss of tax' in the other Member State. This obligation exists when there is

---

[404]  Schilcher/Spies (2013), p. 214; see infra p. 115.
[405]  Muñoz Forner (2011), p. 268.
[406]  Terra/Wattel (2012), p. 424.
[407]  Schilcher/Spies (2013), p. 216; ECJ, 13 April 2000, Case C-420/98 (W.N. v. Staatssecretaris fan Financien), 2000 ECR I-2847, par. 13.

a 'reasonable expectation' without a need for the information to be certain or proven.[408] A loss of tax means an 'unjustified savings of tax' in another Member State.[409]

b)    A person liable to tax obtains a reduction or exemption, which would give rise to an increase of tax or liability in another Member State.

c)    Business dealings between taxpayers of two Member States are conducted through one or more countries in such a way that a saving of tax may result in one or the other Member State or in both. This rule may apply for instance in case of the use of treaty shopping through artificial holding structures or conduit entities.

d)    A competent authority of a Member State has grounds for supposing that a saving of tax may result from artificial transfers of profits within a group of enterprises. This will typically be the case for transfer pricing cases, such as an initial adjustment in one Member State for breaches of arm's length conditions between related enterprises.

e)    Information forwarded to one Member State has enabled it to obtain new information, which may be relevant in assessing liability in the forwarding Member State.

In addition, Member States *may* communicate information voluntarily and spontaneously, which may be useful to the other Member States (Art. 9 par. 2 DAC).

There is a time limit for the exchange. According to Art. 10 par. 1, the Member State must forward the information referred to in Art. 9 par. 1 DAC to the competent authorities of the Member States concerned as quickly as possible, but no later than one month after it becomes available (Art. 10 par. 1 DAC).

### 4.  Automatic exchange of information

The introduction of a mandatory automatic exchange is a major development, even though it came gradually and only for specific items of income. In any event, it already goes beyond the previous instruments already in force. Indeed, under the old EID automatic exchange of

---

[408]  Terra/Wattel (2012), p. 424; ECJ, 13 April 2000, Case C-420/98 (W.N. v. Staatssecretaris fan Financien), 2000 ECR I-2847, paras 22–24.

[409]  ECJ, 13 April 2000, Case C-420/98 (W.N. v. Staatssecretaris fan Financien), 2000 ECR I-2847, paras 22–24.

information was allowed, but only after bilateral (or multilateral) consult-ations between the Member State and in specific cases.[410] There are currently several bilateral agreements on automatic exchange of infor-mation on various types of income and they differ considerably from each other.[411] In addition, the EUSD also provides for an automatic exchange of information (subject to the transitory period for Austria and Luxembourg) but it only covers interests on savings income.[412]

The new DAC introduces a systematic communication of information, without prior request, at pre-established regular intervals for specific categories of income, phased over a defined period of time.[413] As from 1 January 2015, the competent authority of each Member State must communicate information that is available concerning residents in that other Member State in the following *five categories* of income and capital:[414] income from employment, director's fees, life insurance prod-ucts not covered by other EU legal instruments on exchange of infor-mation, pensions, and ownership and income from immovable property.

The information has to be '*available*', which implies that it has to be retrievable in the tax files following the domestic rules for gathering information of the Member State communicating the information (Art. 3 par. 9 DAC).[415] According to commentators, this condition may lead to significant imbalances between the Member States.[416] The Member States must inform the Commission, before 1 January 2014, of the category in respect of which they have information available, and of any changes thereto (Art. 8 par. 2 DAC). In addition, Member States have to indicate to the competent authority if they do not want to receive information regarding in one or all of these categories or that they do not wish to receive information not exceeding a certain threshold (Art. 8 par. 3 DAC). In this case, other Member States are under no obligation to provide this information automatically to this State.[417] In order to avoid 'free-riding', the DAC also includes a provision which motivates States to make some categories available – if a State has no information

---

410 Terra/Wattel (2012), p. 424.
411 Terra/Wattel (2012), p. 424.
412 See supra p. 83.
413 Schilcher/Spies (2013), p. 215.
414 See Art. 29 second sentence DAC.
415 Schilcher/Spies (2013), p. 215.
416 Schilcher/Spies (2013), p. 215; Terra/Wattel (2012), p. 831.
417 Schilcher/Spies (2013), p. 216.

available on any category of income or capital in its tax file, it will be considered to not wish to receive any information.[418]

The European Parliament, in a resolution of 10 February 2010, proposed to also include dividends, capital gains and royalties in the list.[419] This proposal was not accepted, in particular because it would have overruled the EUSD.[420] This could however change in a further step, following the report and the procedure designed in Art. 8 par. 5 DAC. It is more than probable that automatic exchange will be extended to dividends, capital gains and royalties (see Art. 8 par. 5 lit. b DAC). Indeed, on 12 June 2013, the EU Commission delivered a new proposal to expand the scope of automatic exchange of information under the DAC, to cover dividends, capital gains, any other income generated with respect to the assets held in a financial account, any amount with respect to which a financial institution is the obligor or debtor, including any redemption payments and account balance.[421]

The automatic exchange of information will be sent using a standard computerised format and based on the existing format used for the EUSD (Art. 20 par. 4). The communication of information will take place at least once a year, within six months following the end of the tax year of the Member State (Art. 8 par. 6 DAC).

## 5. Other forms of assistance

The Directive also provides for additional forms of assistance, such as (i) the presence of foreign officials, (ii) simultaneous control, (iii) notification of foreign decisions, or (iv) feedback.

To allow *foreign officials* to assist the investigations of the requesting State may be efficient because they usually have a better knowledge of 'what they are looking for' in the requested State.[422] The DAC opens the door for such presence, but with the agreement of the concerned Member States. Indeed, according to Art. 11 DAC, by agreement between the requesting authority and the requested authority, and in accordance with the arrangements laid down by the latter, foreign officials may be present in administrative offices of the requested Member State or during

---

[418]   Ibid.

[419]   OJ C 341 E/90, 16 December 2010; Gabert (2011), p. 343; Muñoz Forner (2013), p. 269.

[420]   Muñoz Forner (2013), p. 269.

[421]   Proposal for a Council Directive amending Directive 2011/16/EU as regards mandatory automatic exchange of information in the field of taxation, COM (2013) 348 final.

[422]   Terra/Wattel (2012), p. 425.

administrative enquiries carried out in the territory of the requested Member State (Art 11 par DAC). In addition, the foreign official of the requesting authority may interview individuals and examine records, as long as it is allowed under the legislation of the requested Member State (Art. 11 par. 2 DAC). A refusal by the person under investigation to submit to the inspection measures of the foreign official duly authorized will be treated as if the refusal were committed in respect of the national authorities (national treatment) (Art. 11 par. 2, second sentence, DAC).[423]

The Directive also provides for *simultaneous control*, agreed by two or more Member States, in their own territory, of one or more persons of common or complementary interest to them, with a view to exchanging information thus obtained (Art. 12 par. 1 DAC). The Member States are free to participate or not in the simultaneous control but it has to explain the reason of its refusal (Art. 12 par. 3 DAC). Each Member State can invite identified independent persons who should be the subject of a simultaneous control and notify the Member States concerned of any cases for which they propose a simultaneous control and give reason for this choice (Art. 12 par. 2 DAC).

Many Member States require notification to taxpayers of all relevant tax decisions. As taxpayers become more and more mobile, it can be difficult for Member States to notify their decisions to a specific taxpayer.[424] Therefore, Art. 13 DAC introduces national treatment of Member States' decisions and instruments on taxes covered by the Directive.[425] At the request of a Member State, the requested Member State shall notify the addressee within its territory of any instrument or decisions from the requesting Member State, as if it were its own decision.[426] Standard forms are provided for in the DAC (Art. 20 par. 3).

Where a Member State has provided information, pursuant to Art. 5 or 9, it may ask the requested State to send *feedback* (Art. 14 par. 1 DAC). Feedback must however be in accordance with the domestic rules on tax secrecy and data protection. Feedback for automatic exchange of information shall be sent once a year in accordance with the practical arrangements agreed upon bilaterally (Art. 14 par. 2 DAC).

Finally, Member States, together with the Commission, will examine and evaluate the cooperation, and *share best practices* and experience (Art. 15 DAC).

---

[423]  Ibid.
[424]  Terra/Wattel (2012), p. 426; Muñoz Forner (2013), p. 271.
[425]  Ibid.
[426]  Terra/Wattel (2012), p. 426.

## E. Secrecy Clause

Under Art. 16 par. 1 DAC, information or communications are covered by the obligation of official secrecy and enjoy the protection under the national law of the requesting Member State (national treatment). Exchange of information according to the DAC is also subject to the provisions implementing Directive 96/46/EC on data protection (Art. 25 DAC).

Contrary to the old EID, the information may however be used for a wide range of purposes.[427] This extension is also in line with Art. 26 par 2 OECD Model DTC.[428] In particular, Member States may use the information for the following purposes:

- For the administration and enforcement of the domestic laws of the Member States concerning taxes covered by the Directive.
- For the assessment and enforcement of other taxes and duties covered by the Recovery Assistance Directive (RAD).[429] This list includes VAT, excise duties and customs duties.
- For the assessment and enforcement of compulsory social security contributions.
- For judicial and administrative proceedings that may involve penalties, initiated as a result of infringements of tax law; the provisions governing the rights of defendants and witnesses in such proceedings must however be respected (Art. 16 par. 1, third sentence, DAC).
- For other purposes for which the use of the information is allowed under par. 1, to the extent that (i) this is possible under the law of the requesting Member State and (ii) the requested State gives its permission. This rule is in line with Art. 26 par. 2 OECD Model DTC. The requested State is obliged to approve the exchange if the information can be used for similar purposes under its domestic rules (Art. 16 par. 2 DAC).
- The requesting State may also forward the information to a third Member State, provided this transmission is in accordance with the rules and procedures laid down in the DAC. The Member State of

---

[427] Ibid.

[428] Muñoz Forner (2013), p. 275.

[429] Council Directive 2010/24/EU of 16 March 201 concerning mutual assistance for the recovery of claims relating to taxes, duties and other measures, OJ L 84/1, 31.3.2010.

origin of the information may oppose such sharing within ten working days of receipt of the communication (Art. 16 par. 3 DAC).

- Finally the information may also be forwarded to a third *non-*Member State under the conditions of Art. 24. In particular, the Member State of origin of the information must give its consent and the receiving non Member State has to give an undertaking that it is prepared to reciprocate in exchanging information (Art. 24 par. 2 DAC).[430]

## F. Limits

The DAC provides grounds for the refusal to provide information, which, in accordance with the recent developments in the global standard for exchange of information, are stricter than the old EID.[431] In particular, contrary to the old Directive, the existence of domestic banking secrecy is no longer a ground for refusal of information (see Art. 18 par. 2 DAC).

First, a Member State will supply information, referred to in Art. 5, provided that the requesting State has exhausted the usual sources of information which it could have used in the circumstances for obtaining the information, without running the risk of jeopardizing the achievement of its objectives (Art. 17 par. 1 DAC). This corresponds to the principle of *subsidiarity*, also contained in Art. 26 par. 1 of the OECD Model DTC and Art. 5 par. 5 lit. g TIEA Model.[432]

Second, a Member State is not obliged to carry out enquiries or to communicate information, if this would be contrary to its *own legislation* (Art. 17 par. 2 DAC). A similar rule existed under Art. 8 par. 1 of the old EID and served as a legal basis for countries, such as Luxembourg or Austria, to refuse the supply of information based on domestic bank secrecy rules.[433] As we have seen, bank secrecy or information related to ownership of interest, are no longer grounds for refusal, according to Art. 18 par. 2 DAC, which corresponds to the OECD standard of Art. 26 par. 5 OECD Model DTC.

Third, according to the principle of *reciprocity*, a requested Member State may decline to provide information where the requesting Member State is unable, for legal reasons, to provide similar information (Art. 17 par. 3 DAC). In other words, a Member State cannot take advantage of

---

[430] Schilcher/Spies (2013), p. 223.
[431] Gabert (2011), p. 345; Terra/Wattel (2012), p. 427.
[432] Muñoz Forner (2012), p. 272.
[433] Terra/Wattel (2012), p. 428.

the wider system of exchange of information of another Member State.[434] As a consequence, a Member State is not obliged to give banking information to Luxembourg or Austria, concerning tax years prior to 2011 (Art. 18 par. 3).[435]

Fourth, supply of information may be refused where it would lead to the disclosure of a commercial, industrial or professional secret or of a commercial process, or of information whose disclosure would be contrary to public policy (Art. 17 par 4 DAC). This rule corresponds to Art. 26 par. 3 OECD DTC.

## G.   Legal Protection of Taxpayers

The rules of legal protection of taxpayers remain a matter of domestic law, as referred to under Art. 16 par. 1 DAC. It follows that, apart from the secrecy clause of that paragraph and the data protection rules of Art. 25 DAC, the persons involved in the exchange of information process have to rely on domestic legislation for their potential rights (notification, right to be heard, right to appeal). The level of protection may also vary considerably among Member States in this respect.

## H.   Most Favoured Nation Clause

An interesting 'most favoured nation (MFN)' clause is granted under Art. 19 DAC. According to this rule, where a Member State provides for a wider cooperation than that granted under the DAC, that Member State may not refuse to provide such wider cooperation to any other Member State wishing to enter into such mutual wider cooperation with that Member State (Art. 19 DAC). This clause is however not applicable within the EU: if two Member States decide to cooperate more extensively, they are not obliged to grant the same to all other Member States.[436]

This MFN could have an important impact on future enhanced cooperation among Member States. Indeed, the rules of the US FATCA are developing rapidly, in particular under the new form of Intergovernmental Agreements (IGA), which introduced a form of reciprocal automatic exchange of information between countries of the world and the United States.[437] When a Member State, such as Luxembourg or

---

[434]   Ibid.
[435]   Terra/Wattel (2012), p. 428; Schilcher/Spies (2013), p. 220.
[436]   Schilcher/Spies (2013), p. 216; Terra/Wattel (2012), p. 428.
[437]   See infra p. 156 ff.

Austria, enters into an IGA with an extended exchange of information, that country should not be in a position to refuse to cooperate with another Member State on similar grounds.[438] In other words, the MFN clause includes a potential for constant improvement of the existing exchange of information rules contained in the Directive. FATCA, with all the IGAs concluded around the world, is in fact accelerating the movement toward a more global automatic exchange of information among Member States.

### I. Coordination

Many different international instruments in the area of international assistance coexist, alongside the DAC, and the question arises as to which is applicable in a particular case.

In fact, the DAC may be characterized as a 'minimum standard' between EU Member States.[439] This rule is confirmed by Art. 1 par. 3 DAC, according to which provisions with a broader scope of mutual assistance than the DAC remain applicable. It follows that Member States are free to choose the most favourable instrument applicable in a particular case. So far the DAC should often prevail, at least under the current rules. Indeed, Art. 26 OECD Model DTC provides for various types of exchange of information but does not include a compulsory automatic exchange. In addition, it includes comparable grounds for refusal to the DAC. TIEAs, as we have seen, generally only include exchange of information upon request. The CMAAT is comparable to the DAC but requires a specific bilateral arrangement between the Contracting States for automatic exchange of information.[440] In cases where such a bilateral arrangement exists, we could however imagine broader rules of exchange of information, for example on a broader scale of income categories and without the phasing of entering into force of the rules. Accordingly, such a bilateral agreement would not be affected by the DAC and would be valid (Art. 1 par. 3 DAC).

A Member State, choosing to exchange information on a wider scale than the DAC with another Member State, is however not obliged to apply the same rules with another Member State because the most favoured nation clause does not apply in EU internal relations.[441] The situation would however be different with the entry into force of bilateral

---

[438]  Muñoz Forner (2011), p. 273.
[439]  Schilcher/Spies (2013), p. 225; Terra/Wattel (2012), p. 419.
[440]  See also Schilcher/Spies (2013), p. 225.
[441]  Schilcher/Spies (2013), p. 225.

IGAs, implementing FATCA, concluded by an EU Member State with a third country.[442]

The rules of the Savings Directive, which provide, subject to the transitory regime for Austria and Luxembourg, for an automatic exchange of information between Member States on interest on savings of individuals prevails over the rule of the DAC, as a *lex specialis*.[443]

### J.    Evolution of the DAC towards the Global OECD Standard of Automatic Exchange of Information

The global acceptance of automatic exchange of information as the new global standard of exchange of information necessitates a new overall coordination and assessment of the instruments of exchange of information in EU law. These changes are going in the direction of an extension of the scope of the DAC, on the one hand, and the repeal of the EUSD, on the other hand. During its meeting of 14 October 2014, the EU Council agreed to implement within the EU the new global standard on AEOI developed by the OECD and endorsed by the G20. As a consequence, the EU Council agreed on a draft directive extending the scope of the mandatory automatic exchange of information, such as interest, dividends and other income, as well as account balances and sales proceeds from financial assets.[444] This proposal would thus amend the DAC and bring it in line with the OECD AEOI standard.

In this respect, the EU Commission has committed to concluding negotiations on new tax agreements with Switzerland, Andorra, Monaco, Lichtenstein and San Marino before the end of this year.

## IV.  THE DIRECTIVE CONCERNING MUTUAL ASSISTANCE FOR THE RECOVERY OF CLAIMS

### A.  Introduction

With globalization and freedom of movement, the need for an efficient system of recovery of tax claims became more and more pressing. Because of taxpayer mobility, Member States had difficulty recovering taxes from debtors, who could easily move outside their territory to

---

[442]   See supra p. 157.
[443]   Schilcher/Spies (2013), p. 226.
[444]   EU Council, Press release of 14 October 2014.

escape recovery procedures.[445] An old Directive on the recovery of claims from operations forming part of the system of financing the European Agricultural Guidance and Guarantee Fund, and of agricultural levies and customs duties was adopted in 1976.[446] This instrument was then modified, first in 1979, to include VAT[447] and excise,[448] and second in 2001 to cover direct taxes.[449] This Directive, including its various amendments, was further codified by a Directive of 2008.[450] These developments were still not sufficient to follow the growing and increasing capital and taxpayer's mobility.

Therefore, instead of amending the existing rules again, a new Directive on mutual assistance for the recovery of tax claims (DRC) was agreed upon on 16 March 2010 and had to be applied from 1 January 2012. In essence, the new Directive extends the scope of mutual assistance for recovery of claims relating to taxes not yet covered by the old Directive and introduces new assistance tools, in particular a new European uniform instrument, in order to make recovery more efficient. On 18 November 2011, the Commission issued an implementing Regulation for the application of the recovery Directive, including, in annexes, a uniform enforcement instrument and a uniform notification form.[451]

It should be noted that, in a similar way to exchange of information in tax matters, the ECJ has also indirectly favoured a more extensive use of cross-border instruments dealing with the collection of taxes between Member States.[452] In fact, according to the ECJ's case law, a discriminatory tax regime cannot as such be justified by the need to safeguard the

---

[445]   Terra/Wattel (2012), p. 429.

[446]   Council Directive 76/308/EEC of 15 March 1976, OJ L 73 of 19 March 1976, p. 18.

[447]   Council Directive 79/1071/EEC of 6 December 1979 amending Directive 76/308/EEC, OJ L 331 of 27 December 1979, p. 10.

[448]   Council Directive 92/108/EEC of 14 December 1992.

[449]   Council Directive 2001/44/EEC of 15 June 2001 amending Directive 76/308/EEC on mutual assistance, OJ L 175 of 28 June 2001, p. 17; Terra/Wattel (2012), p. 429.

[450]   Council Directive 2008/55/EC of 26 May 2008 on mutual assistance for the recovery of claims relating to certain levies, duties, taxes and other measures, OJ L 150, 10.6.2008, p. 28.

[451]   Commission Implementing Regulation No 1189/2011 of 18 November 2011 laying down detailed rules in relation to certain provisions of Council Directive 2010/24/EU concerning mutual assistance for the recovery of claims relating to taxes, duties and other measures, OJ L 302, 19 November 2011, p. 16.

[452]   See supra p. 105.

recovery of tax claims, because the Directive on collection of taxes offers assistance precisely in cross-border situations.[453]

The DRC appears to be the 'most important' legal instrument providing mutual recovery assistance in the EU.[454] In some respects, it appears more efficient than both Art. 27 of the OECD Model DTC and the CoE/OECD CMAAT because it provides for a *uniform instrument* opening the request for collection of tax claims in the requested State.[455] In other aspects, however, the CMAAT is broader than the EU instrument. In particular, the former allows assistance with regard to older claims (up to 15 years), while the latter does not compel Member States to grant assistance for claims below a certain threshold or for claims that are more than five (or ten) years old.[456]

It should be noted that in many aspects, the DRC is coordinated with the new DAC. In particular, when they address similar issues (such as organization, definitions, limitations, secrecy rules, etc.) the two Directives are aligned.[457] We will therefore refer to the previous explanations on corresponding rules.

## B. Scope

The Directive applies to *claims* relating to: a) all taxes and duties of any kind levied by or on behalf of a Member State or its territorial or administrative subdivisions, including the local authorities, or on behalf of the Union; b) refunds, interventions and other measures forming part of the EU agricultural system; c) levies and duties provided under the common sugar market organization (Art. 2 DRC).

It follows that the *material* scope of the Directive is very broad. It includes: a) administrative penalties, fines, fees and surcharges; b) fees for certificates; c) interest and costs relating to the claims for which mutual assistance may be requested (Art. 2 par. 2 DRC). However, the Directive does not apply to compulsory social security contributions, fees not referred to in par. 2, dues of contractual nature or to criminal penalties imposed on the basis of a public prosecution or other criminal penalties not covered by Art. 2 lit. a (Art. 2 par. 3 DRC).

---

[453]   See Schilcher/Spies (2013), p. 234, with references to ECJ of 6 October 2011, C-493/09, Commission v. Portugal, par. 49.

[454]   De Troyer (2014), p. 135.

[455]   De Troyer (2014), p. 136.

[456]   Ibid.

[457]   Terra/Wattel (2012), p. 430.

The definition of *persons* covered by the DRC corresponds to the DAC (Art. 3 par. 11 DAC). It means that Member States may ask for assistance against any debtors, and not only taxpayers.[458] In the case of spontaneous exchange, provided for by Art. 6 DRC, the scope is however limited to information concerning residents of a Member State.[459]

The DRC entered into force on 1 January 2012. All requests made after this date are therefore based on the new Directive. It appears that, absent any specific rule on the relevant taxable period, the date of the tax year to which the request relates is immaterial.[460]

## C. Organization

The rules correspond to the organization system of the DAC.[461] Member States have to name a 'competent authority' for the purpose of the Directive (Art. 4 DRC). This competent authority has then to designate a single central liaison office, which will be responsible for the cooperation under the DRC (Art. 4 par. 2 DRC). In addition, the Member State may also designate liaison departments (Art. 4 par. 3 DRC).

## D. Forms of Assistance

There are four types of assistance in the recovery of claims: exchange of information, notification to the addressee, recovery of tax claims, and precautionary measures.

### 1. Exchange of information
First, the Directive provides for a mandatory exchange upon request of information foreseeably relevant to the applicant authority in the recovery of claims (Art. 5 DRC). For that purpose, the requested authority must arrange for the carrying-out of any necessary administrative enquiries in order to obtain the information. The standard of 'foreseeable relevance' corresponds to the OECD standard of Art. 26 Model DTC.

Second, the Directive also introduces an exchange of information without prior request, where refunds of taxes or duties, other than VAT, relate to a person established or resident in another Member State (Art. 6 DRC). In that case, the Member State from which the refund is to be

---

[458]   See De Troyer (2014), p. 137, who had already argued in this sense under the old Directive.
[459]   Schilcher/Spies (2013), p. 228.
[460]   Ibid.
[461]   Gabert (2011), p. 342.

made may inform the Member State of the establishment or residence of the upcoming refund (Art. 6 DRC). This rule is in fact a spontaneous form of exchange of information, which creates a legal basis for more extensive information on a case-by-case basis.[462] According to Schilcher and Spies, the compulsory spontaneous exchange of information rules provided for by Art. 9 par. 1 DAC should take precedence over the discretionary power granted by Art. 6 DRC ('may').[463]

Third, similar to the DAC, foreign officials may be authorized, by agreement between the applicant authority and the requested authority, to be present in the administrative offices of the requested Member State, to participate in the enquiries, or to assist during court proceedings of that Member State (Art. 7 DRC).

## 2.   Assistance for the notification of documents

At the request of the applicant authority, the requested Member State must notify the addressee of all documents, including those of a judicial nature, which emanate from the applicant Member State and relate to tax claims or its recovery (Art. 8 DRC).

The notification will be effected in accordance with the national laws, regulations and administrative practices in force in the requested Member States (Art. 9 par. 1 DRC). The request must be accompanied by a standard form, which includes information on the name, address of the addressee, purpose of the notification and a description of the attached documents (Art. 8 second sentence, DRC). According to the subsidiarity principle, the request for notification should be made only when the applicant State is unable to notify of the document in accordance with the rules of notification in the applicant State or when this notification would give rise to disproportionate difficulties (Art. 8 par. 2 DRC). In addition, Member States may notify of any document directly by registered mail or electronically to a person within the territory of another Member State (Art. 9 par. 2 DRC).

## 3.   Assistance for recovery

*i)  The request*   Upon request, the requested Member State will recover the claims, which are the subject of an instrument permitting enforcement in the applicant Member State (Art. 10 DRC). The request will be accompanied by a uniform instrument, which reflects the substantial contents of the initial instrument permitting enforcement, and constitutes

---

[462]   Vascega/Van Thiel (2010), p. 235.
[463]   Schilcher/Spies (2013), p. 229.

the sole basis for the recovery and precautionary measures in the requested Member State (Art. 12 par. 1 DRC). As a consequence, it may not be subject to any act of recognition, supplementation or replacement in the requested Member State (Art. 12 par DRC).

*ii) The execution of the request* The requested State will execute the request of recovery according to its own rules, as if it were a claim of its own (national treatment) (Art. 13 par. 1 DRC). The requested Member State will remit to the applicant State the amounts recovered with respect to the claim – including interest according to paras 3 and 4 (Art. 13 par. 5 DRC). It can seek to recover and retain from the persons involved the costs incurred linked to the recovery (Art. 20 par. 1 DRC).

## 4. Precautionary measures
At the request of the applicant authority, the requested Member State must take precautionary measures, if allowed by its national law, to ensure recovery when a claim or instrument permitting enforcement in the applicant Member State is contested at the time of the request, or where the claim is not yet the subject of an instrument permitting enforcement, in so far as precautionary measures are also possible, in similar situations, under the national law of the applicant State (Art. 16 DRC).

The new DRC reinforces the efficiency of the precautionary measures because it does not require any more that the request should be a 'reasoned request' (according to Art. 13 of Directive 2008/55/EEC).[464] In addition, the documents permitting precautionary measures, attached to the request, are not subject to any act of recognition, supplementation or replacement in the requested State (Art. 16 par. 1, second sentence, DRC).

## E.  Disputes

Disputes concerning the claim, the initial instrument permitting enforcement, the uniform enforcement instrument, or of a notification made by the requesting Member State, fall within the competence of the applicant (requesting) Member State (Art. 16 par. DRC). However, disputes concerning the enforcement measures taken in the requested Member

---

[464] Lao (2013), p. 316.

State or the validity of the notification of that State are to be brought before the competent body (courts) of that Member State (Art. 16 par. 2 DRC).

Along the same line, in the *Kyrian* case, which concerned Directive 76/308/EEC of 15 March 1976, as amended by Directive 2001/44/EC of 15 June 2001, the ECJ held that Art. 12 par. 3 of that Directive,

> must be interpreted as meaning that the courts of the Member States where the requested story is situated do not, in principle, have jurisdiction to review the enforceability of an instrument permitting enforcement. Conversely, where a court of that Member State hears a claim against the validity or correctness of the enforcement measures, such as the notification of the instrument permitting enforcement, that court has the power to review those measures were correctly effected in accordance with the laws and regulations of that Member State.[465]

Where a claim or instruments according to par. 1 has been brought before the competent body (court) of the applicant Member State, that State must inform the requested Member State and indicate the extent to which the claim is not contested (Art. 14 par. 4 DRC). As soon as it has received the information, the requested Member State will *suspend* the enforcement unless the applicant Member State requests otherwise, following the rules of par. 3, subparagraph 3 (Art. 14 par. 4 DRC). It means that the requesting Member State has to justify still asking the requested Member State to recover the contested claim, and be ready to be liable for reimbursing any sums recovered and compensation due, should the contestation become subsequently favourable to the debtor (Art. 14 par. 4, subparagraph 3 DRC).

### F. Limits

In principle, when the conditions are met, the requested Member State is obliged to implement assistance in recovery. In particular, the new DRC confirms in accordance with the international standard, that banking secrecy is no longer an obstacle for the assistance. However, the requested Member State is not obliged to *supply information* (Art. 5 DRC):

a)   which it would not be able to obtain for the purpose of recovering similar claims arising in the requested Member State

---

[465]   ECJ, 14 January 2010, C-233/08, *Milan Kyrian* (2010) ECR-I-00177, par. 64; Lao (2013), p. 323.

b)   Which would disclose any commercial, industrial or professional secret. However, this rule cannot be construed that a requested Member State may decline information solely because it is held by a bank, other financial institution, nominee or person acting in an agency or a fiduciary capacity or because it relates to ownership interests in a person (Art. 5 par. 3 DRC).

c)   The disclosure of which would be liable to prejudice the security of or be contrary to the public policy of the requested Member State.

In general, the requested Member State is not obliged to *grant assistance* provided in Arts 5 and 7 to 16 if the initial request for assistance is made in respect of claims which are more than five years old (Art. 18 par. 2 DRC) or the total amounts of the claims covered by the Directive, for which assistance is requested, is less than EUR 1500 (Art. 18 par. 3 DRC). Issues concerning periods of limitation are governed by the law of the applicant Member State (Art. 19 par. 1 DRC). However, suspension, interruption or prolongation of that period is in principle determined by the law of the requested State, unless that law does not provide for suspension, interruption or prolongation, in which case steps taken in the requested State are deemed to have been taken in the requesting State in so far as they would produce suspension, interruption or prolongation under the law of the requesting State (Art. 19 par. 2 DRC).[466]

In addition, the requested Member State is not obliged to grant the *assistance for recovery* (including precautionary measures), if the recovery of the claim would, because of the situation of the debtor, create serious economic or social difficulties in the requested Member State, in so far as the law in that State allows such exception for national claims (Art. 18 par. 1 DRC).

Finally, the Member State may not *make a request for a recovery* if:[467]

- The claim or the instrument permitting enforcement is contested in the applicant Member State, except if the laws of both States allow the action and the requesting State covers any potential damages or refunds if the contestation is subsequently favourable to the debtor (Art. 11 par. 1 in liaison with Art. 14 par. 4, third subparagraph, DRC).[468]
- It has not exhausted its own recovery possibilities within its own jurisdiction, unless it is obvious that there are no assets for recovery

---

[466]   Schilcher/Spies (2013), p. 233.
[467]   Terra/Wattel (2012), p. 432.
[468]   Ibid.

in the applicant State or where recourse to such procedures would give rise to disproportionate difficulty (Art. 11 par. 2 DRC).

## G.  Secrecy Rules

The secrecy rules of the DRC (Art. 23) correspond to the DAC (Art. 16). In particular, any information received by a Member State must be kept secret in the same manner as information received under its domestic law (national treatment).

## H.  Coordination

Similar to the DAC, the DRC confirms that other international rules of recovery of claims are not affected by it (Art. 24 par. 1 DRC). It follows that Member States are free to choose the wider rules of international recovery. Such rules exist either in double taxation treaties including a clause corresponding to Art. 27 OECD Model DTC or in the CMAAT.

# V.  ADMINISTRATIVE COOPERATION IN THE FIELD OF INDIRECT TAXES

## A.  Introduction

On 16 December 1991, the ECOFIN Council adopted the Directive on the abolition of fiscal frontiers (91/680), which had to be implemented as of 1 January 1993.[469] In the meantime, a simplification Directive was also introduced.[470] Following heavy discussions, a final agreement was reached on 19 October 1992 for an approximation of VAT rates, resulting in Directive 92/77/EEC.[471] As a consequence, on 1 January 1993, the EU introduced the European single market, according to which goods, persons, capital and services should be able to circulate freely among

---

[469]   Terra/Wattel (2012), p. 117; Directive 91/680/EEC of 16 December 1991, OJ 1991 L 376, p. 1.

[470]   Terra/Wattel (2012), p. 117; Directive 92/111/EEC, OJ 1992 L 384, p. 47; a further simplification Directive was also 92/77/EEC of 19 October 1992, OJ L 316/1. p. 92.

[471]   See also Torres-Richoud (2013), p. 329.

Member States. Implementing rules for the abolition of fiscal frontiers were also introduced.[472]

Parallel to the Directive on the abolition of fiscal frontiers (92/680), necessary measures in the area of exchange of information were introduced, such as: (i) a regulation on statistics and (ii) a regulation on administrative cooperation.[473] The first measure is a statistical tool, called Intrasat, implementing a methodology for the statistical observation of the transfer of goods between Member States (see infra B.). The second measure, a Regulation of 27 January 1992 on administrative cooperation in the field of indirect taxation,[474] was further modified, leading to a more comprehensive system of administrative cooperation and combating fraud in the field of VAT (see infra C.).

## B.  Intra-Community Trade Statistical Information System

The Regulation on the statistics relating to the trading of goods between Member States was adopted on 7 November 1991.[475] The Regulation introduced the so-called intra-community trade statistical information system (Intrasat), which applies to movement of goods between Member States. Intra-EU statistics record the arrival (corresponding to import) and dispatch (corresponding to export) of movable property by each Member State.[476] As such, Intrasat is closely linked to the VAT system and introduces an electronic reporting tool.[477]

This Regulation was later replaced, on 31 March 2004, by Regulation 638/2004,[478] which simplifies the former regulation and improves the comparability of statistics among Member States.[479]

---

[472]  In fact, since the introduction of the transitional arrangement on 1 January 1993, various Directives have been implemented, which resulted on 28 November 2006 in the adoption of Directive 2006/112/EC on the common system of VAT, recasting the Sixth VAT Directive, which entered into force on 1 January 2007, and has also been modified many times; see Terra/Wattel (2012), p. 173 ff.

[473]  Terra/Wattel (2012), p. 117.

[474]  Council Regulation no 218/1992 of 27 January 1992 on administrative cooperation in the field of indirect taxation, OJ L 024.

[475]  Regulation 3330/91 of 7 November 1991, OJ 1991 L 316, p. 1.

[476]  Terra/Wattel (2012), p. 434.

[477]  Ibid.

[478]  Regulation 638/2004/EC of the European Parliament and of the Council on Community statistics relating to the trading of goods between Member States and repealing Council Regulation (EEC) 3330/91; Terra/Wattel (2012), p. 435.

[479]  Terra/Wattel (2012), p. 435.

## C.  Regulation on the Administrative Cooperation and Combatting Fraud in the Field of VAT

### 1.  Historical developments

As described above, the abolition of fiscal frontiers resulted in a free transfer of movable goods between Member States. This generated notably the transitional system of taxation for intra-Community transfers of goods. This major achievement had to be followed by additional measures in order to combat fraud and foster tax cooperation among Member States.

Regulation 218/92 on administrative cooperation in the field of indirect taxation (VAT) was therefore adopted on 27 January 1992.[480] It established a system of close cooperation between Member States, on the one hand, and between the Member States and the EU Commission, on the other hand. At that time, exchange of information in the field of VAT was also governed by the Directive 77/799/EEC of 19 December 1977 concerning mutual assistance in the field of direct and indirect taxation.[481]

This Regulation, and Directive 77/799, proved however insufficient to effectively combat fraud. In particular, it appears that VAT fraudsters could take advantage of the transitional cross-border VAT rules, which were harmonized at the EU level, but still implemented to a large extent at the level of each Member State.[482] 'Carousel' frauds, in this respect, represent a classic example of VAT fraud.[483] A 'carousel' would typically involve the selling of goods between Member States, where one taxable person is entitled to claim the input VAT, while other taxable persons along the chain have disappeared.[484]

As a result, a new Regulation No 1798/2003 of 7 October 2003 on administrative cooperation in the field of value added tax was adopted.[485] The new Regulation noted that the 'existence of two separate instruments for cooperation on VAT has, moreover, hampered effective cooperation

---

[480]   See supra note 474.
[481]   OJ L 336, p. 15.
[482]   Torres-Richoux (2013), p. 331.
[483]   See Terra/Wattel (2012), p. 180.
[484]   See for instance joined Cases C-354/03, C-355/03 and C-484/03, ECR I-0483; Terra/Wattel (2012), p. 180.
[485]   Council Regulation (EEC) No 1798/2003 of 7 October 2003 on administrative cooperation in the field of value added tax and repealing Regulation (EEC) No 218/92.

between tax administrations'.[486] In addition, 'there is not enough direct contact between local or national anti-fraud offices, with communication between central liaison offices being the rule'. It further added that:

Cooperation is also not intensive enough, in that, apart from the VAT information exchange system (VIES), there are not enough automatic or spontaneous exchanges of information between Member States. Exchanges of information between the respective administrations as well as between administrations and the Commission should be made more intensive and swifter in order to combat fraud more effectively.[487]

The new Regulation introduced several improvements in the cooperation in the field of VAT, namely: the organization of the departments responsible for the administrative assistance and notably the designation of central liaison offices; rules for request of information and for administrative enquiries; time limits for providing information; the presence of foreign officials in administrative offices and participation in administrative enquiries in the requested Member State; simultaneous controls; requests for administrative notification. In addition, the Regulation introduced:[488]

- more possibilities of automatic and spontaneous exchange of information between Member States;
- rules for electronic storage and for the exchange of information by electronic means on specific to intra-community transactions;
- provisions for services supplied by electronic means and telecommunications and radio broadcasting services;
- VAT refunds to taxable persons established in another Member State;
- rules for the relation with the Commission and third States;
- conditions governing the exchange of information (notably, the principle of communication by electronic means, rules of secrecy and purpose of the use of information).

In a report dated August 2008, the EU Commission concluded that, despite the improvement of the legal framework for administrative cooperation in the field of VAT, further changes still needed to be introduced.[489] It appeared in particular that Member States did not make sufficient use of the tools provided for in the rules for administrative

---

486   Regulation 1798/2003, (10).
487   Regulation 1798/2003, (13).
488   Terra/Wattel (2012), p. 437.
489   Terra/Wattel (2012), p. 436; Torres-Richoux (2013), p. 332.

cooperation.[490] Better tools of administrative assistance, such as automatic or spontaneous systems, and faster mechanisms have to be put in place. Last but not least, bank secrecy should not be an obstacle to cooperation in the field of VAT.

As a result, the Council adopted Regulation 904/2010 on 7 October 2010.[491] This new (recast) Regulation supplements the former Regulation 1798/2003 on administrative cooperation on VAT, taking into account all the past amendments of that Regulation and the new amendments that have to be made. The (recast) Regulation introduces more effective measures against cross-border fraud and collection of VAT in cases where the place of taxation is different from the place of establishment of the supplier.[492]

## 2. Scope

*i) Purpose*   In general, the Regulation lays down the conditions under which the competent authorities in the Member States are to cooperate with each other and with the Commission to ensure compliance with the laws on VAT (Art. 1 par. 1 Regulation). To that end, it provides for rules and procedures of cooperation and exchange between Member States that may help to effect a correct assessment of VAT, monitor the correct application of VAT, particularly intra-Community transactions, and combat VAT fraud; it lays down rules to collect and exchange such information by electronic means (Art. 1 par. 1, second sentence, Regulation). The Regulation also describes the conditions under which competent authorities are to assist in the protection of VAT revenue in all the Member States (Art. 1 par. 2 Regulation). This rule is interesting because it reinforces the need for Member States to make use of the instruments provided in the Regulation and also to safeguard revenues of each other. Finally, the Regulation includes rules and procedures for the exchange by electronic means of VAT information on services supplied electronically (Art. 1 par. 4 Regulation).

The Regulation does not affect the application in Member States of the rules on mutual assistance in criminal matters (Art. 1 par. 3 Regulation).

*ii) Competent authorities*   Each Member State must inform the EU Commission of its competent authority for the purpose of the Regulation. Following that, the Commission will make available to the Member

---

[490]   Torres-Richoux (2012), p. 333.
[491]   Regulation (EU) No 904/2010 of 7 October 2010.
[492]   Terra/Wattel (2012), p. 436.

States a list of all competent authorities and publish this information in the Official Journal of the EU (Art. 3 Regulation).

Each Member State will designate a single *central liaison office* to which principal responsibility will be delegated for contacts with other Member States in the field of administrative cooperation. It may also be designated as responsible for contacts with the Commission (Art. 4 par. 2 Regulation). In practice, this central liaison office will be responsible for cooperation on requests by default, i.e. when the requesting Member State does not know which authority to contact, and also has a central role to play in automatic or spontaneous exchange of information.[493]

The competent authority of each Member State may designate liaison departments. The central liaison office will be responsible for keeping the list of those departments up-to-date and making it available to the central liaison offices of the other Member States concerned (Art. 4 par. 2 Regulation). In addition, the competent authority of each Member State may designate competent officials who can directly exchange information on the basis of the Regulation (Art. 4 par. 3 Regulation).

### 3. Forms of assistance

*i) Exchange of information on request* Upon request, the requested authority must communicate the information referred to in Art. 1, including any information relating to a specific case or cases (Art. 7 par. 1 Regulation). The requested authority will implement the administrative enquiries necessary in order to obtain such information (Art. 7 par. 2 Regulation). If however the requested State considers that no administrative enquiry is necessary it shall immediately inform the requesting authority of the reasons thereof.[494] In order to obtain the information sought, the requested authority must proceed as though acting on its own account or at the request of another authority in its own Member State (Art. 7 par. 5 Regulation).

A standard form for request of information and administrative inquiries is prescribed (Art. 8 Regulation). Communication of pertinent information may include reports, statements, and any other documents, or certified copies or extracts thereof (Art. 9 Regulation). The requested information must be provided for as soon as possible, but in any case no later than three months following the receipt of the request (Art. 10 par.

---

[493] Terra/Wattel (2012), p. 438.

[494] As of 1 January 2015, an enquiry into the amounts declared by a taxable person in connection with the supply of goods and services listed in Annex I may be refused solely for limitative reasons (Art. 7 par. 4 Regulation).

1 Regulation). If the requested authority is already in possession of the information, the time limit is reduced to one month (Art. 10 par. 1 second sentence Regulation).

*ii) Exchange of information without prior request (automatic and spontaneous exchange of information)* The competent authorities of each Member State must, without prior request, forward the information to the competent authority of any other Member States in the following cases (Art. 13 par. 1 Regulation):

> a) where taxation is deemed to take place in the Member State of destination and the information provided by the Member State of origin is necessary for the effectiveness of the control system of the Member Sate of destination; b) where a Member State has ground to believe that a breach of VAT legislation has been committed or is likely to have been committed in the other Member State; c) where there is a risk of tax loss in the other Member State.

Case a) corresponds to one of the purposes of the Regulation, which is to ensure the proper functioning of the internal market, and takes into account the fact that Member States also have to provide assistance to other Member States for the correct application of tax for activities carried out in their own territory but owed to another Member State.[495] Cases b) or c) pertain to situations where important fraud risks exist, such as the use of so-called 'phoenix' or 'shadow' companies (which carry out a large number of intra-Community transactions during initial years and then disappear), or VAT refunds for taxable persons outside the EU.[496]

The exchange of information will be either automatic, in accordance with Art. 14, or spontaneous, following Art. 15 (Art. 13 par. 2 Regulation).

The categories of information subject to *automatic exchange*, the frequency of exchanges and practical arrangements will be based on the committee procedure referred to in Art. 58 par. 2 (Art. 14 Regulation).[497] A Member State may however abstain from taking part in the automatic exchange of information with respect to one or more categories where the collection of information for such exchange would require the imposition of new obligations on persons liable for VAT or would impose a

---

[495]    See recital (7) to the Regulation.

[496]    Terra/Wattel (2012), p. 440; Torres-Richoux (2013), p. 339.

[497]    In practice, the procedure will be based on Arts 5, 7, and 8 of Council Decision 1999/468/EC (Art. 58 par. 2 Regulation); see also Torres-Richoux (2013), p. 339.

disproportionate administrative burden on the Member State (Art. 14 par. 1, second sentence Regulation).

As of 1 January 2015, the competent authority of each Member State must, in particular, exchange information *automatically* in order to enable Member States of consumption to ascertain whether taxable persons not established in their territory declare and correctly pay the VAT due with regard to telecommunication services, broadcasting services and electronically supplied services, regardless of whether those taxable persons make use of the special scheme (Art. 14 par. 2 Regulation).

In addition, the Member States must, by *spontaneous exchange*, forward to the competent authorities of the other Member State any information referred to in Art. 13 par. 1, which has not been forwarded under automatic exchange referred to in Art. 14 of which they are aware and which they consider may be useful to those competent authorities (Art. 15 Regulation).

*iii) Feedback* Where a competent authority provides information, on request or spontaneously, it may request a feedback from the requesting authority (Art. 16 Regulation). In this case, the requested authority must, without prejudice to the rules on tax secrecy and data protection applicable in its Member State, send feedback as soon as possible, provided it does not impose a disproportionate burden on it (Art. 16 Regulation).

*iv) Storage* Articles 17 to 24 provide for the rules on storage and exchange of information. Each Member State must store, in electronic systems, specific information, designated in Art. 17 par. 1 (notably, information collected, data on the identity, legal form, and address of the person to whom a VAT ID number has been issued). Member States have to ensure that the information, available in the electronic system, is kept up-to-date, and is complete and accurate (Art. 19). Automated access to the information stored, pursuant to Art. 17, must be granted to the competent authority of any other Member State (Art. 21 Regulation).

*v) Request for administrative notification* According to Art. 25, at the request of the requesting authority, the requested authority must notify the addressee of all instruments and decisions, which emanate from the competent authorities and concern the application of VAT legislation in the territory of the Member State in which the requesting authority is established.

*vi) Presence in administrative offices*     Article 28 par. 1 provides that officials authorized by the requesting authority, with a view to exchanging information, may be present in the offices of the administrative authorities of the requested Member State, or any other place where those authorities carry out their duties, and also must be given copies of the documentation. Officials authorized by the requesting authority may also be present during the administrative enquiries carried out in the territory of the requested Member State (Art. 28 par. 2 regulation). The officials of the requesting authority cannot exercise the powers of inspection, but they may have access to the same premises and documents as the requested authority.

*vii) Simultaneous control*     Member States may agree to conduct simultaneous controls whenever they consider such controls to be more effective than controls carried out by one Member State (Art. 29 Regulation). A Member State must identify independently the taxable person, which it intends to propose for a simultaneous control, notify the competent authority of the other Member State concerned, and give reasons for its choice (Art. 30 par. 1 Regulation). The requested Member State, receiving the proposal, must confirm its agreement or communicate its reason for refusal, in principle within two weeks of receipt of the proposal, but no later than one month (Art. 30 par. 2 Regulation).

*viii) Information to taxable persons*     The competent authorities of each Member State must ensure that persons involved in the intra-Community supply of goods or services and non-established taxable persons supplying telecommunication services, broadcasting services and electronically supplied services, are allowed to obtain, for the purpose of such transactions, confirmation by electronic means of the validity of the VAT identification number of any specified person as well as the associated name and address (Art. 31 Regulation).

*ix) Eurofisc*     In order to promote and facilitate multilateral cooperation in the fight against VAT fraud, Arts 33 to 37 established a network for the swift exchange of targeted information between Member States, called Eurofisc (Art. 33 Regulation). Information exchanged within the network will remain confidential and governed by the secrecy rule of Art. 55 (Art. 34 par. 3 Regulation). In particular, the EU Commission will provide Eurofisc with technical and logistical support but does not have access to the information referred to in Art. 1, which can be exchanged via Eurofisc.

## 4. Special rules

*i) Special schemes for electronically supplied services* The Regulation provides for rules applicable to the special schemes governed by Chapter 6 of Title XII of Directive 2006/112/EC for electronically supplied services. The special schemes refer to non-established taxable persons supplying electronic services to non-taxable persons. The Regulation distinguishes between provisions applicable until 31 December 2014 (Arts 38 to 42) and from 1 January 2015 (Arts 43 to 47).

Until 31 December 2014, the information provided by the taxable person not established in the Community to the Member State of identification, when his activities commence, must be submitted by electronic means (Art. 39 par. 1 Regulation). The Member State of identification must then transmit this information by electronic means to the competent authorities of the other Member States by electronic means within ten days from the end of the month during which the information was received; in the same manner, the competent authorities of the other Member States must be informed of the allocated identification number (Art. 39 par. 2 Regulation). Finally, the Member State of identification must inform without delay by electronic means if a non-established taxable person is excluded from the identification register (Art. 39 par. 3 Regulation).

The return with the details set out in Art. 365 of the VAT Directive 2006/112/EC is to be submitted by electronic means (Art. 40 par. 1 Regulation). The Member State of identification must transmit this information by electronic means to the competent authorities of the other Member States, within ten days from the end of the month during which the information was received (Art. 40 par. 2 Regulation; including details about potential conversion into Euros). If the non-established taxable person does not pay the total tax due, the Member State of identification must ensure that the payment is transferred to the Member States of consumption in proportion to the tax due in each Member State (Art. 41 par. 2 Regulation).

As of 1 January 2015, the rules remain basically the same. However, they have to be adapted in order to take into account Directive 2008/8/EC amending the VAT Directive pertaining to the place of supply of electronic services. From 1 January 2015, the existing scheme for non-established persons is replaced by a 'Special scheme for taxable persons non-established within the Community supplying telecommunication services, broadcasting services or electronic services to non-taxable persons' and, in addition, a 'Special scheme for the telecommunication services, broadcasting services or electronic services supplied by taxable persons established within the Community but not in the Member State of consumption to non-taxable persons' is introduced.[498] In other words, the rules applicable until 31 December 2014 for electronic supply by taxable persons established outside the Community will be extended to taxable persons in another Member State.[499]

Under Art. 46 par. 3, however, concerning payments to be transferred to the Member State of consumption, the Member State of identification is entitled to retain, of the amount due to the Member States of consumption: a) from 1 January 2015 until December 2016 – 30 per cent; b) from 1 January 2017 until December 2018 – 15 per cent; c) from 1 January 2019 – 0 per cent.

*ii) Exchange and conservation of information pertaining to VAT refunds* Where the competent authority of the Member State of establishment receives an application for refund of VAT, pursuant to Art. 5 of Directive 2008/9/EC, and Art. 18 of that Directive is not applicable, it must, within 15 calendar days of receipt and by electronic means, forward the application to the competent authorities of each Member State of the refund concerned, with confirmation that the applicant is a taxable person for the purpose of VAT and that the identification or registration number given by that person is valid for the refund period (Art. 48 Regulation).

The competent authorities of each Member State of the refund must notify by electronic means the competent authorities of the other Member States of any information required by them pursuant to Art. 9 par. 2 of Directive 2008/9/EC (Art. 48 par. 2 Regulation).

*iii) Relation with the Commission and third States* The Member States and the Commission must examine and evaluate how the arrangements for administrative cooperation are working (Art. 49 par. 1 Regulation). The Commission will in particular pool the experience of each Member State with the aim of improving the operation of those arrangements (Art. 49 par. 2 Regulation). The Member State must communicate to the Commission any available information relevant to their application of the Regulation (Art. 49 par. 2 Regulation).

In addition, Art. 50 par. 1 provides for a legal base for exchange of information between Member States, emanating from a non-EU country, in so far as permitted by assistance arrangements with that particular

---

[498]  Terra/Wattel (2012), p. 256.
[499]  Terra/Wattel (2012), p. 443; see also Torres-Richoux (2013), p. 342.

third country.[500] In addition, competent authorities may communicate, in accordance with their domestic provisions on the communication of personal data to third countries, information obtained under this Regulation, provided that the following conditions are met: (i) the competent authority of the Member State from which the information originates has agreed to the communication and (ii) the third country has given an undertaking to provide the cooperation required to gather evidence of the irregular nature of transactions which appear to contravene VAT legislation (Art. 50 par. 2 Regulation).

## 5. Conditions governing the exchange of information

Articles 51 to 57 Regulation rule the conditions governing exchange of information. They provide for (i) conditions on the form of the exchange, (ii) limits to the exchange and (iii) secrecy rules. These rules in essence correspond to the existing ones under the previous Regulation 1798/2003.

*i) Form* As a general rule, all information is to be provided, as far as possible, by electronic means under arrangements to be adopted by the committee procedure referred to in Art. 58 par. 2 (Art. 51 Regulation).

*ii) Limits* Limits are based, in general, on the principles of subsidiarity, the principle of reciprocity, and protection of business or trade secrets (but not banking secrecy). These principles correspond to the potential grounds for refusal to supply information that typically govern international cooperation in tax matters.

The requested authority must supply the information to the requesting authority in another Member State, provided that: 'a) the number and nature of the requests made by the requesting authority within a specific period of time do not impose disproportionate administrative burden on that requested authority; b) the requesting authority has exhausted the usual source which it could have used in the circumstances to obtain the information requested, without running the risks of jeopardizing the achievement of the desired end' (Art. 54 Regulation). The latter is in fact a restatement of the *principle of subsidiarity*, which governs administrative assistance in general.

The Regulation imposes no obligation to have enquiries carried out or to provide information on a particular case, which are contrary to the laws or administrative practice of the *requested* Member) (Art. 54 par. 2 Regulation). In addition, the competent authority of a requested Member

---

[500]  Terra/Wattel (2012), p. 444.

State may refuse to provide information where the *requesting* Member State is unable for legal reasons, to provide similar information (*principle of reciprocity*) (Art. 54 par. 3 Regulation).

The supply of information may also be refused if it would lead to the disclosure of a commercial, industrial or professional *secret* or of a commercial process, or information whose disclosure would be contrary to public policy (Art. 54 par. 4 Regulation).[501] However, paras 2, 3 and 4 cannot be interpreted as authorizing the requested authority to refuse to supply information on a taxable person identified for VAT purposes in the Member State of the requesting authority on the sole grounds that this information is held by a bank, other financial institution, nominee or person acting in an agency or fiduciary capacity or because it relates to ownership interest in a legal person.[502]

*iii) Secrecy rules*   Information communicated or collected in any form, pursuant to this Regulation, is covered by the obligation of official secrecy and enjoys the protection extended to similar information under both (i) the national law of the Member State which received it and (ii) the corresponding provisions applicable to Union authorities (Art. 55 par. 1 Regulation). Such information must only be used in the circumstances provided for in this Regulation (Art. 55 par. 1 in fine Regulation). It may be used (Art. 55 par. 1 in fine Regulation):

- for the purpose of establishing the assessment base or the collection or administrative control of tax for the purpose of establishing the assessment base;
- for the assessment of other levies, duties and taxes covered by Art. 2 of Directive 2008/55/EC of 26 May 208 on mutual assistance for the recovery of claims relating to certain levies, duties, taxes and other measures;
- in connection with judicial proceedings that may involve penalties, initiated as a result of infringements of tax law without prejudice to the general rules and legal provisions governing the rights of defendants and witnesses in such proceedings.

By way of derogation, the competent authority of the requested Member State must permit its use for *other purposes* in the requesting Member

---

[501]   This rule corresponds in substance to the OECD standard applicable under Art. 26 par. 3 lit.c of the OECD DTC Model (see supra p. 33).

[502]   This rule corresponds in substance to the OECD standard applicable under Art. 26 par. 5 of the OECD DTC Model (see supra p. 36).

State, if the information can be used for similar purposes under the legislation of the former (Art. 55 par. 3 Regulation).

Where the requesting authority considers that the information received is likely to be useful to the competent authority of a *third* Member State, it may transmit it to the latter authority; it must then inform the requested authority, which may require that the transmission of the information be subject to its prior agreement (Art. 55 par. 4 Regulation).

Persons duly accredited by the Security Accreditation Authority of the Commission may have access to this information only in so far as necessary for care, maintenance and development of the CCN/CSI Network (Art. 55 par. 2 Regulation).

Any reports, statements and other documents, or certified true copies or extracts thereof, obtained by the requested authority and communicated to the requesting authority, under the assistance provided by this Regulation, may be invoked as evidence by the competent bodies of the Member State of the requesting authority on the same basis as similar documents provided by another authority of that country (Art. 56 Regulation).

Finally, Art. 57 prescribes that for the purpose of applying the Regulation, Member States must take all necessary measures to ensure effective internal coordination between the competent authorities, to establish direct cooperation between the authorities authorized for the purposes of such coordination and to ensure the smooth operation of the information exchange arrangements provided for in the Regulation. This rule is indeed essential for the proper functioning of the administrative assistance in the Regulation. Past reports from the EU Commission have identified that some Member States did not systematically collect or centralize the essential information.[503]

## 6. Coordination
The Regulation applies without prejudice to the fulfillment of any wider obligations in relation to mutual assistance based on other legal provisions, including bilateral or multilateral agreements (Art. 60 par. 1 Regulation). In addition, in case Member States conclude bilateral arrangements on matters covered by this Regulation, they must inform the EU Commission without delay. The Commission must in turn inform other Member States (Art. 60 par. 2 Regulation).

---

[503]  Torres-Richoux (2013), p. 344.

Moreover, the Regulation does not affect the application in the Member States of the rules on mutual assistance in *criminal matters* (Art. 1 par. 3 Regulation).

## D.  Administrative Cooperation on Excise Duties

Administrative cooperation in the field of excise duties has evolved, notably taking into account the necessity to develop more effective rules of assistance in order to combat fraud and the development of a computerized monitoring system in the field of transfer of excise goods.

Council Regulation 2073/2004/EC was adopted on 16 November 2004.[504] The purpose of this Regulation was to reduce national budgetary losses and competition distortions in the movement of products subject to excise duty.[505] It also improved the rules of administrative cooperation contained in Directive 77/799 and on the so-called 'horizontal excise Directive' 92/12/EEC.[506] Confronted with wide significant fraud, especially in the area of tobacco and alcohol excise duty, this Regulation aimed at improving mutual assistance in the field of excise taxes, notably with more direct communications between administrations and promoting more use of electronic monitoring systems.[507]

In particular, the Regulation provides for:[508]

- exchange of information upon request (requested authority must proceed as though acting on its own account);
- time limits for response following a request for information (in general three months);
- spontaneous and automatic exchange of information (notably a compulsory automatic exchange, in cases where there is a risk of serious fraud in a Member State);
- simultaneous audits;
- rules concerning time limits for storage and procedures for exchange of information;

---

[504]   Council Regulation (EC) No. 2073/2004 on administrative cooperation in the field of excise duties, OJ L 359, p. 1.

[505]   Maitro de la Motte (2012), p. 535.

[506]   Terra/Wattel (2012), p. 446. The 'horizontal excise Directive was later replaced by the General Arrangement Directive 2008/118/EC. For a general description, see Terra/Wattel (2012), no 7.2, p. 267 ff.

[507]   COM (2003) 797 final; Terra/Wattel (2012), p. 446, note 40.

[508]   See also Terra/Wattel (2012), p. 447; Maitro de la Motte (2012) p. 536 ff.

- transfer of statistical information to the Commission;
- exchange of information with non-EU countries.

An interesting and original electronic system of 'electronic early warning' is implemented in Art. 23 par. 1 of Regulation 2073/2004.[509] It provides for rapid and direct electronic information or a 'warning message' to the liaison office of the Member State of destination of goods subject to excise duty in case the Member State of departure of the goods has relevant information.

The 2004 Regulation was repealed by a new Regulation No 389/2012 of 2 May 2012, on administrative cooperation in the field of excise duties.[510] This Regulation notably takes into account the introduction of the Excise Movement and Control System (EMCS), in April 2010.[511] The EMCS has been introduced, following Decision No 1152/2003/EC of 16 June 2003 on computerizing the movement and surveillance of excisable products.[512]

The new Regulation adapts the current rules on exchange of information and seeks to replace manual procedures on the movement of excise duties with automated procedures, to the extent the information is electronically available.[513] Many of the rules of Regulation 2004 are however maintained, notably: the single point of contact in each Member State (Arts 3 to 7), information upon request (Arts 8 to 10), the possibility of simultaneous controls (Art. 13) and of the presence of officials of one Member State in the territory of another Member State (Art. 12), rules addressing notification of administrative decisions (Art. 14), exchange of information without prior request (particularly automatic exchange) (Arts 15 to 18), and relations with third countries (Art. 32).

However, the new Regulation enhanced the role of *electronic* means in the exchange of information (Arts 19 to 22). These requirements are met with a more systematic use of the ECMS system. The new Regulation also contains more strict *time limit* rules.

Article 25 includes traditional grounds for *refusal to supply* information, such as: domestic rules (principle of reciprocity); information

---

[509] Maitro de la Motte (2012), p. 540.
[510] Council Regulation on administrative cooperation in the field of excise duties, (EC) No 2073/2004, OJ L 121 p. 1.
[511] Terra/Wattel (2012), p. 447; Parida (2013), p. 430.
[512] Decision No 1152/2003/EC of the European Parliament and of the Council of 16 June 2003, OJ 2003 L 162, p. 5; see Terra/Wattel (2012), p. 266.
[513] Terra/Wattel (2012), p. 447; Maitro de la Motte (2012), p. 542.

which would disclose a commercial or business secret; limits of public policy. However, in accordance with the modern standard, the Regulation confirms that national rules on bank secrecy cannot be a reason to refuse an exchange of information (Art. 25 par. 4).

It also includes a *secrecy* clause and rules for *data protection* and use of the information communicated under the Regulation (Art. 28). In particular, all processing of personal data by Member States under the Regulation is subject to the national provisions implementing Directive 95/46/EC (Art. 28 par. 4). However, the Regulation limits the scope of certain rights and obligations laid down in Directive 95/46/EC, specifically the rights defined in Art. 10, Art. 11 par. 1, Art. 12 and Art. 21, to the extent necessary to safeguard the interest referred to in point (e) of Art. 13 par. 1 of that Directive (Art. 28 par. 4, second sentence). This restriction is made, bearing in mind the potential loss of revenue for the Member States and the crucial importance of information covered by this Regulation for the effectiveness of the fight against fraud.[514]

Finally, according to n. (25) of the recitals:

> The Regulation respects the fundamental rights and observes the principles which are recognized by the Charter of Fundamental Rights of the European Union, in particular the right to protection of personal data (Art. 8). In view of the limits set by the present Regulation, the processing of such data carried out within the framework of this Regulation does not go beyond what is necessary and proportionate for the purposes of protecting the legitimate fiscal interest of the Member States.

---

[514]   Regulation, recital, n. (20).

# 9.   The so-called Swiss 'Rubik' agreements

## I.  INTRODUCTION

As of March 2009, notably, following the global acceptance and implementation of Art. 26 of the OECD Model DTC, discussions started towards moving from exchange of information upon request, as the current standard, to automatic exchange of information. In parallel to these developments, Switzerland developed an alternative model: the so-called 'Rubik' model.[515] The 'Rubik' system is simple in appearance. It is based on a withholding tax, levied at source by the paying agent, which should correspond to the rate of tax in the country of residence of the taxpayer. The amount of tax is then transferred to the State of residence, while preserving the confidentiality of the taxpayer. This system can be seen as a typical 'Swiss compromise', which tries to solve two apparently conflicting principles: confidentiality, on the one hand, and tax compliance in the residence state, on the other hand. After all, under Rubik, the taxpayer involved, having paid his due under the withholding, is deemed compliant in the State of residence, while confidentiality is preserved.

The Rubik agreements, more precisely, are made of a combination of: (i) a regularization mechanism for the past that preserves confidentiality (solution for the past); (ii) a withholding tax, collected by a Swiss paying agent, which enables, for the future, tax due on assets to be settled anonymously (solution for the future). Under the philosophy of the system, the rate of the tax should correspond to the tax that the relevant taxpayer should have been required to pay in his or her State of residence. The Swiss paying agent withholds the tax on Swiss source investment income (dividends, interest, royalties and capital gains), passes it to the Swiss Federal Tax Administration, which then transfers the amount of tax, on an anonymous basis, to the state of residence of the taxpayer.

---

[515]   Lissi/Bukara (2012), p. 42 ff; 103 ff.

At the beginning of the implementation process, the system seemed to have some allies. In a first stage, agreements of this type have been reached with Germany[516] (signed on 21 September 2011, then modified on 5 April 2012), the United Kingdom[517] (signed on 6 October 2011, then modified on 20 March 2012) and Austria[518] (signed on 13 April 2012), all ratified by the Swiss Federal Parliament in May 2012. It is worth noting that the initial versions of the agreements with Germany and United Kingdom were amended by a Protocol in order to make them compatible with the EUSD,[519] especially regarding the tax treatment of interest and the problem of succession.[520]

In a second stage, however, following the refusal by the German Parliament to ratify the agreement in December 2012, the Rubik Agreement with Germany remained ineffective. The Agreements with the United Kingdom and Austria, however, entered into force on 1 January 2013. The same year, a Federal Act on International Withholding Tax (IWTA), regulating the implementation of these Agreements, was also implemented by Switzerland. Negotiations with other States, notably Greece, Italy, and Spain, were still ongoing but it appears that, following the negative vote of the German Parliament, a halt in the development of the 'Rubik' model occurred. The move towards automatic information exchange as a global standard, which had already started in 2012, but became effective in 2013, has also modified the focus. Rubik appears to remain an interesting but probably a more transitory model.

Except for some peculiarities, inherent to the domestic tax laws of the Contracting States (United Kingdom, Austria), the Rubik agreements are built on the same model. They are based on the following three pillars:[521] (i) a regularization mechanism for the past that preserves confidentiality;

---

[516] Agreement between Germany and Switzerland on the future tax treatment of capital investment income and the treatment of previously undeclared funds (21 September 2011), [hereinafter Switzerland-Germany Agreement].

[517] Agreement between the Swiss Confederation and the United Kingdom of Great Britain and Northern Ireland on cooperation in the area of taxation (6 October 2011), [hereinafter Switzerland-United Kingdom Agreement].

[518] Agreement between Switzerland and the Austrian Republic on the future tax treatment of capital investment income and the treatment of previously undeclared funds (13 April 2012), Treaties IBFD [hereinafter Austria-Switzerland Agreement (2012)].

[519] See Oberson (2013), p. 363.

[520] See Waldburger (2012), p. 169.

[521] For more details, see Oberson (2013), p. 368 ff.

(ii) a withholding tax, collected by a Swiss paying agent, which enables, for the future, tax due on assets to be settled anonymously; and (iii) concessions granted to Switzerland.

## II. REGULARIZATION OF THE PAST

### A. Conditions

In order to benefit from the system of regularization of the past, the taxpayer concerned must fulfill the following four cumulative conditions:

(1) be a concerned person in accordance with the Agreement;
(2) hold assets;
(3) with a Swiss paying agent;
(4) within the reference dates set by the Agreement.

*Assets* include all sorts of bankable assets deposited by a Swiss paying agent, notably accounts, securities, and structured products. Items that are not considered assets include the contents of safes, real estate, movable assets and insurance contracts subject to the regulation of FINMA (except for insurance wrappers).

*Swiss paying agents* include, notably, banks and securities dealers, as well as all natural and legal persons residing in Switzerland who accept assets from third parties on a regular basis or pay income or gains or make their payments within the framework of their economic activity. This notion corresponds, in fact, to that defined in the EUSD.

### B. Consequences

When the conditions are met, the taxpayer concerned must communicate in writing his/her choice between a voluntary declaration and a withholding payment to the paying agent.

In regard to a voluntary declaration, the taxpayer concerned authorizes the paying agent to communicate information to the Swiss competent authority, which will in turn transmit it to the foreign authority. The regularization is treated as a voluntary disclosure from the foreign authority with, in principle, a waiver of prosecution, with the exception of serious cases.

The option of a withholding payment is executed by the paying agent through a deduction at source from the assets of the taxpayer concerned. The Swiss paying agent, in particular, computes the levy and transfers to the Swiss competent authority one-off amounts. The *rate* is variable and is calculated according to mathematical formulae that take into consideration various parameters, notably the duration of the banking relationship and the difference between the account's initial and final capital. The rate varies between 21 per cent and 41 per cent for the United Kingdom, and between 15 per cent and 38 per cent for Austria. The paying agent issues a certificate to the relevant person confirming that he/she is no longer liable for the tax on these assets for the periods in question. The certificate has an 'extinctive effect', which includes, without limitation, interest, penalties and extra charges. Regarding criminal investigations, the Switzerland-United Kingdom Agreement (2011) sets the limit in a side letter, which states that, to the extent that the relevant person meets the procedures set out and fully cooperates with the HMRC, it is 'highly unlikely' that he/she would be subject to a criminal investigation.

Should the taxpayer not accept the regularization, he/she must close his/her accounts and transfer his/her assets to a third state, at the latest on the date of implementation of the agreement (Austria), or by 31 May 2013 (United Kingdom).

The Switzerland-United Kingdom Agreement (2011) provides for an upfront payment of CHF 500 million, to be settled by the Swiss paying agents. This payment is intended to be balanced out by subsequent payments and then reimbursed to the paying agents. The agreement with Austria does not provide for such a payment.

On 22 September 2014, the FTA announced having transferred to Great Britain and Austria the total of the taxpayers' declarations and amount of taxes due, following the 'solution for the past', during the period of July 2013 to August 2014. It is interesting to note that the total of tax transferred is 469.5 million GBP, in favour of the United Kingdom, and 738.3 million Euros, in favour of Austria.

Similarly, Switzerland has made a commitment to communicate to the UK and Austrian competent authorities a list of the ten main states or territories to which the concerned persons transferred their closed accounts between the time the agreement was signed and four months from the implementation date of the agreement.

## III. WITHHOLDING TAX ON INCOME AND FUTURE GAINS

Swiss paying agents levy a withholding tax on *income* generated and *gains* realized on the assets of the relevant persons.

The purpose of the agreement is to apply tax rates as close as possible to the rates charged by the state of residence of the relevant person. With regard to Austria, the rate is 25 per cent in respect of all forms of income (including capital gains). In the United Kingdom, the system is more complicated and the rate varies depending on the type of income (dividends 40 per cent, other income 48 per cent, and capital gains 27 per cent).

*Interest* is regulated by the Savings Agreement of 2004. In fact, the two systems are coordinated. As the rate provided in the Savings Agreement (35 per cent) is higher than the Austrian tax rate (25 per cent), the taxpayer can request reimbursement of the overpayment. However, since the UK rate is higher (48 per cent), the Swiss paying agent levies an additional rate of 13 per cent.

*Inheritances* also fall within the scope of the agreements and are subject to a 40 per cent rate (United Kingdom). Austria does not levy such a tax.

Similar to the regularization of the past, the relevant persons are also able to authorize the Swiss paying agent to declare the income and gains concerned to the foreign competent authority through the Swiss competent authority.

## IV. ACCOMPANYING MEASURES

In order to permit the proper functioning of these agreements, accompanying measures have been adopted.[522] They consist fundamentally of implementing mechanisms to ensure that the system will be respected and that, with the exception of the two main options (voluntary disclosure and withholding tax), the persons concerned and paying agents will not circumvent the obligations set out in the agreements.

In order to avoid, in particular, the reintroduction of new untaxed funds by taxpayers who have regulated their situation, the agreements provide for a specific mechanism for the exchange of information that goes beyond that provided by a tax treaty. Thus, according to the Switzerland-United Kingdom Agreement (2011), the Contracting State may submit *specific information requests* in so far as the requesting State's enquiry indicates the identity of the concerned taxpayer and plausible reasons why it is necessary to control the tax situation of this particular taxpayer. In this instance, should the concerned person hold an account in

---

[522] See Weidmann/Suter (2012), p. 127.

Switzerland, the Swiss competent authority communicates the name of the bank concerned and the number of accounts held. However, the number of requests is limited (500 per year). Fishing expeditions are prohibited. The Switzerland-Austria Agreement (2011) does not include such a system. Exchanges of information must be based solely on the tax treaty.

In addition, an *anti-abuse clause* was agreed upon.[523] It provides that Swiss paying agents must not knowingly manage or encourage the use of artificial arrangements whose sole or main purpose is the avoidance of taxation of the relevant persons under the provisions of the Agreement in respect of relevant assets. Any paying agent that does not respect this clause is required to pay to the competent authority an amount equivalent to the tax owed.

## V. CONCESSIONS TO SWITZERLAND

Switzerland's main aim was to achieve, via these agreements, an *effect* sustainably *equivalent* to that of automatic exchange of information. A common declaration to this effect has been made by the relevant states, as well as in Art. 1 of the agreements.

Similarly, these states have declared that they renounce any efforts to actively acquire data stolen from Swiss banks. Moreover, they have committed ('highly unlikely' according to the terms of the agreement with the United Kingdom), not to prosecute the Swiss paying agents and their employees involved in offences committed before the agreements were signed.

Finally, Switzerland has also managed to obtain, even if in a relatively non-binding manner, facilities for the cross-border delivery of financial services by Swiss companies (*access to the market*).[524]

## VI. ASSESSMENT

The Swiss system is based on the paying agent principle, according to which the Swiss financial intermediary has to determine and levy the applicable withholding tax on investment income. It also offers an interesting compromise between effective taxation in the country of

---

[523]   See, for example, Art. 34 of the Switzerland-United Kingdom Agreement.
[524]   See the Memorandum on the Austria-Switzerland Agreement (2012) and the Switzerland-United Kingdom Agreement (2011).

residence while preserving confidentiality. Contrary to the EUSD transitional system, the scope of the withholding tax is much broader since it fundamentally covers most types of investment income. In addition, the withholding tax also includes entities that have been interposed in order to circumvent the duty of the individual beneficial owner. Finally, from a financial standpoint, it offers direct flows of tax to the residence country, which could be welcome by some countries in a difficult financial position.

The Swiss Rubik agreements have however been controversial. Even in Switzerland, some commentators have criticized their complexities combined with high implementation costs for the paying agents. Indeed, in order to be effective, the withholding tax rate has to correspond, for each different category of investment income, to the rate of the residence country. The Swiss paying agent must then correctly characterize each type of investment income and then apply the relevant withholding. Commentators abroad also have diverse opinions. While some were rather enthusiastic,[525] others criticized the system,[526] comparing it with a kind of 'indulgence', or pointing out potential loopholes in the system.[527]

The Rubik system remains in the author's view an interesting attempt to find a compromise between privacy, on the one hand, and tax compliance in the residence state, on the other hand. This proposal was designed to find a long-term alternative solution to automatic exchange of information.[528] The wheel, in the meantime, has clearly moved towards automatic exchange of information as the future global standard.[529] This does not mean that the withholding tax system is bound to disappear. It can already serve as a transitory system towards automatic exchange and represents a potential solution for countries not ready to apply complex automatic exchanges. In this respect, an interesting alternative would be to implement a flat rate withholding tax, independent of the effective rate of tax in the residence of the taxpayer. Such systems, for instance, are in place under the transitory regime of the EUSD, at a rate of 35 per cent on interest on savings, or under FATCA, at a rate of 30 per cent.

---

[525] Rivolta (2012), p. 138.

[526] See Pistone (2013), p. 216 ff.

[527] See Perdelwitz (2011), p. 496.

[528] For a comparison between the Rubik system and automatic exchange of information, see infra p. 176 ff.

[529] See also infra p. 184.

# 10. Foreign Account Tax Compliance Act (FATCA)

## I. INTRODUCTION

The United States has been confronted with billions of dollars of losses every year, as a result of offshore tax evasion.[530] Tax evasion mechanisms have been effective, notably by using bank secrecy rules in other foreign jurisdictions. In order to fight against offshore tax evasion, the United States has introduced various tax enforcement strategies, starting with the Qualified Intermediary, and culminating with the adoption of FATCA in 2010.[531]

As of 2001, foreign financial institutions could enter into a Qualified Intermediary (QI) agreement with the IRS. Under a QI agreement, non-US financial intermediaries agreed to collect information from their customers investing in the United States, identifying whether they are US persons or not, and which of the non-US persons are entitled to a reduced withholding tax at source.[532] Under the QI agreement, the foreign financial intermediary had to determine the identity of their US customers but they did not have to report the identity of non-US clients (including corporations), to the extent that the foreign financial intermediary (QI) concluded that the proper withholding tax was withheld on US source income of the non-US clients.[533]

The QI system was however insufficient to combat offshore tax evasion. Indeed, as of 2000, various banks, and notably LGT and UBS, have been found helping US clients to hide offshore accounts. In the LGT bank, the IRS has identified at least a hundred accounts belonging

---

[530] Blank/Mason (2014), p. 1245; Staff of the Homeland Security and Governmental Affairs Permanent Subcommittee on Investigations, 110th Cong., Tax Haven Banks and U.S. Tax Compliance, 2008, p. 3.

[531] Blank/Mason (2014), p. 1245.

[532] Grinberg (2012), p. 16.

[533] Blank/Mason (2014), p. 1245.

to US persons.[534] More precisely, in the UBS case,[535] following the whistleblowing of Bradley Birkenfeld, it appeared that employees from the bank had been assisting US clients to open hidden offshore accounts, notably by interposing offshore shell companies. The UBS estimated that the QI agreement did not impose a withholding tax because the payments were made to foreign (non-US) entities, even though the bank knew that the beneficial owners of those shell companies were US persons.[536] After a first request pertaining to about 300 accounts, the UBS entered into a deferred prosecution agreement and agreed to disclose the names of 4250 US account holders. Later, starting notably in 2012, other Swiss banks became targets of investigations from the IRS and the United States Department of Justice (DoJ).[537]

As a result of these developments, Congress enacted FATCA on 18 March 2010.[538] The Act introduced Sections 1471 through 1474 in chapter 4 of the Internal Revenue Code (IRC). The IRS also issued the final FATCA regulations in January 2013.

## II. FATCA RULES

### A. In General

#### 1. Introduction
The purpose of FATCA is to ensure that all US direct and indirect owners of offshore accounts report annually to the IRS the value and income of those accounts.[539] The system is designed so that offshore income of US persons is reported and that deposits in offshore accounts are after tax income.[540] FATCA applies to both US direct and indirect owners of accounts, i.e. US account holders and foreign entities with substantial US owners.

#### 2. Withholdable payments to foreign financial institutions (FFI)
Under Section 1471(a) IRC, the withholding agent is required to withhold 30 per cent of any withholdable payment to a foreign financial

---

[534] Gupta (2013), p. 225; Permanent Subcommittee report, op.cit. p. 3 ff.
[535] See supra p. 43.
[536] Blank/Mason (2014), p. 1245.
[537] See infra p. 206 (solving the past).
[538] Hiring Incentives to Restore Employment Act.
[539] Tello (2014), p. 91.
[540] Ibid.

institution (FFI) which does not meet the requirement of Section 1471(b) IRC. Under the latter, FFIs are required to enter into an agreement with the IRS, in order to become participating FFIs.

In particular, participating FFIs are required to identify their US account holders and report, on an annual basis, the name, address and taxpayer identification number (TIN) of each account holder which is a specified US person, and the name, address and TIN of each substantial US owner of a US owned foreign entity, account number, account balance or value and gross receipt and gross withdrawals or payments from the account (Section 1471(c) IRC). A US owned foreign entity with a substantial US owner is an entity, which is more than 10 per cent owned, directly or indirectly, by a US person (Section 1471(d)(3) and 1473(2) IRC). Participating FFIs are also required to withhold 30 per cent of certain payments to a recalcitrant account holder or another financial institution, which does not meet the requirement of FATCA (Section 1471(b)(1)(D) IRC). In particular, the withholding tax applies to payments to non-participating FFIs, in cases where the funding of those payments to the extent attributable to a withholdable payment (*'passthru payment'*).[541] This withholding tax induces foreign FFIs, 'not investing in the US, but investing in or through participating financial institutions', to join FATCA.[542]

In order to identify pre-existing and new account holders, FFIs have to apply due diligence processes, which are similar to the anti-money laundering and know your customer (KYC) rules.[543] Extensive rules have been implemented in the Treasury Regulations to that end. Since the burden of proof rests on the account holder, if the latter cannot prove that he or she is a non-US person, the holder is treated as a so-called 'recalcitrant account holder'.[544]

If foreign law would prevent the FFI from reporting the required information with respect to a US account maintained by such an institution, the participating FFI has to close the account, unless a waiver is obtained from the account holder within a reasonable period of time (Section 1471(b)(1)(F) IRC).

According to Section 1473 IRC, a *withholding payment* means, subject to some exceptions,

---

[541]  See Section 1471(d)(7)IRC; Grinberg (2013), p. 331.
[542]  Grinberg (2013), p. 331; for more details about 'passthru payments', see Harvey Jr. (2011), p. 13 s.
[543]  Treas Regs 1.1471-4(c) 2013; Cavelti (2013), p. 185.
[544]  Cavelti (2013), p. 185.

(i) any payment of interest (including original issue discount), dividends, rents, salaries, wages, premiums, annuities, compensations, remunerations, emoluments, and other fixed or determinable annual or periodical gains, profits, and income, if such payment is from sources within the United States, and (ii) any gross proceeds from the sale or other disposition of any property of a type which can produce interest or dividends from sources within the United States.

A FFI is any financial institution which is a foreign entity. A *financial institution* means any entity that (A) accepts deposits in the ordinary course of a banking or similar business, (B) as a substantial portion of its business, holds financial assets for the account of others, or (C) is engaged (or holding itself out as being engaged) primarily in the business of investing, reinvesting, or trading in securities (as defined in section 475 (c)(2) without regard to the last sentence thereof), partnership interest, commodities (as defined in section 475(e)(2), or any interest (including a futures or forward contract or option) in such securities, partnership interests, or commodities (Section 1471(d)(5) IRC). In addition, the reporting and withholding requirements also apply in principle to US accounts maintained by each other FFI which is a member of the same *expanded affiliated* group as such FFI (Section 1471(e) IRC). An expanded affiliated group is made up of all members of a group, which is owned through 50 per cent ownership determined by either vote or value.[545]

The withholding tax, under Section 1471(a), is however not due on certain payments, to the extent that the beneficial owner of such payments is, according to Section 1471(f) IRC,

(1) any foreign government, any political subdivision of a foreign government, or any wholly owned agency or instrumentality of any one or more of the foregoing, (2) any international organization or any wholly owned agency or instrumentality thereof, (3) any foreign central bank of issue, or (4) any other class of persons identified by the Secretary for purposes of this subsection as posing a low risk of tax evasion.

---

[545] See Section 1471(e)(2) IRC; Treas. Reg. 1.1471-5(i)(2); Tello (2014), p. 100 (describing the transitory rules to alleviate some of the problems of the requirement that each member of the expanded affiliated group must be either a participating FFI or a deemed compliant FFI). It appears that the final Regulations keep 31 December 2015 as the end of the transitory period; Zagaris (2014), p. 1058.

In that context, the Treasury Regulations have implemented the category of '*deemed-compliant*' FFIs.[546]

### 3. Withholdable payments to other foreign entities

Under Section 1472 (a) IRC, the withholding agent must also deduct and withhold a 30 per cent tax on any withholdable payment to a non-financial foreign entity (NFFE), if (i) the beneficial owner of such payment is such entity or any other non-financial foreign entity and (ii) the requirements of subsection (b) are not met with respect to such a beneficial owner, i.e. if a waiver from withholding is not provided.

A NFFE is any foreign entity that is not a financial institution. A *waiver* from the withholding tax exists however, if (i) such beneficial owner or the payee provides the withholding agent with a *certification* that such beneficial owner does not have any substantial US owners, or provides the name, address, and TIN of each substantial US owner of such beneficial owner, (ii) the withholding agent does not know, or have reason to know, that any information provided by the beneficial owner or payee is incorrect, and (iii) the withholding agent reports the information provided (Art. 1472 IRC).

Payments to so-called 'excepted NFFEs' are however not subject to the withholding tax, as long as the NFFE identifies itself as such.[547] Excepted NFFEs are, according to Section 1472 (c) IRC:

(A) any corporation the stock of which is regularly traded on an established securities market,
(B) any corporation which is a member of the same expanded affiliated group as a corporation described in subparagraph A,
(C) any entity which is organized under the laws of a possession of the United States and which is wholly owned by one or more bona fide residents (as defined in section 937(a)) of such possession,
(D) any foreign government, any political subdivision of a foreign government, or any wholly owned agency or instrumentality of any one or more of the foregoing,
(E) any international organization or any wholly owned agency or instrumentality thereof,
(F) any foreign central bank of issue, or
(G) any other class of persons identified by the Secretary for purposes of this subsection, and
(2) any class of payments identified by the Secretary for purposes of this subsection as posing a low risk of tax evasion.

---

[546] See Treas. Reg. 1.1471-5(f); see also Tello (2014), p. 98 f.
[547] Gupta (2013), p. 234.

Excepted NFFEs also include so-called *'active'* NFFEs.[548] An entity is an active NFEE if less than 50 per cent of its gross income from the preceding calendar year is passive income and less than 50 per cent of the weighted average percentage of assets held produce or are held for the production of passive income.[549] If these conditions are met, payments to the active NFFE are not subject to the FATCA withholding.[550]

Payments to nonfinancial group entities may also be exempted from the withholding tax, provided all of its activities consist of owning the stock of one or more subsidiaries that each engage in a non-financial business.[551] The purpose of this rule is to provide relief for foreign holding companies receiving income from their US parent, to the extent that the foreign holding does not engage in financial activities.

## 4. Comments

The FATCA mechanism is both innovative and effective.[552] Under the rules, the foreign entities are divided into two classes.[553] FFIs, on the one hand, and NFFEs, on the other hand.

If the FFI, anywhere in the world, refuses to comply with the FATCA rules, it will be subject to a 30 per cent withholding tax on US source payments, notably dividends, interest, fixed or determinable annual or periodical (FDAP) income and gross proceeds from sale of assets that generate US dividends or interest (Sections 1471(a) and 1473(1)). To avoid this withholding tax, FFIs must enter into an agreement with the IRS and report information on each US account held by US persons or by a non-US entity with substantial US owners (Section 1471(c) IRC).[554]

A NFFE, however, is not required to enter into an agreement with the IRS, but has similar due diligence requirements to identify the substantial US owners.[555] In particular, the NFFE has to provide the withholding agent with a certificate that confirms that it has no US owners, or identify the name, address and TIN of each substantial US owner (Art. 1472(b) IRC). However, as a result of the various exceptions, notably the 'excepted NFFE', including the 'active NFFE' categories, it appears that

---

[548] See Treas. Regs., Section 1.1472-1(c)(iv).
[549] See Treas. Regs, Section 1.1472-1(c)(1)(iv); Tello (2014), p. 99; see also Gupta (2013), p. 234.
[550] Tello (2014), p. 99; Gupta (2013), p. 234.
[551] Gupta (2013), p. 235; Tres. Regs. 1.1471-5(e)(5)(i).
[552] Blank/Mason (2014), p. 1246.
[553] Tello, (2014), p. 91.
[554] Blank/Mason (2014), p. 1246.
[555] Tello (2014), p. 91.

most NFFEs will not be subject to the complex FATCA requirements, other than to confirm their excepted status to the withholding agents.[556]

The FATCA provisions are also innovative, in several ways.[557] First, the scope of the withholding tax is much broader than before because it covers all kinds of returns from financial investment accounts, including gross proceeds from sales. Second, the disclosure requirements encompass accounts, regardless of whether they generate US source income or are held by an affiliate of a participating FFI. Third, it also requires reporting on accounts held by a foreign entity, notably if more than 10 per cent of the equity is held by a US person (Section 1471(d)(1)(A).

The FATCA regime also introduces new requirements to identify account holders. A delicate issue indeed is the requirement to identify pre-existing account holders, from before the entry into force of the system. In order to implement this, following a lengthy process, the Treasury Department issued detailed final regulations in order to respond to the various concerns raised by different industries, notably insurance and asset managers.[558]

An interesting development, in this context, is that the FATCA regime does not allow FFIs to rely on documentation provided by the customers, but requires additional due diligence processes based on indicia of US ownership in the files.[559]

Finally, in order not to disrupt markets, some statutory provisions were also introduced, such as the 'grand-father' provisions that exempt from withholding certain pre-existing obligations.[560]

## III. INTERGOVERNMENTAL AGREEMENTS (IGA)

### A. Introduction

FATCA, as a unilateral tax enforcement measure with extraterritorial effects, has raised criticism and concerns.[561] By definition, FATCA is targeted against offshore accounts of US persons (and foreign entities owned by US persons). In order to be implemented, foreign entities, and notably FFIs, which have to comply with FATCA, are usually in other

---

[556] Tello (2014), p. 99.
[557] Morse (2012), p. 535 s.
[558] Tello (2014), p. 92.
[559] Morse (2012), p. 536.
[560] Tello (2014), p. 92.
[561] See the various references by Blank/Mason (2014), p. 1246.

jurisdictions. In order to force them to comply, FATCA introduced a 'carrot and stick' mechanism, by imposing a withholding tax on non-cooperative foreign entities.[562]

However, an important impediment to the implementation of FATCA is the potential conflict between the various requirements, in particular reporting, and domestic privacy rules.[563] For example, in the EU, the EU Data Protection Directive would prevent any EU state from collecting and disclosing data as to whether an account holder is a US citizen or resident.[564] The same issue would also occur under other data privacy or bank secrecy laws of other states.

The solution to this problem became the intergovernmental agreement (IGA).[565] On 7 February 2012, the US Treasury and five EU states (so-called G5), namely France, Germany, Italy, Spain and the United Kingdom, announced that they had developed a model IGA, the so-called Model 1 IGA, which in essence would solve the conflict of laws issue, by requiring local FFIs to disclose the FATCA required information to their local tax authorities, rather than to the IRS.[566] The local tax authorities would then pass on the information to the IRS through automatic exchange of information, under a tax treaty, a TIEA or the CoE/OECD Multilateral convention on Mutual Assistance in Tax Matters.[567] It should be noted that this draft model provided for a reciprocal form of automatic exchange of information. The first Model 1 IGA was published on 26 July 2012. On 14 September 2012, the first IGA Model 1 was concluded with the United Kingdom. This IGA follows the Model published on 26 July 2012. Currently, there are more than a hundred Model 1 IGAs signed.

After the announcement of the development of an IGA Model 1 by the G5 and the United States, Japan and Switzerland entered into negotiations, which resulted in the design of a so-called Model 2 IGA.[568] This Model 2 was published on 14 November 2012. Under this Model, local

---

[562] Cavelti (2013), p. 186

[563] Tello (2014), p. 92; Blank/Mason (2014), p. 1246; Grinberg (2013), p. 331.

[564] Tello (2014), p. 92.

[565] Tello (2014), p. 92; Grinberg (2013), p. 331.

[566] US Treasury, Joint Statement from the United States, France, Germany, Italy, Spain and the United Kingdom Regarding an Intergovernmental Approach to Improving International Tax Compliance and Implementing FATCA (7 February 2012); Tello (2014), p. 92.

[567] Tello (2014), p. 93.

[568] Tello (2014), p. 93; for a comparison of Model 1 and 2 IGAs, see Somare/Wöhrer (2014), p. 397 ff.

FFIs would be allowed to enter into an agreement directly with the IRS and report the required information on US accounts directly to the IRS.

An IGA, like a TIEA, is treated in the US like an executive agreement and not a tax treaty.[569] As a consequence, it does not require the Senate's approval.

## B.   Model 1 IGA

Under a Model 1 IGA, FFIs have to report the US account holders directly to their local tax authority, which then passes on the information to the IRS, through a double tax treaty, an IGA, or another multilateral convention. As a consequence, the United States does not impose the 30 per cent withholding tax and the FFIs are no longer obliged to enter into an agreement directly with the IRS. In addition, simplification rules are included. As of 15 September 2013, it appeared that ten Model 1 IGAs had been signed; they included an extensive list of FATCA partner exempt entities and accounts under Annex II.[570] However, future IGAs will probably not include such a detailed list of tax-exempt entities.[571]

Under the initial version, as a follow up to the 7 February 2012 statement, the United States may agree to provide similar reporting on the US accounts of the other country's residents (*reciprocal* version).[572] It would imply that the United States would agree to establish a domestic reporting system under which US financial institutions ('UFI') would identify their customers and report information about foreign account holders to the IRS, which would then pass it on to the partner states.[573] The extent to which such an effective reciprocal system will be put in place will be one of the main issues of the implementation of IGAs in the future. In any event, it seems that the reciprocal version of the Model 1 IGA would only be available to jurisdictions with which the United States has a double taxation treaty, or a TIEA, and where Treasury and the IRS have agreed that the recipient State has 'robust protections and practices in place, to ensure that the information remains confidential and that it is used solely for tax purposes'.[574]

Another version of Model 1, however, is non-reciprocal. The main difference here is that the IGA foreign partner will have to collect and

---

[569]   Tello (2014), p. 93.
[570]   Ibid.
[571]   Ibid.
[572]   Tello (2014), p. 93; Cavelti (2013), p. 187.
[573]   In the same vein, Cavelti (2013), p. 187.
[574]   Zagaris (2014), p. 1055.

report information about US accounts holders while the United States will not need to reciprocate.[575] Such a type of IGA should be interesting for countries with limited (or no) income tax and that favour privacy.[576]

## C. Model 2 IGA

### 1. In general

Under the Model 2, FFIs are authorized to enter into an agreement directly with the IRS and to apply the FATCA implementation rules. In addition, an exchange of information system is put in place between the Contracting States, so that eventually recalcitrant account holders are disclosed. The main difference between Model 2 and 1 is that Model 1 gives a legal basis for FFIs in the Contracting State to enter into an agreement with the IRS and report directly information about US account holders.[577]

So far, the United States has entered into Model 2 IGAs with Bermuda, Japan and Switzerland.

### 2. The United States IGA with Switzerland[578]

Under the United States/Swiss IGA, Swiss FFIs are authorized to enter into an agreement with the IRS and to report information about US account holders (Art. 3 Agreement). Such registration and reporting is not regarded as a violation of Art. 271 of the Swiss Criminal Code (Art. 4 Agreement).

Under Art. 5, exchange of information about US accounts and on amounts paid to non-participating FFIs will take place according to Art. 26 of the 1996 double taxation treaty (DTC) between Switzerland and the United States, as amended under the Protocol of 2009. However, requests for information exchange cannot be made before the entry into force of that Protocol and to information pertaining to the period beginning before the entry into force of the Agreement (Art. 5 par. 1 *in fine* Agreement).[579]

---

[575]　Zagaris (2014), p. 1056.

[576]　Ibid.

[577]　Tello (2014), p. 94.

[578]　See Accord entre la Suisse et les Etats-Unis d'Amérique sur leur coopération visant à faciliter la mise en oeuvre du FATCA, of 14 February 2013, which entered into force on 2 June 2014, RS 0.672.933.63.

[579]　As of today, even though the Protocol has been ratified by Switzerland and signed and transmitted to the US Senate, it has not yet been ratified by the United States, see also Tello (2014), p. 94. In the meantime, we wonder whether a specific exchange of information agreement, such as modified TIEA, could not

These requests will take the form of so-called 'group requests', which are admissible under Art. 26 of the DTC. This rule takes into account the recent developments in favour of group requests, following the July 2012 position of the OECD.[580]

In addition, the FTA is required to respond to a request for information within eight months after the request (Art. 5 par. 3 lit. c Agreement). If that deadline is not respected, the account is regarded as recalcitrant until the information is provided and the withholding tax is due after the eight month period expires (Art. 7 par. 2 Agreement).[581] Finally, in accordance with Swiss law, the amount of tax withheld on payments to financial accounts has to be borne by the account holder (Art. 7 par. 2 *in fine* Agreement). This rule is important because it allowed the Swiss FFIs to pass on the cost of any withholding tax to a recalcitrant account holder.[582]

There is a most-favoured nation clause in Art. 12 should the United States grant a more favourable regime, for part. C (Obligations of the United States) and Annex I of the Agreement, to any other jurisdiction. In addition, according to Art. 13, the door remains open to negotiate a Model 1 reciprocal IGA with the United States. It appears recently that Switzerland wishes to renegotiate the Agreement and is moving towards such a Model 1 IGA. In our view, a Model 2 IGA can be understood because at the time of the negotiations the 'Rubik' strategy was at the forefront of the Swiss policy. Now that the path has moved towards AEOI, the Model 2 IGA with its unilateral approach does not make much sense.

### D.  Other FATCA Models

The Treasury Department is also willing to enter into 'free-standing' IGAs with countries that do not have tax information exchange rules with the United States.[583] This could take the form of either a Model 1 (but non reciprocal) or a Model 2 IGA.

---

be adopted between the two States during the transitory period before the ratification of the 2009 protocol.

[580]  See also supra p. 22.
[581]  Tello (2014), p. 94.
[582]  Ibid.
[583]  Ibid.

# IV. ISSUES

## A. A Major Development

FATCA represents a major achievement. It includes all the essential features of a new global standard for exchange of information.[584] Indeed, FATCA has precipitated the movement and efforts towards multilateral information exchange. It could also help to improve the development within the EU, in particular towards broadening the scope of both the EU DAC and EUSD, which have been slowly adapted, after considerable efforts from some states attempting to preserve their bank secrecy.[585]

Some challenges are however still ahead. First, the issue of reciprocity appears to be critical. Second, it is also important that the new rules, in order to become a global standard, cover the most important financial places in the world,[586] and are implemented effectively in an equivalent way (level playing field).

## B. Reciprocity

One of the main challenges for the future implementation of the FATCA model is reciprocity. Indeed, under the initial Model 1, the United States 'acknowledge the need to achieve equivalent levels of reciprocal automatic information exchange'.[587]

The extent to which the United States may introduce such reciprocal rules of domestic reporting, under the current regime, remains to be analysed. The implementation of such rules is yet essential for the global development and acceptance of FATCA.[588] Indeed, reciprocity under FATCA would imply that US financial institutions would have similar reporting obligations towards account holders resident in the IGA partner.

Currently, the United States exchanges information with treaty partners and with the parties to the CMAAT. Basically, information for these exchanges of information is collected by the US withholding agent and includes the name of the beneficial owner, the amount paid, the type of income and the tax withheld.[589] It is however not clear to what extent an

---

[584] Blank/Mason (2014), p. 1248.
[585] Ibid.
[586] Cavelti (2013), p. 188.
[587] Reciprocal IGA, Model 1; Cavelti (2013), p. 188.
[588] See also Cavelti (2013), p. 189.
[589] Tello (2014), p. 95. This information is collected under Form W-8BEN.

effective exchange of information occurs, 'because there is no uniform method of providing the information to the treaty partner'.[590] In addition, if the US financial institutions also have to apply FATCA rules for payments to entities, they would be confronted with the issue of accounts held by LLCs and, in particular, Delaware limited liability companies (LLCs) for which beneficial ownership information is lacking.[591] Indeed, there are limits to obtaining information because the rules about identification of beneficial ownership of corporations, LLCs or other entities are governed by state governments in the United States.[592] It appears that many states do not require ownership information to be provided, either at the time of incorporation or subsequently.[593] This problematic situation is however well known, including at the OECD Global Forum.[594] The peer review, in particular, identified issues concerning ownership information on Delaware entities and LLCs in general. Even if the IRS used its powers to inquire about ownership information in these cases, the effectiveness of these powers would be limited if the information is not held by a person within the jurisdiction of the United States.[595]

The situation is however evolving. Developments have already occurred in the area of interest on deposits from non-resident aliens. The implementation of the *final interest reporting regulations*, on 17 April 2012, has obliged US banks and other US payers of bank deposits to report interest earned by non-resident alien individuals, who reside in a country with an exchange of information agreement.[596] It should be mentioned that it is only the reporting on individual owners of bank deposits which is required, and not on deposit interests earned by corporations or a foreign government.[597] Revenue Procedure 2012-24 provides a list of countries with which the United States has in effect an income tax or other convention relating to the exchange of tax information. Financial institutions that maintain deposits of resident customers

---

[590] Tello (2014), p. 95.

[591] Blank/Mason (2014), p. 1249.

[592] Zagaris (2014), p. 970.

[593] Ibid.

[594] See OECD, Global Forum on Transparency and Exchange of Information for Tax Purposes Peer Reviews: United States 2011, nn. 38, 87; Blank/Mason (2014), p. 1249; Zagaris (2014), p. 970.

[595] OECD, Peer Review United States, June 2011, n. 39; Zagaris (2014), p. 970.

[596] Tello (2014), p. 95.

[597] Ibid.

in those countries will have to report the interest earned on those deposits, as of 1 January 2013.[598] There is also a list of countries with which the Treasury and the IRS have determined that automatic exchange of information on deposit interest is appropriate. Currently, only Canada is on this list. This list should also include in the future the countries that concluded an IGA Model 1 (reciprocal agreement) with the United States.

It should be mentioned that the Florida and Texas Bankers Association have challenged the reporting requirements of the recent bank deposit interest regulations. Their challenge was however defeated by the US District Court for the District of Columbia, on 13 January 2014.[599]

Information exchanged under the deposit interest regulation is however not equivalent to FATCA.[600] First, FATCA applies to a broader scope of income than interest, such as dividends, rent, and other FDAP income, including gross proceeds from gains. Second, the reporting of interest only applies to individuals, while FATCA in particular requires identification of the US owners of corporations.[601] It remains to be seen in the future the extent to which the acknowledgment in favour of reciprocity made by the United States under the February 2012 joint statement will evolve.

The implementation of rules similar to FATCA in the United States will furthermore have to face strong political opposition, in particular from the financial sector. The scope of the reciprocity required towards the United States by FATCA partners is also not clearly defined as of today.

## C. FATCA as a New Standard

It is interesting to note that, despite wide criticism, FATCA had a major influence on tax systems around the world as a new and different model to fight against tax fraud and the use of non-disclosed offshore accounts. This influence emerged from the model itself, which started as a unilateral statute to be transformed into a bilateral IGA, sometimes even providing for an (albeit asymmetric) reciprocity.

FATCA started then to be implemented as a model for other jurisdictions. In particular, the United Kingdom has introduced 'son of

---

598    Tello (2014), p. 95; the report will be made on Form 1042-S.
599    *Florida Bankers Association et al. V. United States Department of Treasury et al*, US District Court of Columbia, Civil Action n. 13.529.
600    See also Cavelti (2013), p. 189.
601    Tello (2014), p. 96; Cavelti (2013), p. 190.

FATCA' legislation or agreements with Crown dependencies or overseas territories.[602]

At the same time, FATCA has accelerated efforts toward multilateral information exchange.[603] In particular, at the EU level, FATCA was viewed as an opportunity to redefine and broaden the scope of existing Directives, notably the Savings and the Administrative Assistance Directives. The most-favoured nation clause of the EU Directive on Administrative Assistance, in particular, could lead to a major broadening of the scope of the Directive by introducing the rules of FATCA to all other EU countries.[604]

The same is true for OECD Model, which is implementing a new global standard of automatic exchange of information. On 21 July 2014, the OECD publicized the new Standard for automatic exchange of financial account information in tax matters. In the introduction, the OECD mentions that the Common Reporting Standard,

> with a view to maximizing efficiency and reducing cost for financial institutions, draws extensively on the intergovernmental approach to implementing FATCA. While the intergovernmental approach to FATCA reporting does deviate in certain aspects from the CRS, the differences are driven by the multilateral nature of the CRS system and other US specific aspects, in particular the concept of taxation on the basis of citizenship and the presence of a significant and comprehensive FATCA withholding tax.[605]

---

[602] Blank/Mason (2014), p. 1247.
[603] Blank/Mason (2014), p. 1248.
[604] See infra p. 116.
[605] OECD, Standard for Automatic Exchange of Financial Account Information in Tax Matters, July 2004, n. 5 ad Introduction.

# 11. Towards automatic exchange of information

## I. HISTORICAL PERSPECTIVE

The first attempt to implement a global system of automatic cross-border exchange of information can be traced back to the 1927 Draft Model Convention of the League of Nations.[606] This Model was later modified in the 1943 Mexico Draft and 1946 London Draft of the League of Nations.

Exchange of information rules were later incorporated in the OECD Model DTC of 1963. At this stage, the focus of the Model relied on exchange of information upon request. The OECD Model, however already includes the various forms of exchange of information, including automatic exchange; such a system is still allowed, under Art. 26 OECD Model DTC, but is not compulsory.[607] The CMAAT, developed by the OECD and the European Council, introduced in 1988 the possibility of automatic exchange, which however necessitates a specific agreement between the competent authorities of the participating states. The Nordic Convention on mutual administrative assistance in tax matters also provides for automatic exchange of information.

In the EU, various instruments have been developed as tools against international tax fraud in the area of both direct and indirect taxation. In particular, the EUSD, adopted in 2004, provides for automatic exchange of information on savings interests paid by an EU paying agent to an individual resident in another EU Member State. A transitional system of withholding tax was allowed in Austria, Belgium and Luxembourg. Equivalent measures have also been adopted with selected third countries. The EU also introduced further the DAC, in 2012, which provides for mandatory automatic exchange of information, as of January 1 2015, on five specific categories of income and wealth, namely income on employment, director's fees, life insurance products, pension and income and wealth from immovable property. In 2014, the EU also proposed to

---

[606] Dean (2008), p. 609; Parida (2013), p. 425; see supra p. 30.
[607] See OECD Commentary to Art. 26 DTC Model, n. 9 ad Art. 26.

modify the DAC to provide for automatic exchange of information on specific additional categories of income.

The United States introduced the FATCA in 2010. The FATCA rules entered into force in July 2014 and provide for a unilateral form of identification and automatic reporting on US persons by FFI. The FATCA rules were further complemented by intergovernmental agreements (IGA), with various models,[608] which introduced an enhanced bilateral cooperation, sometimes – at least for Model 1 IGAs – with a reciprocal commitment to automatic exchange of information.

An alternative model to automatic exchange of information was developed by Switzerland in 2012. Under the so-called Rubik agreements, which were adopted between Switzerland and the United Kingdom and Austria, Swiss paying agents would levy a final withholding tax which is designed to correspond to the rate of income tax in the country or residence of the beneficial owner of the income.

The 'big bang' of 2009 has provoked a major development in the field of global transparency and exchange of information. Most countries, including jurisdictions with strong bank secrecy rules, have agreed to adopt the international standard for information exchange.[609] At this time, the minimum global standard was still focusing on an exchange of information upon request of information foreseeably relevant for the implementation of domestic laws of the Contracting States, without the possibility to refuse to supply it based on domestic bank secrecy rules. Progress was still being made at the G20, the OECD, the EU, and the Global Forum on Transparency and Exchange of Information for Tax Purposes in improving transparency and exchange of information upon request.[610]

Later on, especially as of 2012, the political focus started to move in favour of automatic exchange of information. It appears that the implementation of FATCA in the United States put great pressure in this direction. In this respect, the joint statement of 5 February 2012 between the G5 (France, Germany, Italy, Spain and the United Kingdom) and the United States, which announced their intention to develop a system of multilateral automatic exchange of information, in order to implement the FATCA rules, can be described as a *turning point*.[611] A little more than a year after this joint statement, namely on 19 April 2013, the G20 Finance Ministers and Central Bank Governors endorsed automatic exchange of

---

[608]  See supra p. 156 ff.
[609]  Oberson (2013), p. 21.
[610]  OECD, Standard of AEIO (2014), n. 2 ad Introduction.
[611]  In this sense, Tello/Maherbe (2014), p. 1.

information as the future new standard. On 6 September 2013, the G20 leaders committed to automatic exchange of information as the new international standard. In February 2014, the G20 Finance Ministers and Central Bank Governors endorsed the Common Reporting Standard for automatic exchange of information, which was then published in July 2014.

## II. FORMS OF AUTOMATIC EXCHANGE OF INFORMATION (AEOI)

### A. Legal Basis

There are currently about *five* main international instruments in force that provide a legal basis for automatic exchange of information.

First, double taxation treaties based on Art. 26 of the OECD Model DTC, the UN or the US Models, provide for three different forms of exchange of information: upon request, spontaneous and automatic. Automatic exchange of information is however an option and is not compulsory. It follows that, from a bilateral standpoint, countries that wish to implement automatic exchange of information simply have to introduce a competent authority agreement (CAA), according to the OECD Common Reporting Standard described later[612] in order to implement AEOI.

Second, TIEA models, in either a bi- or multilateral form, may also serve as a basis for automatic exchange of information. These instruments are especially effective with countries with no DTC, in the form of an OECD or UN Model, because they do not have a comprehensive income tax system. However, according to Art. 5 of the TIEA Model, these treaties typically provide for exchange of information upon request only. Subject to an agreement between the Contracting States, automatic exchange may however also be included under this type of Model.[613]

Third, according to Art. 6 of the CMAAT, automatic exchange of information is allowed between Contracting States in respect of specific cases and in accordance with the procedures *mutually agreed* between the states. It means that Contracting States, in order to implement automatic exchange of information, may do so simply by entering into mutual CAA. Indeed, automatic exchange of information under the CMAAT is

---

[612] See infra p. 188.
[613] See OECD Commentary to TIEA n. ad; Parida (2013), p. 430.

based on a separate agreement between the competent authorities of the Contracting States. In this respect, the adoption of a multilateral CAA, in the form developed in the OECD standard of AEOI, may also be facilitated under the CMAAT. In its recent publication describing the international standard for AEOI, the OECD indicated that the CMAAT is a much more efficient instrument in order to establish a global automatic exchange, notably because of its global reach.[614] The mutual CAA adopted between the contracting parties, based on the legal basis of the CMAAT, will then activate and 'operationalize' the automatic exchange between the participants.[615] This is the step that has notably been taken, on 29 October 2014, by the 51 jurisdictions, which have signed a multilateral competent authority agreement in Berlin, during the meeting of the Global Forum, and have committed to exchange information as of 2017.

Fourth, AEOI may also be based, between EU countries, on the EU Directives. For direct tax purposes, notably, the domestic rules implementing the EUSD form such legal basis (to the exception of the transitory withholding tax system) for savings income paid by EU paying agents to individuals in other Member States. According to Art. 9 EUSD, the competent authority of the source state is obliged to automatically communicate information on savings income covered by the directive to the competent authority of the EU State of residence of the individual beneficial owner of the income.[616] The EU DAC, in Art. 8, also provides for a mandatory AEOI on five categories of income and wealth. At the EU level various legal bases also exist in the field of VAT and excise tax.[617]

Fifth, following the implementation of FATCA, IGAs also serve as a legal basis for automatic exchange. In this respect, we tend to believe that the more promising models are IGAs based on Model 1, which include a reciprocal exchange. As the OECD recognized, there is even a possibility of entering into multilateral IGAs in order to introduce a global standard of AEOI.[618]

---

[614]   OECD, Standard AEOI 2014, n. 11 ad Introduction.
[615]   Ibid.
[616]   See also Parida (2013), p. 429.
[617]   See supra p. 126 ff.
[618]   OECD, Standard AEOI 2014, n. 16 ad Introduction.

## B. Main Features and Functioning of the Various Models

### 1. Introduction

In order to enhance international administrative cooperation and fight against offshore tax evasion, four different models have emerged:[619] (i) the OECD, based on a bilateral or a multi-lateral approach; (ii) the EU system focusing on the paying agent (EUSD and later automatic exchange directive on specific income); (iii) the US FATCA system requiring identification and reporting rules on FFI and (iv) the Swiss Rubik system of anonymously withholding tax.

All these systems have in common that they tend to focus on the financial intermediaries (also called paying agents) as tax collectors. While these four basic models do present major differences, which we are going to analyse further, it remains that they are all based on the same premises and, according to Grinberg, represent a 'remarkable shift' from 'a dispute about whether financial intermediaries should function as cross-border tax intermediaries to a dispute about how financial intermediaries should perform that role'.[620]

### 2. The EU system

The European system of taxing offshore accounts and other assets held by EU residents is based on two different directives.

Under the EUSD, as a general rule, EU paying agents are required to disclose automatically, to their national competent authority, interest payments on savings (as defined under EUSD) to an individual beneficial owner, resident in another EU state. The competent authority will then forward the information to the competent authority of the EU residence jurisdiction. As a compromise, Austria, Belgium and Luxembourg were allowed, during the so-called transitory period, to levy a withholding tax (currently 35 per cent) instead of automatic reporting. In addition, specific third countries, and notably Switzerland, had to adopt equivalent measures.[621] Currently a withholding tax on interest from savings (instead of automatic reporting) is applied, under the EUSD, by Austria, Luxembourg, and under bilateral agreements by Switzerland, Andorra, Liechtenstein, San Marino, and Monaco. Ten associated EU territories also apply the rules of the EUSD.[622]

---

[619] See also Grinberg (2012), p. 327 ff.
[620] Grinberg (2012), p. 343.
[621] See supra p. 89.
[622] See supra p. 89.

The EUSD is based on the *paying agent* system. This is the paying agent, resident in the EU (or in the country associated or bound by a bilateral agreement), which has to implement the rules of the EUSD and notably determine whether or not payments are subject to reporting. Then, under the ordinary rule, the paying agent automatically reports the savings income to its tax administration, which then forwards the information to the tax administration of the country of residence of the individual taxpayer resident in another EU state. Alternatively, under the applicable regime (notably for Austria and Luxembourg, and the five connected third states), the paying agent has to levy 35 per cent on the interest payment to the individual taxpayer resident in another EU state. The country of source keeps 25 per cent of the proceeds and refunds 75 per cent to the country of residence of the individual taxpayer. As Morse describes it, the EUSD is based on a bank-to-bank source government-to-residence government (B2G2G) approach.[623]

The new and interesting paying agent system was rather revolutionary. It has introduced one of the first systems of global automatic exchange of information on interest from savings accounts within the EU network. In addition, it focuses on the financial intermediary, in the EU (and connected jurisdictions), who becomes a sort of agent of the tax administration. The combination of a general automatic reporting with a transitional withholding regime can be explained by competition between financial centres. In particular, it appears that Austria, Belgium and Luxembourg wanted to ensure that competing financial centres, such as Switzerland, would be obliged to apply equivalent rules. The focus on countries with close ties with the EU and not on other financial centres such as Hong Kong or Singapore has sometimes been described as the 'Mercedes' length principle'.

The EUSD, however, has many weaknesses.[624] First, its scope is limited to interest on savings income. In order to address offshore accounts, the rules should include all sorts of investment income. Second, the system only covers paying agents that are inside the network, i.e. resident in the EU or in an associated or connected jurisdiction. In order to be really effective, the paying agent system should be adopted by the whole world, including notably other offshore financial centres such as Delaware, Singapore, Dubai or Hong Kong.[625] EU individuals could easily circumvent the rules of the EUSD by investing funds in a

---

[623]  Morse (2012), p. 538.
[624]  See Morse (2012), p. 538 ff; Cavelti (2013), p. 193 ff.
[625]  In this sense also Böckli (2000), p. 552.

jurisdiction outside the network covered by the EUSD system. Third, the EUSD only applies to interest payments to individual, beneficial owners of the payments. In particular, it does not apply to legal entities and allows paying agents to treat corporations as beneficial owners.[626]

As one commentator has demonstrated, in order to apply, the EUSD scope of application requires, like a 'gare de triage', a cumulative check-list analysis whether the payment is: (i) interest from savings; (ii) paid by a paying agent; (iii) the paying agent is resident in the EU; and (iv) the beneficiary is an individual resident in another EU state.[627] The automatic reporting (retrospectively, if applicable, of the withholding tax) only applies if all these conditions are met.

In order to close some of the loop-holes of this system, a proposal was presented to expand the scope of payments subject to reporting to specific financial instruments that serve as substitute for interest and to also include payments not only to individuals but to entities under a look-through approach based on anti-money laundering legislation.[628]

Following the developments in the area of international assistance in tax matters, and also in order to address some of the deficiencies of the EUSD, the EU adopted the DAC. The DAC introduced a global auto-matic exchange of information between EU countries on five specific categories of income and wealth, namely employment income, director's fees, life insurance products, pensions and ownership and income from immovable property. But the system, as we have seen, may lead to imbalances between the states, since competent authorities must exchange information that is *available*, which means retrievable in the tax files in accordance with domestic rules of information gathering.[629] In addition, according to Art. 8 par. 3 DAC, EU Member States have to indicate to the competent authority and to the EU Commission if they do not want to receive any information in one or all of these categories. Finally, if one Member State does not provide information in one or all of these categories, it will be considered that this state does not want to receive any information from the other states, which also demonstrates that the DAC has only been designed as an instrument for selected information.[630]

It follows that the DAC is not directly based on the paying agent system because the exchange of information is designed to go between

---

[626] EUSD, Art. 4 par. 2; Morse (2012), p. 539.
[627] See Böckli (2000), p. 542.
[628] Morse (2012), p. 540.
[629] Schilcher/Spies (2013), p. 215.
[630] Terra/Wattel (2012), p. 832; Muñoz Forner (2013) p. 269.

EU Member States, which have to have specific information available. The information will be gathered in each EU Member State, according to domestic law, about various types of taxpayers (employers, companies, insurance companies, real estate owners, etc.). Following the classification of Morse, the EU DAC is therefore more based on a source government-to-residence government (G2G) approach.

The new global system clearly goes in the direction of a global system of automatic exchange. Contrary to the EUSD, there is no transitory withholding tax system allowed. For these five types of investment income and wealth, automatic exchange is mandatory.

The EU DAC, however, is still not fully comprehensive in the area of automatic exchange of information. First, contrary to the EUSD, the territorial scope of the DAC is narrower that the EUSD, since the rules are in force only within the EU, despite the fact that other competing financial centres do not necessarily apply equivalent rules. In other words, the requirement of equivalent measures implemented by associated territories or five competing countries in Europe, notably Switzerland, is not applicable here. This restricted territorial scope may in part be explained by the development, since March 2009, resulting in the implementing of the OECD global standard of exchange of information by competing EU financial centres.[631]

Second, the DAC system is broader in material scope than the EUSD but still does not apply to many forms of investment income, such as dividends, royalties or capital gains. A pending proposal intends to expand the scope of the DAC and require automatic reporting on three additional types of income.[632]

The DAC still represents a major path on the road toward global exchange of information. In addition, it contains a most favoured nation clause that inherently provides for self-development of the DAC. Indeed, according to Art. 19 DAC, an EU Member State, which has a wider cooperation relationship with a third country, may not refuse to provide such wider cooperation to another Member State.[633] It follows that EU Member States entering into IGAs with the United States must extend the wider rules offered by this agreement.

---

[631]   See supra p. 8 ff.

[632]   See EU Commission proposal of 12 June 2013, COM (2013) 348 final; see supra p. 118.

[633]   Muñoz Forner (2013), p. 273.

## 3. The FATCA system

The essential feature of the FATCA regime, as designed in 2010, is to compel FFIs or NFFEs to report to the IRS all US persons (account holders), including US beneficial owners. Failing to do so, the FFIs or NFFEs will be subject to a 30 per cent withholding tax on investment income (including gross proceeds from sale) from the United States,[634] and this is regardless of whether those payments are made to US or non-US accounts at the FFI.[635] The purpose of FATCA is in fact to solve the problem of US taxpayers evading tax on income from offshore accounts.[636] As Morse characterizes it, FATCA follows a bank to residence-government (B2G) approach.[637] In many aspects, the pro-visions of FATCA are very innovative and have pushed existing law and practices in new directions.[638] In particular, the scope of the rules is very large and the withholding tax applies to all types of income from investment (FDAP income) and from the gross proceeds from the sale of securities. In addition, the fact that the requirement for disclosure applies regardless of whether the accounts generate US source income or are held at an affiliate of a participating FFI changes the nature of the withholding tax.[639] Here the tax is more a tool to force compliance of foreign entities with US accounts. Furthermore, FATCA also covers accounts held by a foreign entity if a US person holds more than 10 per cent of the equity; in other words, contrary to the QI regime, FATCA refuses to presume that a corporation is a taxpayer and beneficial owner.[640]

Finally, an important aspect of FATCA is that it is extra-territorial in nature. It targets foreign entities (FFI or NFFE) and it also applies if the foreign country has banking secrecy or data protection rules, which would prevent the financial entity from reporting.[641] This is the reason why, in order to be effective, the cooperation from the foreign country is required. As a result, the intergovernmental agreement approach (IGA) has been implemented. The IGA has transformed the unilateral character of FATCA into a bilateral (perhaps even multilateral) system of cooperation.

---

[634] See also Blank/Mason (2014), p. 1246; Cavelti (2013), p. 183.
[635] Morse (2012), p. 530.
[636] Morse (2012), p. 529.
[637] Morse (2012), p. 530.
[638] Morse (2012), p. 535.
[639] Ibid.
[640] Morse (2012), p. 536; IRC Sec. 1471(d)(1)(A).
[641] Cavelti (2013), p. 186.

## 4. The OECD system

In 2006, the OECD started to work on a project to improve the system of reduced source country withholding tax under a double taxation treaty.[642] It resulted, following the development of 2008, in a report of the Informal Consultative Group (ICG Report), which fundamentally recommended that OECD countries develop systems similar to QI.[643] The ICG project would however go further in some respects and notably abandon the anonymous withholding component of the QI system.[644] The project was later developed under the so-called Treaty Relief and Compliance Enhancement (TRACE) project.[645]

The amendments of the CoE/OECD CMAAT in 2011, which adapted to the changes of the OECD standard in Art. 26 Model DTC and was opened also to non-OECD members, provided further, as we have seen, a clear legal basis for automatic exchange of information.

Following the Cannes Summit of the G-20 in 2011, the OECD started to work actively with G-20 countries to develop a new single standard for automatic exchange of information. After various G-20 meetings, the OECD proposal was endorsed, notably during the July 2013 and September 2013 meetings. This resulted in the implementation of a common reporting standard (CRS) for automatic exchange of information.[646] The CRS was then published in July 2014.

## 5. The Swiss anonymous withholding alternative approach

The Swiss model, based on an anonymous withholding system, was clearly designed as an equivalent alternative for automatic exchange of information.[647] The so-called Rubik system is a compromise solution between two apparently conflicting rules: (i) the legitimate right to tax offshore accounts of the residence country and (ii) the protection of privacy of the foreign investor. To solve this contradiction, the system introduces a final withholding tax on offshore investment income as a

---

642    Grinberg (2012), p. 331.
643    Grinberg (2012), p. 332.
644    Grinberg (2012), p. 332.
645    OECD, Report of the informative consultative group on the taxation of collective investment vehicles and procedures for tax relief for cross-border investors and possible improvements to procedures for tax relief for cross-border investors, 2009 (TRACE Project).
646    OECD, Report to the G20: 'Automatic Exchange of Information: What it is, How it works, Benefits, What remains to be done', Paris 2012; see infra p. 188.
647    See in particular, the recital to the treaties with Germany, United Kingdom and Austria.

substitute for reporting in a residence country. The rate of the tax should however correspond to the rate which should have been paid in the residence country. The Swiss paying agent withholds the tax on Swiss source investment income (dividends, interest, royalties and capital gains), passes it to the Swiss Federal Tax Administration, which then transfers, on an anonymous basis, the tax to the residence country of the taxpayer.

As we have seen, the agreement with Austria and United Kingdom, which entered into force on 1 January 2013, provides a solution for the past and a solution for a future. The solution for the past corresponds to a sort of tax amnesty, with a lump-sum anonymous withholding tax to clear up undeclared taxable periods before the relevant period defined under the agreement. The solution for the future corresponds to the anonymous withholding system described above.[648] Alternatively, the taxpayers may voluntarily authorize their banks to disclose the information, instead of having to subject the income to the withholding tax. The tax is levied on investment income received by *individuals*, resident in the treaty partner (UK or Austria), but only includes entities, such as trusts, fiduciary accounts and domiciliary companies that can be attributed to the individual (look-through approach).[649]

The Swiss system is based on the paying agent principle, according to which the Swiss financial intermediary has to determine and levy the applicable withholding tax on investment income. It also offers an interesting compromise between effective taxation in the country of residence while preserving confidentiality. Contrary to the EU transitional system, the scope of the withholding tax is much broader since it covers fundamentally most types of investment income. In addition, the withholding tax also includes entities that have been interposed in order to circumvent the duty of the individual beneficial owner. Finally, from a financial standpoint, it offers direct flows of tax to the residence country, which could be welcome by some countries in a difficult financial position.

The Swiss Rubik agreements are rather complex and imply high implementation costs for the paying agents. Indeed, in order to be effective, the withholding tax rate has to correspond, for each different category of investment income, to the rate of the residence country. The

---

[648] For more details, see supra p. 146.
[649] See also Cavelti (2013), p. 199. Discretionary trusts are however excluded from the scope of the agreement.

Swiss paying agent must then correctly characterize each type of investment income and then apply the relevant withholding.

## C. Comparison of Automatic Exchange vs. Withholding Models

### 1. Commonalities

Despite their differences, both systems of automatic exchange and final withholding have a *common goal*: to fight against international tax avoidance.

Contrary to the usual system of exchange of information upon request, which remains the most frequent system endorsed by the OECD standard of Art. 26, both systems also provide for an *automatic* and *standardized* mechanism of tax cooperation between states.[650] While this is obvious for the automatic exchange of information, it is also a common feature of the withholding tax. In this case, the paying agent has to determine its obligations under the treaty and automatically withhold the tax due on the investment income. The tax is then automatically transferred to the country of residence of the taxpayer.

There are also similarities in the use of financial intermediaries as agents to implement the rules of international assistances in tax matters. While it is common that financial intermediaries serve as auxiliaries for domestic tax authorities, it is a profound change in the system that financial intermediaries serve as agents for foreign tax authorities.[651] Under the double taxation treaty between the United States and Switzerland, there was already an embryonic form of cooperation from the Swiss financial institution in favour of the United States, under the so-called, additional withholding tax. Under this system, in order to secure the correct amount of withholding tax, the Swiss bank had to levy an additional withholding tax in order to ensure that the client would only receive 70 per cent.[652] After the introduction of the QI system, such additional tax still applies but only for Swiss taxpayers.[653] But this system was of limited scope and not as far reaching as the new international trend towards using the financial intermediary as an agent for a foreign tax administration, such as the EUSD, FATCA or the Swiss Rubik models.

In both systems, the financial intermediaries (or paying agents) must: (i) identify the relevant taxpayers; (ii) determine the tax liability and

---

[650] Cavelti (2013), p. 201.
[651] Cavelti (2013), p. 200; Grinberg (2012), p. 322.
[652] See Oberson/Hull (2011), p. 144.
[653] Oberson (2014), p. 174.

(iii) apply the implementation rules. The level of due diligence rules and know your customer principles may differ, depending on the model applicable but this as such is not a difference between the two systems. This rule is also true under the Swiss system because the paying agent has to identify the beneficial owner of the investment income. But should the system be designed differently, so that a flat-rate withholding tax would apply, irrespective of the residence of the taxpayer, the withholding tax would then not require the determination by the paying agent of the beneficial ownership of the investment.[654]

## 2. Differences

There are however major differences between the two systems. Perhaps the most important one is a matter of principle: the withholding tax mechanism preserves the *privacy* of the taxpayer and does not disclose his or her identity to the tax administration of residence. By contrast, in a system of automatic exchange, the identity, residence, income and other information, are routinely transferred to the residence tax authorities. In other words, the withholding system assists the residence country in the collection of tax and, in a way, levies it for the account of the tax administration, while the automatic exchange, however, assists the residence country in the relevant information required to later correctly tax resident taxpayers. As Cavelti has demonstrated, finally, the issue at stake fundamentally refers to questions of tax morality, and differences of perception toward the weight of privacy, on the one hand, and the power of the government, on the other hand.[655]

Another major difference, sometimes described as the main advantage of the automatic system, is the limited scope of the withholding tax on investment income, and notably its inability to cover changes in *principal*.[656] 'Anonymous withholding is triggered only when interest, dividends or capital gains are earned in a foreign accounts, whereas automatic information reporting can be structured both to report on income and gains and to measure the growth of principal in a foreign account'.[657] In addition, business or income from enterprises, including fraudulent deductions, or fictitious intercompany loans, are not covered by the withholding tax.

---

[654] Cavelti (2013), p. 206.
[655] Cavelti (2013), p. 210 ff.
[656] Cavelti (2013), p. 201; Grinberg (2012), p. 348 ff.
[657] Grinberg (2012), p. 348.

Even if the rate of the withholding tax is designed to correspond to the domestic residence rate, the withholding tax fails to take into consideration the global economic capacity of the resident taxpayer. As long as the domestic rate is proportional, this is not a major issue, but if the rate on investment income in the country of residence is proportional, the withholding tax does not match the real economic capacity of the taxpayer. This could lead to the consequence that taxpayers who are not taxed at the maximum rate in their country of residence would, most likely, move into voluntary disclosure.[658] In this case, the withholding tax does not replace automatic exchange.

The implementation costs of the two systems, notably the operational requirement, seem to be comparable.[659] Both require identification by the financial intermediary of the relevant taxpayer, its domicile, and reporting requirements. However, according to the withholding tax system, the *collection* of tax is done directly by the financial intermediary and then transferred to the tax administration of the residence country. By contrast, under an automatic reporting, the collection has to be achieved by the tax administration of the residence country, based on the data transferred. In this aspect, the withholding tax appears to be more burdensome, in the sense that it requires a careful analysis of the characterization rules and rates of tax under the treaty, including potential changes under the law of the domestic residence state.[660] In fact the more treaties with foreign countries, the more difficult it is to apply the withholding tax system. This aspect should however be balanced with the high administrative costs and requirements that an automatic system implies, such as technology, matching of information and language issues.

### 3. Overall assessment

The main advantage of the withholding tax system is that the tax is immediately transferred to the residence state, under the intermediation of the paying agent in the source state. This could be especially helpful for residence countries in difficult financial situations or that cannot afford the large infrastructure required for automatic reporting.

For some policy makers, the respect of privacy also is an important advantage of this system, while others take the opposite view. Indeed, automatic exchange tends to have a deterrent effect against tax evasion. It

---

[658]   Cavelti (2013), p. 207.
[659]   Ibid.
[660]   Grinberg (2012), p. 351; Cavelti (2013), p. 207.

deters rather than detects.[661] Privacy, for those who favour the deterrent effect of automatic exchange, is therefore seen as a disadvantage of the system.[662]

However, the withholding taxes present major disadvantages. First, their scope of application (investment income) is too narrow and neither covers an increase of principal nor takes into account the economic capacity of the taxpayer. The system of automatic exchange does not discriminate among various sources of income. Second, the implementation of the withholding tax is quite complex and difficult to secure with many treaty partners. By contrast, the automatic exchange of information system, provided its design is clear and based on suitable standards, can be put in place as an efficient system, using electronic database and matching possibilities in the country of residence.[663]

Third, as a global standard, the system of automatic exchange is clearly more suitable.[664] The recent developments, notably in the G20, the EU, the USA and OECD, have in fact showed that the path has gone towards automatic exchange of information as the new global standard.[665] This does not mean that the withholding tax is bound to disappear. It can still apply as a transitory system towards automatic exchange and as a limited alternative for countries not ready to implement complex automatic exchange. In this respect, the Swiss Rubik Model, at the most, could serve 'as a model for a bilateral solution between a selected number of countries'.[666] A simpler alternative could be to implement a flat-rate withholding tax, independent of the residence of the taxpayer.[667]

---

[661]   Parida (2013), p. 433.

[662]   Cavelti (2013), p. 209.

[663]   See Parida (2013), p. 432.

[664]   Same opinion as Cavelti (2013), p. 209, with the precision that technically the automatic exchange is superior provided the information that is exchanged is not overly broad.

[665]   See infra p. 184.

[666]   Cavelti (2013), p. 214.

[667]   In this respect, Avi-Yonah has proposed a global uniform withholding tax on portfolio investments, along the lines of the EUSD transitory system, see (2000), p. 1667 ff.

### D.   The Impact of Anti-Money Laundering (AML) Legislation

### 1.   Introduction
Parallel to the developments in exchange of information, global rules against AML have been introduced. The links between AML rules and exchange of information in tax matters have started to accelerate in two different ways. First, the rules of identification of AML legislation may serve to help identify beneficial owners, or controlling persons, for tax purposes. Second, tax crimes have become predicate offences for AML purposes as well.

### 2.   Identification of the beneficial owner
AML legislation includes sophisticated rules to identify beneficial owners of financial institutions. While the purpose of AML rules is different than exchange of information, the international or domestic implementations legislation may help to identify the persons hiding or controlling complex structures.

In Europe, Directives 2005/60/EC of 26 October 2005 and 2006/70/EC of 1 August 2006 on the prevention of the use of the financial system for the purpose of money laundering and terrorist financing,[668] introduced customer due diligence (CDD) on financial intermediaries, in order to identify the beneficial owner of complex structures. The beneficial owner is the natural person who ultimately owns or controls the customer and/or the natural person on whose behalf a transaction or activity is being conducted. In addition, each Member State must form a Financial Intelligence Unit (FIU), which has the power to: (i) control intermediaries and professionals in their CDD; (ii) collect information on the beneficial owners and (iii) cooperate and exchange information with FIU of other Member States.

Under the *Jyske* case of the ECJ,[669] the Court judged that the EU AML Directives did not preclude legislation of a Member State from requiring credit institutions to communicate the information required for AML purposes directly to the FIU of the Member State where the institution carries out their activities in that State under the freedom to provide services. In that case, Jyske, a branch in Gibraltar of the Danish bank NS Jyske Bank, operated in Spain, under the rules on the freedom to provide services, that is to say, without being established there. The Spanish FIU considered that there was a risk that Jyske was being used for money

---

[668]   OJ L 309, 25.11.2005, p. 15; OJ L 214, 4.8.2006, p. 29.
[669]   ECJ 25 April 2013, C-212/11, *Jyske Bank Gibraltar Ltd.*

laundering purposes, in the sense that it was creating Gibraltar corporations ultimately intended to prevent detection of the identity of the actual and final owner of property acquired in Spain, and of the origin of the monies used for the purposes of such acquisition.

It appears that the concept of beneficial owner, in the AML context, is rather broad and does not necessarily correspond to the notion of beneficial owner, or controlling person, used under tax rules. However, there is a clear trend in recent exchange of information rules to refer also to the AML criteria in order to identify the beneficial owner.

For example, under the proposal of 13 November 2008 amending the EUSD,[670] a new definition of beneficial owner would be introduced in order to close existing loopholes. Under these rules, paying agents would be required to look through specific entities outside the EU, on the basis of information already available to them (notably AML information),[671] which could determine the ultimate ownership of interest payments. In this case, there is a direct link between AML identification and tax rules.

In the same vein, a Resolution of 21 May 2013, of the EU Parliament on the fight against tax fraud, tax evasion and tax havens, proposes a modification of the EU AML Directive with a view to introducing a public government register of the beneficial ownership of companies, trusts, foundations and other similar legal structures.[672]

Under FATCA, a FFI is required to identify and report information about US account holders. Especially for new accounts, opened after July 2014, the regulations permit to rely on documentation that complies with AML/KYC rules.[673] The same is true for the due diligence rules following the OECD Common Reporting Standard of automatic exchange of information,[674] which also refer, especially for high value pre-existing accounts, to new individual accounts and for all entity accounts, to the documentation obtained by the reporting financial institution pursuant to AML/KYC procedures.[675] In particular, the OECD Standard refers to AML/KYC procedures for the determination of the

---

[670] COM 2008 727 final.

[671] See Cosentino (2013), p. 300.

[672] See EU European Parliament legislative resolution of 11 March 2014 on the proposal for a directive of the European Parliament and of the Council on the prevention of the use of the financial system for the purpose of money laundering and terrorist financing, A7-0150/2014.

[673] Treas. Regs. 1.1147-4(c)(3)–(4); Tello (2014), p. 100.

[674] See infra p. 194.

[675] See OECD, Standard AEOI, p. 34 (individual account), 38 and 41 ff. (entity account).

controlling persons of so-called passive non-financial entities (NFE) holding accounts.[676] The term 'controlling person' corresponds in fact to the *beneficial owner*, as described in Recommendation 10 and the Interpretative Note of the FATF.[677] As a consequence, the OECD confirms the link between the identification for AEOI and AML purposes by mentioning that the term 'controlling person' must 'be interpreted in a manner consistent with such Recommendations, with the aim of protecting the international financial system from misuse including with respect to tax crimes'.[678]

### 3.  Tax crime as a predicate offense of AML

The relevance of AML information for tax purposes will even increase under the recent evolution of AML legislation, towards considering tax crime as a predicate of money laundering.

Under the FATF Recommendation No 3 of February 2012, serious tax crimes (direct or indirect) are indeed to be included as a predicate of money laundering.[679] The definition of 'tax crime' is however a matter of domestic law.

Following that trend a proposal on 5 February 2013 of a new EU Directive on the prevention of the use of the financial system for the purpose of money laundering and terrorist financing is pending.[680] Under this proposal, criminal activity, as a predicate offence, would include, notably, tax crimes, related to direct and indirect taxes, which are punishable by deprivation of liberty or a detention order for a maximum of more than one year or, as regards those States which have a minimum threshold for offences in their legal system, all offences punishable by deprivation of liberty or a detention order for a minimum of six months (Art. 3 par. 4 lit f draft Directive).

In this framework an interesting question is whether this information, stemming from AML enforcement, may be passed on to the tax authorities. It seems that so far states have different domestic rules in this context.

---

[676]  See infra p. 196.

[677]  See FATF/OECD Recommendations, February 2012; OECD Standard CRS, Commentary, n. 132 on Section VIII.

[678]  OECD Standard CRS, Commentary n. 132 on Section VIII.

[679]  See FATF/OECD, International Standards on Combating Money Laundering and the Financing of Terrorism and Proliferation, The FATF Recommendations, February 2012.

[680]  COM (2013) 45 final.

In any event, following the OECD Model DTC, if information received by a State appears to be of value for other purposes than those referred to under Art. 26 par. 2, the receiving State may not use the information for those other purposes. However, a Contracting State may wish to allow the sharing of information to other law enforcement agencies and judicial authorities on certain high priority matters (AML, corruption, terrorism) but should provide for a specific treaty norm which would require (i) that such information may be used for other purposes under the laws of both States and (ii) the competent authority of the supplying State authorizes such use.[681]

---

[681] OECD Commentary n. 12.2 ad Art. 26 (added on 15 July 2005).

# 12. Automatic exchange of information (AEOI): the OECD Common Reporting Standard

## I. INTRODUCTION

After the huge developments in exchange of information, after March 2009, political pressures started to grow in favour of automatic exchange of information. On 7 February 2012, after the adoption of FATCA in the United States, the G5 (France, Germany, Italy, Spain and the United Kingdom) announced that they were willing to develop a model multi-lateral automatic tax information exchange system with the United States.[682] This was a 'game changer for the information reporting regime'.[683]

Then, on 19 April 2013, the G20 Finance Ministers and Central Bank Governors endorsed automatic exchange as the new standard. At the G8 summit in June 2013, the OECD presented the report 'A Step Change in Tax Transparency',[684] which broadly fixed the steps to implement a global system of automatic exchange.[685] G8 leaders agreed to work together with the OECD and the G20 to implement these recommendations.[686] On 6 September 2013, the G20 Leaders committed to automatic information exchange as the new global standard. The OECD, following this mandate to develop the model further, released a Model Competent Authority Agreement (Model CAA) and the Common Reporting Standard (CRS). The G20 Finance Ministers and Central Bank Governors in Sydney endorsed the standard, on 22 and 23 February 2014. On 6 May 2014, 47 countries, including all OECD Members, adopted a joint Declaration on automatic exchange of information, notably welcoming

---

[682] See supra p. 157.
[683] Radcliffe (2014), p. 160.
[684] OECD, A Step Change in Tax Transparency, Statement on the Pilot Multilateral Automatic Information Exchange Facility.
[685] See also Radcliffe (2014), p. 161.
[686] OECD, Standard AEOI, n. 3 ad Introduction.

the OECD Standard.[687] By May 2014, over 60 jurisdictions had committed to implement the standard.[688]

On 21 July 2014, the OECD published the standard for automatic exchange of financial account information in tax matters (Standard AEOI). This global model is not intended to restrict existing or different types of automatic exchange system but sets out a *minimum standard*.[689] The CRS draws extensively from the intergovernmental agreement implementing FATCA, taking into account however the multilateral nature of the CRS system and deviating from specific US aspects, such as the taxation based on citizenship and the presence of a comprehensive withholding tax.[690]

> Given these features, that the intergovernmental approach to FATCA is a pre-existing system with close similarities to the CRS, and the anticipated progress towards widespread participation in the CRS, it is compatible and consistent with the CRS for the US to not require the look through treatment for investment entities in Non-Participating Jurisdictions.[691]

On 29 October 2014, at the meeting of the Global Forum in Berlin, 51 countries, including the so-called 'early adopters' group, committed to conclude a multilateral competent authority agreement on automatic exchange of financial information. All these countries have either signed or expressed their intention to sign the CMAAT and expressed their intention to implement the OECD CRS standard of AEOI. For this group, it is expected that the first exchange of information will take place in 2017.[692] Another group of 60 countries is expected to enter into mutual agreements to implement the CRS one year later and therefore should start to automatically exchange information with contracting partners as of 2018. The United States, during this meeting, has indicated that it will

---

[687] See Declaration on Automatic Exchange of Information in Tax Matters, adopted on 6 May 2014 (Annex 6 to the OECD Standard AEOI).

[688] See OECD, Joint Statement by the Early Adopters Group (19 May 2014); OECD, Standard AEOI, n. 3 ad Introduction.

[689] OECD, Standard AEOI, n. 5 ad Introduction.

[690] Ibid.

[691] Ibid.

[692] More precisely, according to the Joint Statement of the early adopters group, September 2014, the first exchange of information in relation to new accounts and pre-existing individual high value accounts should take place by the end of September 2017, while information about pre-existing individual low value accounts and entity accounts should either first be exchanged by the end of September 2017 or September 2018 depending on when financial institutions identify them as reportable accounts.

be undertaking automatic information exchange pursuant to FATCA from 2015 and has entered into AGIs in order to do so.[693]

## II.  MAIN FEATURES

### A.  General Principles

According to the OECD three features are essential for a model of AEOI to be effective.[694] First, the model must be designed with residence jurisdictions' tax compliance in mind. Second, it needs to be standardized, so as to benefit the maximum number of residence jurisdictions. Indeed: 'A proliferation of different and inconsistent models would potentially impose significant costs on both government and business to collect the necessary information and operate the different models.'[695] Third, the model needs to have a global reach.

### B.  The Success Factors of the Model

The OECD Report to the G20: 'Automatic Exchange of Information: What it is, How it works, Benefits, What remains to be done',[696] also summarizes three main success factors for a model of an effective exchange of information: (1) a common reporting standard; (2) legal and operational basis for the exchange of information; and (3) common and compatible technical solutions.

### 1.  Common standard

The model requires a common standard on the information to be reported by financial institutions and exchanged with residence jurisdictions.[697] According to the OECD Standard AEOI, the reporting regime needs to have a broad scope across three dimensions: (i) financial information (it covers different types of investment income, including interest, dividends and similar types of income, and also information on account balances); (ii) account holders subject to reporting (it should not only include

---

[693]   See OECD, Global Forum on Transparency and Exchange of Information for Tax Purposes, AEOI: Status of Commitments, as of 29 October 2014 (available at www.oeced.org/newsroom).

[694]   OECD Standard AEOI, n. 6 ad Introduction.

[695]   Ibid.

[696]   OECD, Paris 2012.

[697]   OECD Standard AEOI, n. 8 ad Introduction.

individuals, but also limit possibilities to use interposed legal entities or arrangements; in other words, it should require financial institutions to look through shell companies, trusts or similar arrangements); (iii) financial institutions required to report (reporting should be required not only by banks, but other financial institutions, such as brokers, certain collective investment vehicles and certain insurance companies).[698]

Due diligence procedures also have to be implemented and followed by financial institutions in order to identify reportable accounts and obtain the accountholder identifying information that is required to be reported for the account.[699]

## 2. Legal and operational basis

There are currently different legal bases or systems of automatic exchange of information. Article 26 of the OECD Model DTC provides for a bilateral model of exchange of information. Under the current Model, automatic exchange of information is allowed but not required. Another form of bilateral automatic exchange of information also exists under the IGA concluded between the United States and numerous countries in order to implement FATCA. These types of bilateral treaties may serve as the basis for automatic exchange of information.

According to the OECD, it is however more efficient to establish automatic exchange of information on the basis of a multilateral exchange of instruments, such as the OECD CMAAT, as amended in 2011.[700] Indeed, this model provides for all forms of exchange of information, contains rules of confidentiality and use of information and allows for the automatic exchange. Under the OECD CMAAT, automatic exchange of information however requires a 'separate agreement' between the competent authorities of the Contracting States, which can be entered into by two or more parties, with automatic exchange taking place on a bilateral basis.[701] Such mutual agreement will take the form of a competent authority agreement (CAA), which can be bilateral or multilateral.

In other words, the functioning of the system, from a legal standpoint, would rely on an international agreement (ideally the OECD or the CMAAT), under which automatic exchange of information would be implemented following a competent authority agreement between the participants to the automatic exchange.

---

[698] OECD Standard AEOI, n. 9 ad Introduction.
[699] OECD Standard AEOI, n. 10 ad Introduction.
[700] OECD Standard AEOI, n. 11 ad Introduction.
[701] Ibid.

### 3.   Common or compatible technical solutions

A common or compatible system for reporting and exchanging information is critical in a standardized automatic exchange system.[702] The OECD standard entails a schema to be used for exchanging information in relation to the IT aspects of data safeguards and confidentiality, and transmission and encryption.[703]

## III.   THE STANDARD ON AUTOMATIC EXCHANGE OF FINANCIAL INFORMATION

### A.   In General

The global standard is the result of a combination between: (i) a model competent authority agreement (Model CAA) and (ii) the CRS on reporting and due diligence for financial account information.

In order to implement the standard, participating countries are required to follow the respective steps.[704] First, the CRS has to be implemented into domestic law. It means that financial institutions have to apply the due diligence and reporting rules in order to identify and report to their domestic competent authority. Second, the participating State has to enter into a competent authority agreement (CAA) in order to activate the automatic exchange of information with another State. Such a CAA must be based on an international instrument, such as a double taxation treaty, or a multilateral convention, such as the OECD CMAAT.

These two steps could also be achieved through a multilateral competent authority agreement, based on the OECD CMAAT, or a multilateral IGA covering the CRS and reporting obligations.[705] For EU Member States, EU legislation could also form the legal basis of the CRS among Member States.

### B.   The Common Reporting Standard

#### 1.   In general

The CRS entails rules that require (i) financial institutions to (ii) report information on (iii) reportable accounts and to follow (iv) due diligence procedure.

---

[702]   OECD Standard AEOI, n. 13 ad Introduction.
[703]   OECD Standard AEOI, n. 13 ad Introduction; see also Annex 3.
[704]   OECD Standard AEOI, n. 16 ad Introduction.
[705]   Ibid.

*Financial institutions* covered are not only banks but also custodial institutions, depositary institutions, investment entities and specified insurance companies, unless they present a low risk of tax evasion.[706]

*Information* to be reported is financial information with respect to reportable accounts, which includes interest, dividends, account balance or value, income from certain insurance products, sale proceeds from financial assets and other income generated with respect to assets held in the account or payments made with respect to the account.[707]

*Reportable accounts* are accounts not only held by individuals, but also entities (which includes trusts and foundations) with a requirement to look through passive entities to report on controlling persons.[708]

*Due diligence procedures* to be performed by reporting financial institutions are described in Sections II to VII of the CRS.

## 2. General reporting requirements

According to Section I (A), but subject to the exceptions of paragraphs C through F, each reporting financial institution must report the information described with respect to each reportable account of such reporting institution. The information to be exchanged,[709] according to Section 2, par. 2, with respect to each reportable account, is:

1. the name, address, jurisdiction(s) of residence, TIN(s) and date and place of birth (in the case of an individual) of each reportable person that is an account holder and, in the case of an entity that is an account holder and that after application of due diligence procedures consistent with Sections V, VI and VII, is identified as having one or more controlling persons that is a reportable person, the name, address, jurisdiction(s) of residence and TIN(s) of the entity and the name, address, jurisdiction(s) of residence, TIN(s), date and place of birth of each reportable person.
2. the account number;
3. the name and identifying number (if any) of the reporting financial institution;

---

[706] OECD Standard AEOI, n. 20 ad Introduction.
[707] Ibid.
[708] Ibid.
[709] The list of information corresponds to the information that has to be reported under the CAA, except that the residence of each reportable person that is an account holder, or of controlling persons, also has to be reported.

4.   the account balance or value as of the end of the relevant calendar
     year or other appropriate reporting period or, if the account was
     closed during such year or period, the closure of the account;
5.   in the case of a custodial account: (a) the total gross amount of
     interest, dividends and other income generated with respect to the
     assets held in the account, in each case paid or credited to the
     account during the calendar year or other appropriate reporting
     period; and (b) the total gross proceeds from the sale or redemption
     of financial assets paid or credited to the account during the
     calendar year or the other appropriate reporting period with respect
     to which the reporting financial institution acted as a custodian,
     broker, nominee, or otherwise as an agent for the account holder;
6.   in the case of any depositary account, the total gross amount of
     interest paid or credited to the account during the calendar year or
     other appropriate reporting period; and
7.   in the case of any account not described in subpar. A (5) or (6), the
     total gross amount paid or credited to the account holder with
     respect to the account during the calendar year or other appropriate
     reporting period with respect to which the reporting financial
     institution is the obligor or debtor, including the aggregate amount
     of any redemption payments made to the account holder during the
     calendar year or other appropriate reporting period.

The information reported must identify the *currency* in which each
amount is denominated (Section I par. B).

There are some *exceptions* to these reporting requirements, namely:

- The TIN(s) or date of birth is not required to be reported if such
  information is not in the records of the reporting financial institution and is not otherwise required under domestic law (Section I.
  C). The reporting financial institution is however required to use
  'reasonable efforts' to obtain the TIN(s) and date of birth with
  respect to pre-existing accounts by the end of the second year
  following the year in which such accounts were identified (Section
  I. C).
- The TIN is not required to be reported if (i) a TIN is not issued by
  the relevant reporting jurisdiction or (ii) the domestic law of the
  relevant reporting jurisdiction does not require the collection of the
  TIN (Section I. D.).
- The place of birth is not required to be reported unless the reporting
  financial institution is otherwise required to obtain and report it under

domestic law and it is available in the electronically searchable data maintained by the reporting financial institution (Section I. E.).

- Finally, there is an exception for the reporting of gross proceeds from the sale or redemption of financial assets (Section I. F.). Indeed, it may be more difficult for reporting financial institutions to obtain that information, so that jurisdiction may consider introducing such reporting gradually.[710]

### 3. General due diligence requirements

In general, an account is treated as reportable beginning as of the date it is identified as such pursuant to the due diligence procedures in Section II through VII and, unless otherwise provided, information must be reported annually in the calendar year to which the information relates (Section II. A.). The balance or value of an account is determined as of the last day of a calendar year (Section II. B.).

The use of *service providers* is allowed to fulfil the reporting and due diligence requirement, as contemplated by domestic law, but these obligations remain the responsibility of the reporting financial institution (Section II. D.).

The due diligence procedure makes a distinction between individual accounts, on the one hand, and entity accounts, on the other hand. Further, the CRS also distinguishes between pre-existing and new accounts, based on the fact that obtaining information on pre-existing accounts is both more costly and difficult than upon account opening.[711] These distinctions correspond to FATCA.[712] However, each jurisdiction may allow reporting financial institutions to apply the due diligence procedures for new accounts to existing accounts, and the procedure for high value accounts to lower value accounts (Section II. D.).

### 4. Due diligence for individual accounts

*i) Preexisting accounts* For pre-existing individual accounts, financial institutions are required to review accounts, without application of any de minimis threshold, and then to distinguish between higher and lower value accounts. However, a cash value insurance contract or annuity contract is not required to be reviewed, identified or reported, provided the reporting financial institution is effectively prevented by law from

---

[710] OECD CRS Commentary, n. 35 ad CRS.
[711] OECD Standard AEOI, n. 21 ad Introduction.
[712] Radcliffe (2014), p. 163.

selling such a contract to residents in the reporting jurisdiction (Section III.A.). A lower value account means a pre-existing individual account with an aggregate balance or value that does not exceed 1,000,000 USD (Section VIII. C. 14.).

For *lower value accounts*, the financial institution has to apply a permanent residence address test, based on documentary evidence. If the reporting financial institution has in its records a current residence address, it may treat the individual account holder as being resident of the jurisdiction in which the address is located (Section III. B. 1.). If however, the reporting institution does not rely on a current residence address for the individual account holder, based on documentary evidence, it has to review electronically searchable data for any of the six the *following indicia* and then apply the procedure of subparagraph B.3 to 6 (Section III B. 2. lit. a to f):

a.    identification of the account holder as a resident of a reporting jurisdiction;
b.    current mailing or residence address in a reporting jurisdiction;
c.    one or more telephone numbers in a reporting jurisdiction and no telephone number in the jurisdiction of the reporting financial institution;
d.    standing instructions to transfer funds to an account maintained in a reporting jurisdiction;
e.    effective power of attorney or signatory authority granted to a person with an address in a reporting jurisdiction;
f.    a 'hold mail' instruction or 'care of' address in a reporting jurisdiction if the reporting financial institution does not have any other address on file for the account holder.

If none of the indicia are discovered in the electronic search, then no further action is needed (until a change of circumstances modifies the analysis) (Section III. B. 3.).

If, however, any of the indicia listed in subparagraph B.2 lit. a to e are discovered in the electronic search (or there is a material change of circumstances) then the reporting financial institution must treat the account holder as a resident for tax purposes of each reporting jurisdiction for which an indicium is identified, unless it elects to apply subparagraph B 6 (Section III. B.4.). It appears that the electronic indicia search is broadly the same as for FATCA.[713] In particular, telephone

---

[713]    Radcliffe (2014), p. 164.

numbers could pose practical problems and create many 'false positive' answers, in cases where a person, working in a different state than their country of residence, gives a work phone number.[714] Indeed, according to Section III.B.4, the taxpayer could be regarded as resident in both (working and residence) states.

If a 'hold mail' or 'care of' address is discovered in the electronic search and no other address and none of the other indicia are identified for the account holder, then the reporting financial intermediary must, in the order most appropriate to the circumstances apply the paper record search described in subparagraph C 2, or seek to obtain from the account holder a self-certification or documentary evidence to establish the residence of the account holder. If the paper search fails to establish an indicium and the attempt to obtain the self-certification or documentary evidence is not successful, the reporting financial institution must report the account as an *undocumented account* (Section III B. 5).

Notwithstanding a finding of indicia, under subparagraph B. 2, a reporting financial institution is not required to treat an account holder as a resident of a reporting jurisdiction if:

a) the account holder information contains a current mailing address, one or more telephone numbers in the reporting jurisdiction or standing instructions to transfer funds to an account in the reporting jurisdiction, and the reporting jurisdiction obtains: (i) a self-certification from the account holder; and (ii) documentary evidence establishing the account holder's non-reportable status.

b) the account holder information contains a currently effective power of attorney granted to a person with an address in a reporting jurisdiction, and the reporting financial institution obtains: (i) a self-certification from the account holder; and (ii) documentary evidence establishing the account holder's non-reportable status.

In summary, for lower value accounts, the financial institution must apply a permanent residence test based on documentary evidence or the financial institution would need to determine the residence on the basis of an indicia search.[715] A self-certification (and/or documentary evidence) would be needed in case of conflicting indicia, in the absence of which reports would be made to all reporting jurisdictions for which indicia have been found.

---

[714] Ibid.
[715] OECD Standard CRS, Introduction n. 21.

For *higher value accounts*, enhanced due diligence procedures apply. They include an *electronic record* search (for any of the indicia described in subparagraph B.2) and a *paper record* search, unless the reporting financial institution's electronic database includes fields for, and captures the information described in subparagraph C.3. If the electronic database does not capture all of this information, then the reporting financial institution must also review the current customer master file, the relevant documents (listed in subparagraph C.2. lit. a to e) associated with the account and obtained by the financial institution within the last five years for any of the indicia described in subparagraph B.2. The relevant documents include, inter alia, most recent documentary evidence related to the account, the account opening contract, the most recent documentation obtained pursuant to AML/KYC procedures or other regulatory purposes, and any power of attorney or standing instructions to transfer funds (Section III. C.2).

In addition to the electronic and paper record search, the reporting financial institution must treat as a reportable account any high value account assigned to a *relationship manager* if the latter has actual knowledge that the account holder is a reportable person (Section C.4.).

If none of the indicia listed in subparagraph B. 2 are discovered in the enhanced review, and the account is not identified as held by a reportable person in subparagraph C 4 (actual knowledge test), no further action is needed (unless there is a material change of circumstances). If however indicia are discovered, then rules similar to the lower account apply (See Section III. B.).

*ii) New accounts*    For new individuals' accounts, a self-certification is always required (including a confirmation of its reasonableness) without a de minimis threshold (Section IV.). The confirmation of reasonableness of self-certification is based the information obtained by the reporting financial institution in connection with the opening of the account, including any documentation collected pursuant to AML/KYC procedures.

## 5. Entities

*i) Pre-existing accounts*    For pre-existing accounts, the participating jurisdictions may choose to allow participating financial institutions to apply a threshold such that pre-existing accounts below 250,000 USD (or equivalent) are not subject to review (Section V. A.).

Then, for pre-existing accounts, reporting financial institutions must apply review procedures to determine whether the account is held by one or more *reportable* persons, or by a *passive non-financial institution* (NFE) with one or more *controlling* persons who are reportable persons (Section V.D.).

First, the financial institution must determine whether the entity itself is a *reportable* person. The analysis can be done on available information based on anti-money laundering (AML) and/or KYC procedures. If the information indicates that the account holder is a resident in a reporting jurisdiction, the reporting financial institution must treat the account as a reportable account, unless it obtains a self-certification from the account holder, or reasonably determines based on information in its possession or that is publicly available, that the account holder is not a reportable person (Section V.D.1.b).

Second, the reporting financial institution has to determine if the entity is a *passive NFE* with one or more controlling persons who are reportable persons (see Section V.D.2). A passive NFE and an active NFE are further defined in Section VIII D. 7, 8 and 9). In particular, a passive NFE is either (i) an NFA that is not active, or (ii) an investment entity (described in A(6)(b)) that is not from a participating jurisdiction (Section VIII D. 8). It follows in particular that if the entity account holder is an investment entity sited in a jurisdiction, which has not signed the CRS, it will be characterized as a passive NFE.[716] If any of the controlling persons of a passive NFE is a reportable person, the account must be treated as a reportable account. In making these determinations, the following tests are applicable (in the most appropriate order under the circumstances):

(a)  Passive NFE. In order to determine whether or not the account holder is a *passive* NFE, the financial institution must obtain either a self-certification from the account holder, or may rely on information in its possession or that is publicly available. It appears that the most relevant criterion is likely to be the reference to the non-financial entity's income and assets, corresponding to the FATCA approach.[717]

(b)  Determining the controlling person. If the entity is a passive NFE, the financial institution has then to identify the *controlling persons* of this entity. According to the OECD Standard, the term 'controlling persons' means 'natural persons who exercise control over any Entity: In the case of a trust, such term means the settlor, the

---

[716]  Radcliffe (2014), p. 166.
[717]  Radcliffe (2014), p. 165.

trustees, the protector (if any), the beneficiaries or class of beneficiaries, and any other natural person exercising ultimate effective control over the trust, and in the case of legal arrangement other than a trust, such term means persons in equivalent or similar positions'.[718]

For this determination, the financial institution may rely on information collected and maintained according to AML/KYC procedures. It should be mentioned in this regard, that the definition of the term 'controlling person' corresponds to the *beneficial owner*, as described in Recommendation 10 and the Interpretative Note of the FATF.[719] In other words, the term 'controlling person' must be interpreted in a manner consistent with the FATF Recommendations.[720]

The OECD Commentary gives more guidance in order to define the controlling person of entities. For a *legal person*, the controlling person will usually be the natural person who ultimately has a controlling ownership interest in the entity (e.g. any person owning more than 25 per cent of the legal person); where no natural person exercises such ownership interest, the controlling person will be the natural person who exercises control through other means; absent such control, the controlling person will be the natural person who holds the position of senior manager official.[721] In the case of a *trust*, the controlling persons are the settlor, trustee, protector (if any), beneficiaries or classes of beneficiaries or any other natural persons exercising ultimate effective control; however the settlor, trustee, protector and beneficiaries or classes of beneficiaries 'must always be treated as Controlling Persons of a trust, regardless of whether or not any of them exercises control over the trust'.[722] For entities similar to trusts, such as *foundations*, controlling persons are identified through similar due diligence procedures as those applicable to trusts.[723]

(c)   Determining the reportable person. In order to determine whether a controlling person of a passive NFE is a reportable person, the financial institution may rely either (i) on information maintained

---

[718]   OECD Standard CRS, Section VIII (D.6).
[719]   See FATF/OECD Recommendations, February 2012; OECD Standard CRS, Commentary, n. 132 on Section VIII.
[720]   OECD Standard CRS, Commentary n. 132 on Section VIII.
[721]   OECD Standard CRS, Commentary, n. 133 on Section VIII.
[722]   OECD Standard CRS, Commentary, n. 134 on Section VIII.
[723]   OECD Standard CRS, Commentary, n. 135 on Section VIII.

and collected pursuant to AML/KYC procedures for accounts with an aggregate value that does not exceed 1,000,000 USD or (ii) on a self-certification.

*ii) New accounts*  For new accounts, fundamentally the same assessment rules apply, without the threshold. In addition, a self-certification is required to determine whether the entity is a reportable person.

## C.  The Model Competent Authority Agreement (Model CAA)

### 1.  Introduction

The Model CAA is the link between the international agreement (typically the CMAAT or a double taxation treaty), which allows the automatic exchange between Contracting States, and the CRS.[724] The CAA will materialize the possibility offered by the international instrument between the states parties to the agreement. It provides for the modalities of the automatic exchange between the participating states.

The OECD Model CAA is drafted as a *bilateral* reciprocal agreement. The OECD however recognizes that a CAA could also be implemented as a *multilateral* competent authority agreement.[725] But it has to be acknowledged that, even if the agreement were multilateral, exchange of information would still be done on a bilateral basis.

Some jurisdictions may also wish to enter into *non-reciprocal* bilateral agreements.[726] This Model would correspond, from a legal standpoint, to the United States Model 1(b) IGA. This solution would be suitable for participating jurisdictions with no income tax, such as tax havens. A non-reciprocal version of the Model CAA could also be implemented with developing countries that may face capacity and technical problems in implementing automatic exchange of information.[727] A non-reciprocal version of the Model CAA is included in Annex 2.

Section 1 provides for the relevant *definitions* applicable under the CAA. The CRS is not defined in the Model CAA but in the multilateral version. In fact, it is possible that the CRS, including IT modalities, will be updated from time to time, as a result of more experience from participating jurisdictions, or in the multilateral context, different dates of

---

[724]  OECD, Commentary CAA, n. 1 ad 1.
[725]  Indeed, a multilateral version of the CAA is included in Annex 1. In fact, on 29 October 2014, at the meeting of the Global Forum in Berlin, 51 States and territories signed a multilateral CAA which would implement AEOI.
[726]  OECD, Commentary CAA, n. 3 ad 1.
[727]  Ibid.

signature, following updates of the CRS.[728] To address this situation, the CRS is defined as 'the standard for automatic exchange of financial information developed by the OECD, with G20 countries, presented to the G20 in 2014 and published on the OECD website'.[729] In addition, a capitalized term not otherwise defined will have the meaning that it has at that time under the law of the jurisdiction applying the agreement, such meaning being consistent with the meaning set forth in the CRS (Sec. 1 par. 2). Any term not otherwise defined in the CAA or the CRS will, unless the context requires otherwise, or the competent authorities agree to a common meaning, have the meaning that it has at that time under the law of the jurisdiction applying the agreement, but any meaning under the applicable tax laws of that jurisdiction will prevail over a meaning given under other laws of that jurisdiction (Sec. 1 par. 2 *in fine*).

## 2. Automatic exchange of information

According to Section 2, pursuant to the provision of the relevant international instrument and subject to the reporting and due diligence rules consistent with the CRS, each competent authority must *annually* exchange with the other competent authority, on an *automatic* basis, the information obtained, which is specified in par. 2.

The information to be exchanged, according to Section 2, par. 2 Model CAA, with respect to each reportable account, is:

a) the name, address, TIN(s) and date and place of birth, in the case of an individual, of each reportable person that is an account holder and, in the case of an entity that is an account holder and that, after application of due diligence procedures, is identified as having one or more controlling persons that is a reportable person, the name, address and TIN(s) of the entity and the name, address, TIN(s), date and place of birth of each reportable person.

b) the account number;

c) the name and identifying number (if any) of the reporting financial institution;

d) the account balance or value as of the end of the relevant calendar year or other appropriate reporting period or, if the account was closed during such year or period, the closure of the account;

---

[728] OECD, Commentary CAA, n. 3, n. 6 ad Section 1.
[729] Ibid.

e)  in the case of a custodial account: (1) the total gross amount of interest, dividends and other income generated with respect to the assets held in the account, in each case paid or credited to the account during the calendar year or other appropriate reporting period; and (2) the total gross proceeds from the sale or redemption of financial assets paid or credited to the account during the calendar year or the other appropriate reporting period with respect to which the reporting financial institution acted as a custodian, broker, nominee, or otherwise as an agent for the account holder;

f)  in the case of any depositary account, the total gross amount of interest paid or credited to the account during the calendar year or other appropriate reporting period; and

g)  in the case of any account not described in subpar. 2 (e) or (f), the total gross amount paid or credited to the account holder with respect to the account during the calendar year or other appropriate reporting period with respect to which the reporting financial institution is the obligor or debtor, including the aggregate amount of any redemption payments made to the account holder during the calendar year or other appropriate reporting period.

The tax laws of the jurisdiction exchanging the information will be relevant to determine the amount and character of payments made with respect to a reportable account (Section 3.1.). The information exchanged will identify the currency in which each relevant amount is denominated (Section 3.2.).

Information must be exchanged within nine months after the end of the calendar year to which it relates (Section 3.3.). The first year is left blank in the Model and is for the participating jurisdiction to insert.[730] In addition, information is only required to be exchanged with respect to a calendar year if both jurisdictions have in effect legislation that requires reporting with respect to such calendar year that is consistent with the scope of exchange provided for in Section 2 and in the CRS (Section 3 par. 3, second sentence). Subject to its domestic law, however, a jurisdiction may choose to exchange with respect to earlier years.[731] In this respect, the Commentary gives the following example:[732] assume that A and B sign the Model in 2015 and agree that information will be exchanged with respect to 2016 and subsequent years. A has legislation in place that requires reporting in 2016 but B provides notice that it has

---

[730]  OECD, Commentary CAA, n. 2 ad Section 2.
[731]  OECD, Commentary CAA, n. 3 ad Section 2.
[732]  OECD, Commentary CAA, n. 4 ad Section 3.

legislation in effect to provide reporting with respect to 2017. In this case, both A and B will only have an obligation to provide information with respect to 2017 but A may choose, under its domestic law, to send information to B in 2016.

There is however an exception with respect to how the year's gross proceeds, described in Section 2. 2. lit. e, are to be reported (Section 3.4). Taking into account that it may be difficult for reporting financial institutions to obtain the total gross proceeds of sale or redemption of property, the jurisdiction may choose a gradual introduction of the reporting.[733]

The exchange will use a common reporting standard schema in extensible mark-up language and the competent authorities will agree on one or more methods for data transmission including encryption standards (Sections 3.5 and 6). The relevant schema and its use are described in the CRS user guide, in Annex 3 of the Standard.

### 3.  Collaboration on compliance and enforcement
The competent authorities will collaborate on compliance and enforcement (Section 4). In particular, a notification will be done when one competent authority has reason to believe that an error may have led to incorrect or incomplete information reporting or there is non-compliance by a reporting financial institution with the reporting requirement and due diligence procedures consistent with the CRS. The notified competent authority 'will take all appropriate measures available under its domestic law to address the errors or non-compliance'. According to Section IX of the CRS, each jurisdiction must have rules and administrative procedures in place to ensure effective implementation and compliance with the reporting and due diligence procedures.

Section 4 does not contemplate a direct contact between the competent authorities from one jurisdiction with a reporting financial institution in the other jurisdiction.[734] However, as an alternative, two competent authorities may allow for such contact. If they do agree, the Commentary provides for an optional alternative language that would replace Section 4 and allow competent authority to make a direct inquiry to a reporting financial institution in the other jurisdiction.[735]

However, contrary to the FATCA rules, the Standard AEOI does not contemplate any form of withholding tax in case of non-compliance with

---

[733]  OECD, Commentary CAA, n. 5 ad Section 3.
[734]  OECD, Commentary CAA, n. 3 ad Section 4.
[735]  Ibid.

the rules.[736] This could become an issue in the future if competing financial centres do not comply with the standard or apply it in an ineffective way. It appears that the Global Forum on Transparency and Exchange of Information for Tax Purposes will monitor and review the implementation of the standard in this respect.[737]

## 4. Confidentiality and data safeguards

Confidentiality of taxpayer information has always been a fundamental cornerstone of tax systems. Both taxpayers and tax administration have a legal right to expect that information exchanged remains confidential. In order to have confidence in their tax systems and comply with their obligations under the law, taxpayers need to know that the often sensitive financial information is not disclosed inappropriately, whether intentionally or by accident. Citizens and governments will only trust international exchange if the information exchanged is used and disclosed only in accordance with the instrument on the basis of which it was exchanged.[738]

Based on that premise, the Model CAA provides for confidentiality rules and data safeguards on the information exchange.

All information exchanged is subject to the *confidentiality* rules provided under the underlying international instrument (OECD CMAAT or DTC), including the provisions limiting the use of the information (Section 5.1.).

Many jurisdictions, including the EU, have also introduced rules on the *protection of personal data*, including taxpayer information. These rules include, inter alia, rights to information access, correction, redress, and the existence of a mechanism to protect the data subject's rights.[739] According to par. 1 of Section 5 the supplying competent authority may, to the extent needed to ensure the necessary level of protection of personal data, specify in the CAA the particular safeguards that must be respected, as required by its domestic law (Section 5.1).[740] It follows that the receiving competent authority must treat the information in compliance not only with its own domestic law, but also with the additional safeguards that may be required to ensure data protection under the domestic law of the supplying authority.[741] However, the specification of

---

[736] Radcliffe (2014), p. 162.
[737] Ibid.
[738] OECD, Commentary CAA, n. 1 ad Section 5.
[739] OECD, Commentary CAA, n. 4 ad Section 5.
[740] OECD, Commentary CAA, n. 4 ad Section 5.
[741] OECD, Commentary CAA, n. 4 ad Section 5.

the safeguards may not be necessary if the supplying competent authority is satisfied that the receiving competent authority ensures the necessary level of data protection.[742]

Since the international underlying instruments on exchange of information prohibit that information should not be exchanged if the disclosure of such information would be contrary to public order, certain jurisdictions may require their competent authorities to specify such limitations.[743] For instance, these jurisdictions could specify that information supplied may not be

> used or disclosed in proceedings that could result in the imposition and execution of the death penalty or torture or other severe violations of human rights (such as for example when tax investigations are motivated by political, racial, or religious persecution) as that would contravene the public policy of the supplying jurisdiction.[744]

Any *breach of confidentiality* or failure of safeguards and any sanction and remedial actions imposed will be notified (Section 5.2). The notice must itself respect the confidentiality rules and also be in accordance with the domestic law of the jurisdiction where the breach or failure has occurred.[745] It should be noted that non-compliance with the confidentiality and data protection rules would be considered significant non-compliance and would justify an immediate suspension of the CAA (see Section 7).[746]

## 5. Consultation, amendments and term of the agreement

In case of difficulties in the implementation or interpretation, a competent authority may request *consultations* to develop appropriate measures to ensure that the agreement is fulfilled (Section 6.1).

The agreement may be *amended* by written agreement of the competent authorities (Section 6.2).

It is interesting to note that a competent authority may *suspend* the exchange of information under the agreement, by writing, in case of 'significant non-compliance' by the other competent authority with this agreement. Non compliance, includes, inter alia, non compliance with the confidentiality and data safeguard provisions of this agreement and the

---

[742]　OECD, Commentary CAA, n. 4 ad Section 5.
[743]　OECD, Commentary CAA, n. 5 ad Section 5.
[744]　OECD, Commentary CAA, n. 5 ad Section 5.
[745]　OECD, Commentary CAA, n. 6 ad Section 5.
[746]　Ibid.

international instrument, failure to provide timely or adequate information or defining the status of entities or accounts as non reporting financial institutions and excluded accounts in a manner that frustrates the purposes of the CRS (Section 7.2).

Finally, either competent authority may *terminate* this agreement by giving notice of termination in writing to the other competent authority (Section 7.3). Such termination will become effective on the first day of the month following the expiration of a period of 12 months after the date of notice of termination. The termination of the underlying international instrument under which the CAA is concluded would lead to the automatic termination of the CAA.[747]

---

[747] OECD, Commentary CAA, n. 8 ad Section 7.

# 13. Solving the past

## I. INTRODUCTION

The move towards AEOI is now widely accepted. Following exchange of information upon request, embodied in numerous DTC and TIEAs around the world, new developments in international exchange of information, as designed under FATCA, the EU Directives, and the OECD CRS described above, seem to aim at 'mass compliance' of all taxpayers.[748]

Going in that direction implies that non-compliant taxpayers, all over the world, must find a way to regularize their situation. Even if the new AEOI rules may not necessarily have a retroactive effect, as soon as the existence of offshore accounts is disclosed to the Contracting State of residence of the taxpayer, it would be a matter of domestic law to define the scope of investigations, including penalties for the relevant tax evader.

The traditional mechanism, which has been widely used by many states, including in the EU, is to open the gate for a tax amnesty. This system, which as such raises many legal issues, remains a transitory domestic solution, which we do not intend to develop here. There are however other interesting possibilities that have been introduced, in an international perspective, which are worth mentioning, namely the Swiss 'Rubik' system, the Liechtenstein LDF Facility, and the United States DoJ Programme for Swiss banks.

## II. THE SWISS 'RUBIK' AGREEMENTS

The 'Rubik' system has already been described above.[749] Primarily designed as an alternative solution for the AEOI (solution for the future), it also includes a 'solution for the past'.

Under this system, the taxpayer concerned has the choice between a voluntary declaration and a withholding payment by the Swiss paying

---

[748] Vanistendael (2014), p. 1149.
[749] See supra p. 143.

agent. The withholding option is executed by the paying agent through a deduction at source from the assets of the taxpayer concerned (one-off amount). The rates applicable, varying between 21 per cent and 41 per cent for the United Kingdom, and between 15 per cent and 38 per cent for Austria, were calculated according to mathematical formulae, taking into consideration various parameters, such as the duration of the banking relationship and the difference between the account's initial and final capital. The amount of the tax is then transferred to the country of residence of the taxpayer (Austria, or the United Kingdom). The relevant person receives also a *certificate* that he/she is no longer liable for the tax on these assets for the periods in question. The certificate has an 'extinctive effect', which includes, without limitation, interest, penalties and extra charges.

## III. THE LIECHTENSTEIN DISCLOSURE FACILITY (LDF)

An interesting alternative to the Rubik agreement for solving the past is represented by the Liechtenstein-United Kingdom agreement on cooperation in tax matters, of 11 August 2009 (so-called LDF).[750] Under the system, UK taxpayers can opt for voluntary disclosure and pay the outstanding taxes for the previous ten years (i.e. from March 1999) and have the opportunity, under specific conditions, to pay the tax through a simplified rate of 40 per cent on the income.[751] There is a fine of 10 per cent but in the event of a complete and voluntary disclosure no criminal investigation will be instigated.

The major difference with Rubik is that, under the LDF system, the name of the taxpayer is thus disclosed to HMRC. From the perspective of the move towards AEOI, this aspect represents an advantage in comparison to the Rubik system.

---

[750] The Liechtenstein Disclosure Facility (LDF) is an agreement reached between the Government of Liechtenstein and the United Kingdom (HMRC) on 11 August 2009, valid from 1 September 2006 to 5 April 2015, which consists of three parts: a joint declaration, a memorandum of understanding and a TIEA; see Langer (2013), p. 449, 462.

[751] Langer (2013), p. 464.

## IV.  THE UNITED STATES DOJ PROGRAM FOR SWISS BANKS INVOLVED IN TAX EVASION WITH US TAXPAYERS

Following the UBS case, and based on information stemming from various sources, such as domestic voluntary disclosure programmes, whistleblowers or other investigations within financial institutions, the DoJ started criminal and administrative procedures against various Swiss banks, including bankers or financial intermediaries, who were involved in assisting fraudulent US taxpayers.

With a view to finding a global solution to this problematic situation, the DoJ announced, on 29 August 2013, a programme which offered Swiss banks, suspected of having participated in some tax evasion schemes, the opportunity to collaborate with the DoJ and implement a settlement on the issue.[752] In a nutshell, the programme allows eligible Swiss banks to avoid criminal prosecution in the US, in exchange for extensive disclosure of information and, in some cases, penalties.[753]

The participating banks are divided into four categories. The *first* pertains to Swiss banks (at that time 14), which are already being investigated by the DoJ and cannot as such participate in the programme. For banks of category 1, the fine is fixed on an individual basis. Indeed, an investigation was already under way before the programme was established. The negotiations are in general targeted towards obtaining a Deferred Prosecution Agreement, like UBS did in 2010, combined with a fine of 780 million dollars. Recently however, on 19 May 2014, Credit Suisse did not obtain a DPA and had to pay a fine of 2.6 billion dollars for helping US tax evaders.

The *second*, and in fact the most important category in practice, is designed for Swiss banks that have reason to believe that they have US non-declared customers. These banks may request a Non Prosecuting Agreement (NPA). For this category, the amount of fine corresponding to the penalty increases depending on the date of the opening of the account. The fine is levied according to the amount of undeclared US accounts, according to a range varying from 20 per cent to 50 per cent. The penalty is 20 per cent of the highest aggregate value for accounts in existence on 1 August 2008. The penalty increases to 30 per cent on accounts opened between 1 August 2008 and 28 February 2009. The

---

[752]  Joint Statement between the U.S. Department of Justice and the Swiss Federal Department of Finance, 29 August 2013.
[753]  See Michel/Matthews (2013), p. 1.

dates were chosen because they correspond to the execution of the Deferred Prosecution Agreement with UBS.[754] This rule is based on the fact that, after the UBS settlement, Swiss banks still involved in assisting US tax evaders were quite aware of the situation and their potential liabilities. For US accounts opened after 28 February 2009, the penalty goes up to 50 per cent of the maximum aggregate value of all such accounts. Penalties may still be reduced if the bank demonstrates that the account was not an undeclared account, was disclosed by the Swiss bank to the IRS, or was disclosed to the IRS through and announced offshore voluntary disclosure programme or initiative following notification by the Swiss bank of such a programme or initiative prior to the execution of the NPA.[755]

Swiss banks that believe they have nothing to worry about are part of the *third* category. Finally the *fourth* category corresponds to banks that are deemed compliant under the FATCA regulations. Categories 3 and 4 may request a Non-Target Letter. No penalties are due for category 3 or 4.

Participating banks must obtain from the Swiss Government, the Federal Council an authorization to cooperate with the DoJ of the United States, consisting of a derogation to Art. 271 of the Swiss Criminal Code (right to disclose information to a foreign State). A model decision has been prepared by the Federal Council in order to grant authorization to cooperate, under specific conditions. The information that Swiss banks must provide in the programme also includes the names of bank employees or third parties (financial intermediaries) who have participated in the tax evasion. This particular requirement is one of the most criticized parts of the programme and has been subject to much controversy in Switzerland. Indeed, the contours of the 'participating' definition are rather vague. As a consequence, some banks have forwarded thousands of names, including persons with auxiliary functions, just because their names appeared somewhere in an email or a document related to a US customer.

A first deadline, of 31 December 2013, has expired for Swiss banks wishing to obtain a NPA and therefore participate in the second category. In practice, a surprisingly high number of banking institutions (106) have announced their willingness to participate in the programme. Negotiations are under way. Banks wishing to participate in categories 3 and 4,

---

[754] Michel/Matthews (2013), p. 3.
[755] See Program for Non Prosecution Agreements or Non Target Letter for Swiss Banks, 29 August 2013, II (category 2) par. H.

requesting a Non-Target Letter, may submit letters of intent no earlier
than 1 July 2014 and no later than 31 October 2014.[756]

The names of US account holders will further be obtained by requests
for information (including 'group requests') under the applicable double
taxation treaty between the United States and Switzerland of 1996, and
the Protocol amending it as of 23 September 2009, based on the standard
of Art. 26 OECD Model DTC of foreseeable relevance.[757] Until the
protocol of 2009 is ratified by the United States, the standard applicable
to the exchange of information remains however the concept of 'tax fraud
and the like'.

---

[756]   DoJ Program, op.cit., III (category 3) B; IV (category 4) B.
[757]   Joint Statement, n. 4; Michel/Matthews (2013), p. 4.

# 14. Legal protection of the taxpayer

## I. INTRODUCTION

Taxpayers, either as subject to tax or information holders, are required to comply with different obligations of reporting, determination, computation and payments of taxes. With the global development of information exchange, the scope of these duties has increased both domestically and internationally. During these tax proceedings, taxpayers are however protected by various rights, which are founded either in the domestic provisions of the countries involved, (notably, constitutional rules such as the equality of treatment, the right to privacy, or procedural rights such as the right to be heard), or in the international instruments (treaties, EU Directives, etc.).

In general, these various rights, depending on the applicable rule of law, may grant each taxpayer a fair process in the exchange of information proceedings, basic privacy protection in the transfer of data, and procedural rights, based on the rule of law and features of a State of Law 'Etat de droit'. The extent to which those rights do apply in the context of international exchange of information is however quite controversial and highly dependent upon: (i) the type of legal instrument applicable for the exchange of information and: (ii) the domestic law of the states involved.

The issue at stake is also exacerbated by the fact that, until recently, little attention had been given to the protection of taxpayers' rights and those of other persons involved in the process of international assistance.[758] Nowadays, the issue has however attracted much more attention, in parallel with the global development of transparency and automatic exchange of information. Indeed, the more global the exchange of information, the greater the risk of breaches of confidentiality, privacy and secrecy provisions, or even abuse in the use of data obtained, for purposes not related to the purpose of the exchange. Currently, many tax administrations 'have confidentiality standards that do not pass the

---

[758] See, in particular, Calderón (2000), p. 462 ff.; Malherbe (1991).

OECD test, and even those tax administrations that do have a confidentiality policy and rules and tests are notorious for losing confidential information to the public at large'.[759]

In this chapter, we are therefore going to analyse to what extent rules for protection of taxpayers may be applied in the context of exchange of information. We will start with a general description of existing taxpayer protection rules (II). Then, we will show how these protection rights apply under international tax treaties, in particular secrecy provisions and limits to the exchange (III). We will further focus on human rights at the ECHR level, such as the protection of privacy or family (IV), data protection rules at the EU level (V) and specific constitutional and procedural rules which may be of relevance, during and after the exchange of information process (VI). Finally, we will analyse how the legal protection of the taxpayer is implemented during the exchange of information process, distinguishing between substantive and procedural rules (VII).

## II.  RIGHTS OF THE TAXPAYERS IN GENERAL

Taxpayers, like any human beings, benefit from constitutional rights granted by the various Constitutions of their state of residence. The precise contours of these constitutional rights may vary between states, but as a rule the Constitution would guarantee the right of dignity, the right of free development of personality, the right to privacy and the right of equality of treatment.

The rights to privacy and due process, including to a fair trial, are also granted by the European Convention on Human Rights (ECHR), notably Art. 6 ECHR and, at the EU level, by the EU Charter. The scope of application of Art. 6 ECHR to tax disputes, in general, and exchange of information, in particular, is however not clearly settled today, as we will discuss later.[760] EU law, according to the data protection directive, also provides for the freedom of movement of data and the protection of data for the persons involved.

Domestic law, either at the constitutional or legislative level, also provides for various procedural rights, which can be applicable during or after the exchange of information process. Each modern state is a State of

---

[759]   Vanistendael (2014), p. 1153.
[760]   See infra p. 226.

Law, warranting equality of treatment, due process, and various protection rules, such as the right of good faith, the right to be heard, the right to appeal to an independent court and the right to a fair trial.

International instruments serving as legal bases for the international exchange of information (bilateral or multilateral treaties, EU Directives, IGAs) may also entail, although not precisely, rules for the protection of the taxpayers involved. As we will see further, these rules provide for secrecy in exchange of information, for rights of refusal to provide the exchange and sometimes for procedural limitations.

Finally, despite these variations on the scope of existing taxpayers' rights, based on various OECD publications in this context, a *'minimum standard'* would consist of the following:[761]

- the right to be informed and heard;
- the right of appeal (to an independent court);
- the right to pay an exact amount of tax;
- the right to certainty;
- the right to privacy (proportionality and respect of privacy in tax investigations and process);
- the right to confidentiality and secrecy (the information should stay confidential within the administration).

## III.  PROTECTION OF THE TAXPAYER UNDER INTERNATIONAL TAX TREATIES

### A.  In General

Exchange of information between tax authorities of different states is in principle only permitted if authorized by rules of international law. In general, these rules will be international tax treaties (bilateral or multilateral) or, for EU Member States, rules of EU law such as Regulations or Directives. As such, these international rules are in general concluded by states (or EU competent authorities) acting in order to defend their interest.

As a whole, the rules of exchange of information usually have a double function. First, and notably in the treaty context, they are designed to implement the protection against double taxation. For example, in order

---

[761]  Brokelind (2011), p. 121; OECD, Tax Administration in OECD and Selected Non-OECD Countries, 2008.

to apply the credit on a foreign withholding tax on dividends, interest or royalties, the state of residence of the taxpayer needs to be able to obtain relevant information on the effective amount of foreign tax withheld. This traditional function has however evolved. Indeed, the second and today probably main function of the exchange of information rules is to fight against tax avoidance. This is true under major information clauses such as Art. 26 of the OECD Model DTC, under which the requesting State may ask for information that is foreseeably relevant to its domestic taxation. But it is even more valid under recent developments in the EU, such as the EUSD and the DAC, and the move in favour of AEOI as the new global standard.

The first function, in part, is also in the interest of the taxpayers involved because it protects them from potential multiple taxation. The second function, however, is not as such designed to protect the taxpayers involved but clearly takes care of the interest of the states in order to fight against tax evasion, with a view to safeguarding their respective revenues. In this context, however, it appears that the interest of the taxpayers also needs to be taken into account because exchange of information notably implies transfer of personal data and also potentially confidential information (trade secrets, professional secrets, client-attorney privileged information, etc.).

In his dissertation, Schenk-Geers, after having analysed in detail the various exchange of information rules, comes to the conclusion that 'governments, in fulfilling their obligation to exchange information with Contracting States, also have a legal duty to weigh the interests of the taxpayers supplying the information'.[762] We concur with this opinion. Each time a state is interpreting a rule of exchange of information, the position of the taxpayer involved should also be taken into account, at least when the rules leave sufficient discretion to weigh his or her position in the balance of interests.

In addition, specific rules also offer, directly or indirectly, protection to the taxpayer. This is in particular the case for the principle of subsidiarity (infra B.), the requirement of foreseeably relevance (infra C.), and the secrecy rules (infra D.), which, while directly targeting states, also have an indirect impact on the taxpayer. The limits of Art. 26 par. 3 also include protective rules (infra E.). Finally, procedural rules also are essential elements of the protection of taxpayers' rights in a State of Law. In general, these rules are reserved by the international instruments and are part of domestic law (infra F.).

---

[762]   Schenk-Geers (2009), p. 300.

## B. Principle of Subsidiarity

Following this general rule of international assistance, a requesting State should first try to obtain the relevant information under its domestic law before asking for the assistance of a foreign state. This principle is implicit in the OECD Model DTC.[763] A similar principle may also be found in the TIEA Model or the CMAAT.

The principle of subsidiarity is mainly in the interest of the requested State. It prevents potential burdensome research that could have been avoided by proper measures of the requesting State. However, the rule also protects the interest of the taxpayer. It reduces the scope of investigations abroad and ensures that the requesting State really needs the information. The question however arises as to how the taxpayer can make sure that this principle is followed by the requesting State. It appears that the protection against potential violation of the principle of subsidiarity is a matter of domestic law.

## C. Foreseeable Relevance

According to Art. 26 par 1 of the OECD Model DTC, the competent authorities of the Contracting States must exchange such information as is *foreseeably relevant* for carrying out the provisions of a double tax convention or to the administration or enforcement of the domestic laws concerning taxes of every kind, insofar as the taxation thereunder is not contrary to the convention. The standard of 'foreseeable relevance' is intended to provide for exchange of information in tax matters to the widest possible extent and, at the same time, to clarify that Contracting States are not at liberty to engage in 'fishing expeditions' or to request information that is unlikely to be relevant to the tax affairs of a given taxpayer.[764]

In other words, the prohibition of fishing expeditions appears the 'ultimate boundary' of the permissible exchange of information upon request.[765] It is however a rather vague concept, as, for example, the case law pertaining to the UBS saga has demonstrated.[766] The OECD Manual on Exchange of Information characterizes fishing expeditions as 'speculative requests for information that have no apparent nexus to an open

---

[763]  OECD Commentary, n. 9(a) ad Art. 26.
[764]  OECD Commentary, n. 5 ad Art. 26.
[765]  Dourado (2013), p. 11.
[766]  See supra p. 43 ff.

inquiry or investigation'. The delimitation between a permissible foresee-ably relevant request, on the one hand, and a forbidden fishing exped-ition, on the other hand, is therefore delicate and has become even more problematic recently with the modification of the OECD Commentary, in 2012, allowing for group requests. Indeed, according to the OECD, the standard of foreseeable relevance can also be met in cases dealing with several taxpayers. In the latter case, it will still be more difficult to establish that the request is not a fishing expedition, so that it is required that the requesting State provides a 'detailed description' of the group and the specific facts and circumstances that have led to the request, and explanation of the applicable law and why there are reasons to believe that the taxpayers in the group have been noncompliant.[767]

In any event, not only is the dividing criteria to distinguish between permissible requests and fishing expeditions not legally clear, but also the consequences of the violation of the standard are not clearly defined. Indeed, according to the OECD, if a request constitutes a fishing expedition, Contracting States are not obliged to provide information in response to a request.[768] This rule seems to stress that the prohibition of fishing expeditions aims at protecting the requested tax administration, which implies that the latter would have the choice to go beyond the standard.[769] But if the prohibition also aims to protect taxpayer's rights, the decision to go beyond such prohibition would constitute a violation of the standard, unless the rights of taxpayers are duly safeguarded.[770] This interpretation would then militate for adequate procedural rules in favour of the taxpayers involved in order to protect their legitimate rights in the process. This is already the case in the domestic law of various states. This would mean, at least, that the taxpayers would have the right of notification (subject to exceptions), the right to be heard, and finally the right to appeal to an independent court.

## D.  Secrecy Rules

### 1.  The OECD Model DTC
The secrecy rules of Art. 26 par. 2 OECD Model DTC have been examined above.[771] In a nutshell, according to Art. 26 par. 2 of the OECD Model DTC, the competent authorities must keep information

---

767  OECD Commentary, n. 52. Ad Art. 26.
768  OECD Commentary, n. 6 ad Art. 26.
769  Dourado (2013), p. 12.
770  Ibid.
771  See supra p. 24.

received within the exchange of information process as *confidential*. At the outset, it should be mentioned that this clause tends to protect the interest of the Contracting States. In particular, it tends to ensure a proper confidence from both administrations under a reciprocal assistance.[772] This provision is however also aimed at protecting the taxpayer involved.[773] Indeed, the domestic laws on secrecy in tax matters, which are designed to safeguard individual rights for the protection of taxpayers, result in an extension of protection of international law.[774]

Furthermore, it should be reminded that the 'autonomous approach' of the 1963 version of the secrecy clause[775] has been replaced, since 1977, by a new version, which refers to the secrecy standard of the requesting State. According to Art. 26 par. 2, the requesting State should apply the secrecy standard which corresponds to its domestic rules. This 'equality of treatment' of the information, in the requesting State, facilitates the treatment of information in that State, but has the effect that the secrecy standard of the requested State is no more relevant to this information. In other words, once the information is passed onto the requesting State, its new standard applies, and there is no certainty that the rules of the requested States will still apply.[776] A lesser standard in the requesting State is however not a reason for refusing the exchange of information.[777]

The requirement for the requesting State to protect such information in the same manner as under its domestic law on secrecy in tax matters is a treaty obligation for that State.[778] It implies that a breach of the domestic rule on secrecy would simultaneously breach international law, which means that the Contracting State would be entitled to counteract by imposing sanctions available under international law.[779]

---

[772] OECD Commentary, n. 11 ad Art. 26.

[773] See also Koppensteiner (2011), p. 239, which admits that secrecy rules also protect the taxpayer, but the latter may invoke them only to the extent that he is aware of the process.

[774] Engelschak in: Vogel/Lehner (2008), n. 50 ad Art. 26.

[775] In 1963, the rule provided that 'any information so exchanged shall be treated as secret and shall not be disclosed to any person or authorities other than those concerned with the assessment or collection of the taxes which are the subject of the Convention'. This clause is autonomous, in the sense that it is especially not dependent on the level of protection granted by the requesting State; Rust (2012), p. 181.

[776] Rust (2012), p. 181.

[777] Rust (2012), p. 181; Engelschak, in: Vogel/Lehner (2008), n. 51 ad Art. 26.

[778] Engelschak, in: Vogel/Lehner (2008), n. 50 ad Art. 26.

[779] Ibid.

The current standard also restricts the number of persons or authorities to which the information may be *disclosed*. In addition, these persons may only use the information for the *purpose* specified. These treaty rules may restrict broader rules of domestic law, which would provide for the possibility to disclose the information to more persons or for other purposes.[780]

In principle, information received by a Contracting State may not be disclosed to a third country, unless a specific provision of a DTC allows such disclosure.[781] Furthermore, under the latest version of the OECD Commentary (2014) the information may be passed on to a third state by the requesting State, only under the authorization of the requested party. This authorization constitutes an additional safeguard to the data protection of the taxpayer.[782]

The information may also be communicated to the taxpayer, his proxy or to the witnesses.[783] This interpretation is in accordance with the text of the MC, which refers to persons 'concerned with the assessment or collection' of the taxes, to which the taxpayers undoubtedly belong.[784] The secrecy rule refers to 'any information received under par. 1', which includes not only the information transferred but also the information received, i.e. information contained in the request. Therefore the request made may be passed on to the *taxpayer*.[785]

Persons authorized, according to Art. 26 par. 2 OECD Model DTC, may also use the information to disclose it in public court proceedings or in judicial decisions. According to commentators, this rule refers only to court proceedings within the meaning of the third and fourth sentence of Art. 26 par. (2) that is, cases dealt with by fiscal courts or in penal proceedings for fraud or other tax offences.[786] However, as soon as the information has been disclosed, it becomes common knowledge and is not subject any more to the restriction on the uses to which it may be put under Art. 26.[787]

---

[780] Rust (2012), p. 181; Engelschak, in: Vogel/Lehner (2008), n. 52 ad Art. 26.

[781] OECD Commentary, n. 12.2 ad Art. 26.

[782] Vegh (2002), p. 398; Rust (2012), p. 187.

[783] OECD Commentary, n. 12 ad Art. 26; Engelschak, in: Vogel (1998), n. 52 ad Art. 26.

[784] Rust (2012), p. 184; see also supra p. 26.

[785] Rust (2012), p. 184.

[786] Engelschak, in: Vogel (1997), n. 52 ad Art. 26.

[787] Ibid.

This rule was further modified on 17 July 2012, when an additional sentence was added, which now allows the use of information for other purposes, for instance to combat money laundering, corruption, and terrorism financing.[788] But this extended use is subject to two cumulative conditions: (i) the information may be used for such other purposes under the laws of both States and (ii) the competent authority of the supplying State authorizes such use.

In summary, it appears that the secrecy rules, which are crucial for the proper functioning of the information exchange, includes many conditions and restrictions on the scope of persons to receive the information, and the possibility of using or transferring it, inside or outside the administration, which are also designed to protect the taxpayers involved. By entering into the exchange of information process, both the requesting and requested States have to make a series of choices, decisions, and balancing of interests, which have to take into account the potential rights of the various persons involved.

## 2. TIEA

Under Art. 8, information received by a contracting party must be treated as confidential and may be disclosed only to the persons or authorities (including courts or administrative bodies) in the jurisdiction of the contracting party concerned with the assessment or collection of, the enforcement or prosecution in respect of, or the determination of appeals in relation to, the taxes covered by this agreement. This clause is rather similar to the OECD Model but contains differences.[789] In our context, the main difference is that it provides for an autonomous concept of secrecy, which is not dependent upon the law of the requesting State.[790] It is interesting to note that according to the Commentary, this tax secrecy provision is intended to protect the *legitimate interests* of the taxpayer.[791]

## 3. CoE/OECD Multilateral Convention

The secrecy rule, while rather similar to Art. 26 OECD Model DTC, is somewhat more restrictive. Any information obtained by a contracting party must be treated as secret in the same manner as information obtained under the domestic law of the requested State, or under the conditions of the applicant State if such conditions are more restrictive (Art. 22 par. 2). This means that the higher standard of the domestic law

---

[788] OECD Commentary, n. 12 ad Art. 26.
[789] See supra p. 63.
[790] Sota, in: Günther/Tüchler (2013), p. 99.
[791] TIEA Commentary, n. 94 ad Art. 8; Rust (2012), p. 186.

between the requesting and requested State will prevail. This clause, as of 2010, also goes further in that it states that the requested State may ask the requesting State to apply the secrecy standard of the requested State to the extent needed to ensure the necessary level of protection of personal data.[792]

Because of its multilateral character, the CMAAT should open up the possibility to extend the exchange of information between more than two states.[793] The passing on of the information received to a third state is only possible subject to a prior authorization by the competent authority of the supplying state (i.e., state from where the information originates) (Art. 22 par 4 *in fine*).[794]

## 4. IGA

IGAs also include rules for the protection of secrecy. The content of the clause will depend on the types of IGA (Model 1 or 2) and in particular whether a pre-existing TIEA or DTC is in force between the Contracting States. If there is a pre-existing TIEA or DTC, the TIA provides that all information exchanged is subject to the confidentiality and protections provided by the applicable treaty (see Art. 3 par. 7 IGA Model 1B).

Absent such TIEA or DTC, the IGA includes a confidentiality clause, which is more restrictive than the OECD Model and non-reciprocal.

On the one hand, the competent authority of the FATCA partner must treat the information received from the United States as confidential and may only disclose such information as may be necessary to carry out its obligation under this agreement; the information may also be disclosed in connection with court proceedings related to the performance of the obligations of the FATCA partner under the agreement (Art. 9 par. 1 IGA Model 1B, no TIEA/DTC).

On the other hand, according to Art. 9 par. 2 IGA, Model 1b,

> Information provided to the US competent authority must be treated as confidential and may be disclosed only to persons or authorities (including courts and administrative bodies) of the government of the United States concerned with the assessment, collection or administration of, the enforcement or prosecution in respect of, or the determination of appeals in relation to US federal taxes or the oversight of such functions. Such persons or authorities shall use such information only for such purposes. Such persons may disclose the information in public court proceedings or in judicial decisions. The information may not be disclosed to any other person, entity,

---

[792]  Rust (2012), p. 187.
[793]  Pross/Russo (2012), p. 364.
[794]  Wittman (2013), p. 193.

authority, or jurisdiction. Notwithstanding the foregoing, where [FATCA Partner] provides prior, written consent, the information may be used for purposes permitted under the provisions of a mutual legal assistance treaty in force between the Parties that allows for the exchange of information.

## 5. Model CAA following the OECD standard of AEOI

The OECD Common Reporting Standard (CRS) of AEOI will be implemented under competent authorities agreements (CAA) between the participating states. The signing of such a CAA will be based on existing legal instruments, such as the CMAAT, a DTC, or even an IGA.[795] It follows that confidentiality and data safeguards rules, under the CAA, will be based on the existing legal instrument allowing such international exchange.

This rule is confirmed by Section 5.1. of the OECD Model CAA. In addition, the competent authorities may include domestic law rules, to the extent needed to ensure the necessary level of protection of personal data (Section 5.1. OECD Model CAA). It follows that the

Competent Authority receiving the information shall treat the information in compliance not only with its own domestic law, but also with the additional safeguards that may be required to ensure data protection under the domestic law of the supplying Competent authority. Such additional safeguards ... may for example relate to individual access to the data.[796]

## 6. Comments

In general, information exchanged between Contracting States must remain secret. However, the confidentiality limit under the OECD Model DTC does not grant a sufficient protection of the taxpayer because the standard refers to the *domestic law* and only provides for a non-discrimination protection.[797] In other words, according to the standard, the Contracting State must treat the information received in the same manner as it treats it under its domestic law. It follows that different protection rules, including procedural rights, will be applicable in the various states.[798] As a consequence, an *autonomous* treaty rule of confidentiality should be preferred. This was the case of the 1963 version of the OECD Model DTC. An autonomous version of such clause is also present under the TIEA Model and the IGA (in the absence of a TIEA or DTC).

---

[795] OECD, Standard AEOI, n. 16 ad Introduction.
[796] OECD, Standard AEOI, Commentary Model CAA, n. 4 ad Section 5.
[797] Dourado (2013), p. 15.
[798] Dourado (2013), p. 15; Rust (2012), p. 181.

Even under the current clause of the OECD Model DTC, the standard still puts some limits to the domestic law, in the sense that it restricts both (i) the persons to whom information may be disclosed and (ii) the purposes of the use of information. These limits have been modified over the time. Recent changes, notably in 2012, have in particular allowed the use of the information for other purposes than tax purposes, subject to two cumulative conditions (the law of both states allows it and the requested States authorizes such use). We see here that this rule is also in the interest of the taxpayer. Should the requesting State not respect confidentiality, the requested State may then refuse to supply the information and as a consequence protect the interest of the taxpayer.[799] In other words, the supplying state has a 'duty of care' to protect the interest of the taxpayer, but its decision is discretionary and there is no guarantee that the requested State will then refuse the supply.[800]

In addition, even in cases where the treaty includes an autonomous confidentiality clause (such as Art. 8 of the TIEA Model), there is no clear answer in case of breach of such confidentiality.[801]

As a conclusion, we should not only recommend the inclusion of an autonomous clause in treaties but also favour the inclusion of clarification rules, which are sometimes included in treaties.

### E.   Limits to the Exchange

#### 1.   In general
The various limits to the exchange of information have already been described above. Article 26 par. 3 OECD Model DTC, provides in particular for three exceptions to the obligation to supply information. They are designed to protect the sovereignty and good relationships between the Contracting States. However, in some respects, they also protect the taxpayers. The protection, as a whole, appears to be reduced because the limits mentioned in these provisions, notably Art. 26 par. 3 OECD Model DTC, deal exclusively with the *obligations* to supply information under international law but leave it to the requested State's *discretion*.[802] If the requested State supplies the information, it still remains under the treaty limits.[803]

---

799   Dourado (2013), p. 16; Schenk-Geers (2009), p. 107.
800   Dourado (2013), p. 16, Schenk-Geers (2009), p. 107.
801   Dourado (2013), p. 16.
802   Engelschalk, in: Vogel (1997), n. 99 ad Art. 26.
803   Engelschalk, in: Vogel (1997), n. 99 ad Art. 26.

## 2. Principle of reciprocity

As we have seen, a Contracting State should not be obliged to carry out administrative measures that are contrary to the practice or the law of that or the other Contracting State, or to supply information which is not obtainable under the law or the normal course of the administration of that or the other Contracting State (Art. 26 par. 3 lit. a and b OECD Model; subject however to the exception of Art. 26 par. 5 OECD Model). This rule has two dimensions: first, a state cannot be requested to take a measure that it cannot implement under its domestic law; second it cannot request to the other state a measure that the former would not be in a position to obtain under its domestic rule. In other words, a Contracting State cannot take advantage of the system of exchange of information of the other Contracting State if it is wider than its own.[804] For instance, a requested State would be allowed to decline a request if a similar request would have been precluded under the rule against self-incrimination in the requesting State.[805] Similar rules are found in the TIEA Model.[806]

## 3. Protection of trade, business or professional secrets

A Contracting State is not obliged to supply information which would disclose any trade, business, industrial, commercial or professional secret or trade process (Art. 26 par. 3 lit. c OECD Model). According to the OECD, the secret mentioned in this provision should not be taken in too wide a sense; in particular, the Contracting State should carefully weigh if the interests of the taxpayer really justify its application.[807] This is interesting because it demonstrates in this context, that the interest of the taxpayer has to be taken into account in the discretionary power of decision granted to the requested State.[808] This interpretation is also confirmed by the definition of a trade or business secret, which desig-nates: 'facts and circumstances that are of considerable economic import-ance and that can be exploited practically and the unauthorised use of which may lead to serious damage (e.g. may lead to severe financial hardship)'.[809]

---

[804]  OECD Commentary, n. 14.1. ad Art. 26; see supra XO.

[805]  OECD Commentary, n. 15.2. ad Art. 26.

[806]  See TIEA Commentary n. 19.5 ad Art. 26.

[807]  OECD Commentary, n. 19 ad Art. 26.

[808]  See also Schenk-Geers (2009) p. 109.

[809]  OECD Commentary, n. 19.2 ad Art. 26; see also Engelschak, in: Vogel (1997), n. 110 ad Art. 26.

In addition, a state may decline information relating to confidential communications between attorneys, solicitors or other admitted legal representatives in their role as such and their clients (*client-attorney privilege*).[810] This rule is also found in the TIEA Model.[811]

### 4. Public policy and use of stolen data

A state cannot be obliged to supply information, the disclosure of which would be contrary to public policy (ordre public) (Art. 26 par. 3 lit c OECD Model). At first, this rule appears to be fundamentally in the interest of the state. For example, the supply of information, which would constitute a state secret, such as information held by the secret service, could be declined if the disclosure of such would be contrary to the vital interest of the requested State.[812] But in other cases, should a tax investigation from a requesting State be motivated by political, racial, or religious persecution,[813] the refusal would also be in the interest of the taxpayer concerned.

An interesting issue in this context pertains to an exchange of information from a requesting State based on stolen data (CD, electronic tools, etc.). When the conditions are met, the requested State has to supply the information obtainable, namely information that is in the possession of its authorities or that can be obtained domestically under the investigation powers foreseen by law.[814] In this context, it is disputable whether a state can use information obtained illegally. The opinions are contrasting. According to Dourado, Art. 26 OECD Model DTC does not contain any prohibition in this context, as long as the confidentiality clause is respected and the prohibition of the use of such evidence in the requesting State depends on the latter's domestic law.[815] By contrast, Steichen argues that the override of Art. 26 par. 3 lit. c (public policy) should not be possible in such a case. Indeed, the public policy doctrine is understood as part of the body of principles that underpin the operation of legal systems in each state.[816]

We also tend to restrict the use of stolen data as evidence. It is the author's view that the use of stolen data, obtained within the framework

---

[810] OECD Commentary, n. 19.3. ad Art. 26.
[811] See supra p. 63.
[812] OECD Commentary, n. 19.5. ad Art. 26.
[813] Ibid.
[814] OECD Commentary, n. 16 ad Art. 26; Dourado (2013), p. 17.
[815] Dourado (2013), p. 17; see also Engelschalk, in: Vogel (1998), n. 21 ad Art. 26.
[816] Steichen (2012), p. 25.

of an exchange of information under a double taxation treaty, violates the good faith principle granted in Art. 26 of the Vienna Convention.[817] This rule is indeed implicit in Art. 26 of the OECD Model DTC, so that an express mention appears not to be necessary. It is worth mentioning here that in Switzerland, a draft proposal of the Federal Law on administrative assistance in tax matters (IAAT), presented in early 2013, would have disallowed the use of stolen data, but only if it was *actively* obtained by illegal behaviour under Swiss law. The consultation process, which took place between August and September 2013, demonstrated however, a strong opposition to such a proposal, so that it was finally deleted.[818]

### F. Procedural Rights

In the *international* context, however, the OECD Model DTC does not entail any specific instrument to protect the taxpayer.[819] According to Art. 3 of the CMAAT, 'Any Party may, by a declaration addressed to one of the Depositaries, indicate that, according to its internal legislation, its authorities my inform its resident or national before transmitting information concerning him, in conformity with Articles 5 and 7'. It follows that as a general rule, while the international instruments do not provide any specific rule of taxpayer protection, they do not prohibit them. A few procedural rules may however be found in some DTCs, typically under a protocol. For instance, some DTCs provide, usually in the Protocol, procedural rights such as notification rights and appeal possibilities.[820]

## IV. EUROPEAN COURT OF HUMAN RIGHTS (ECHR)

The European Court of Human Rights (ECHR) protects various rights, which are of relevance in the context of exchange of information.

First, the ECHR guarantees the right of every natural or legal person to the peaceful enjoyment of his possessions (Art. 1 of Protocol No 1). This also includes protection against confiscatory taxation.

---

[817] Oberson (2012), p. 17.
[818] See Federal Council, Message sur la modification de la loi sur l'assistance administrative fiscale, du 16 octobre 2013.
[819] Pistone/Gruber (2012), p. 109.
[820] See for instance, Protocol 9 of the German/Mexican DTC, quoted by Koppensteiner (2012), p. 254.

In the *N.K.M.* case of 14 May 2014,[821] the applicant, a former civil servant, was subject to a subsequent tax on severance benefits, at a rate of 98 per cent on payments exceeding 3.5 million Hungarian forints. Overall it corresponded to a tax burden of approximately 52 per cent on the entirety of the severance, as opposed to the general income tax rate of 16 per cent.

The ECHR confirmed that the impugned taxation represented an interference with the applicant's right to peaceful enjoyment of possessions.[822] In particular, according to the Court, interference, including one resulting from a measure to secure payment of taxes, 'must strike a "fair balance" between the demands of the general interest of the community and the requirements of the protection of the individual's fundamental rights'.[823] Further, the interference must be compatible with the rule of law and be sufficiently accessible, precise and foreseeable in its application. The notion of 'foreseeability' implies also that 'the applicable law must provide for minimum procedural safeguards commensurate with the importance of the principle at stake'.[824] The Court concluded that the present measure entailed an excessive and individual burden on the applicant's side, which could not be justified by the legitimate public interest, relied on by the government.

Second, according to Art. 8 par. 1 ECHR, everyone has the right to respect for his *private* and family life, his home and his correspondence. An interference with the exercise of this right is only possible if it is in accordance with the law and necessary in a democratic society in the interest of national security, public safety or the economic well-being of the country, for the prevention of disorder or crime, for the protection of health or morals, or for the protection of the rights and freedoms of others (Art. 8 par. 2 ECHR).

In the *Michaud* case, of 6 December 2012, the ECHR confirmed that the requirement for lawyers to report to administrative authorities information concerning another person, which came into their possession through exchanges with that person, constitutes an interference with the right to respect their private life, which includes activities of a professional nature.[825] However, the Court found this infringement justified. The obligation was based on the law and, even if the professional secrecy is one of the fundamental principles on which the administration of

---

[821]  ECHR, *N.K.M. v. Hungary*, 14 May 2013, n. 66529/11.
[822]  *N.K.M.* case, n. 45.
[823]  *N.K.M.* case, n. 42.
[824]  *N.K.M.* case, n. 48.
[825]  ECHR *Michaud v. France*, 6 December 2012, 12323/11.

justice in a democratic society is based, the obligation to report forms part of a series of international instruments intended to prevent money laundering activities and such obligation does not constitute a disproportionate interference with the professional privilege of lawyers.

In *F.S. v. Germany*,[826] the EHCR found that the exchange of information under the old Exchange of Information Directive (77/799/EC) was not a violation of Art. 8 ECHR because, in accordance with Art. 8 par. 2, it was based on the law and justified as a necessary measure in a democratic society to achieve the prevention of crime.

In the context of tax assessment and enforcement, an infringement of Art. 8 ECHR will often be present.[827] The tax return of individuals includes notably information about their personal status (spouse, children), sometimes their religious status (for taxes levied by churches), their medical expenses, houses, their memberships of clubs or associations, charitable gifts, etc. These reporting requirements may be justified by the principle of ability to pay and the necessity to share equally and in a fair way the tax burden among taxpayers.[828] However, the principle of proportionality also requires a balance of the different interests involved, which should imply that the tax authority must respect the secrecy of information.[829]

In our view, this rule is also applicable in the context of international exchange of information. The secrecy rule, in this context, can be seen as a requirement based on the principle of proportionality. This also requires a proper system of protection against violation of this rule. Indeed, the state is obliged to find a 'fair balance' between the legitimate interest of the state to obtain this information and the conflicting right to privacy of the individual.[830] It means that by implementing the domestic rule of international assistance in tax matters, the state has to find a right and proportionate balance, which includes adequate right of protection. This especially includes the right to be informed of the exchange of information.[831] In general, it requires that the taxpayer should be informed that a request has been sent, at the beginning of the exchange of information process. Following the principle of proportionality, it is only if overriding public interest is present that the notification to the taxpayer could occur at a later stage.

---

[826]  *FS v. Germany*, No 30128/96, 27.11.1996.
[827]  Rust (2012), p. 178.
[828]  Rust (2012), p. 179.
[829]  Ibid.
[830]  Koppensteiner (2012), p. 250.
[831]  See also Koppensteiner (2012), p. 251.

Third, Art. 6 ECHR also guarantees the right to a fair trial. As a rule, tax issues are outside the scope of this provision, to the extent that they cannot be characterized as 'civil rights' or 'criminal charges'. Since the *Ferrazzini* case, the ECHR confirmed the exclusion of taxes from the meaning of 'civil rights', because 'tax matters still form part of the hard core of public authority prerogatives with the public nature of the relationship between the taxpayer and the community remaining predominant'.[832] Despite, numerous criticism, notably from Baker,[833] the ECHR has confirmed its position in later judgments.[834]

The concept of criminal controversies however, may fall within the competence of the EHCR provided they include a criminal tax charge. Following the *Engel* case, the notion of 'criminal' covers any penalty, having regard to the following non-cumulative criteria: (i) the legal classification of the offence under domestic law, (ii) the nature of the offence and (iii) the nature and degree of severity of the possible penalties.[835] For instance, the ECHR considers that the determination of a liability to penalties of incomplete tax returns is a determination of a 'criminal charge' within the meaning of Art. 6 ECHR.[836] As a result, all the legal and procedural guarantees provided by criminal law, namely the right to a fair trial, apply to that determination. In the *J.B.* case, in particular, the ECHR held that the taxpayer involved in such proceedings had the right to remain silent and thus could not be fined by the tax administration for not having returned a bank certification (*self-incrimination*).[837] In the *Ravon* case, the Court also admitted that the right to a fair trial, according to Art. 6 ECHR also applied to the pre-litigation phase, namely the tax determination.[838]

---

[832]  *Ferrazzini v. Italy*, No. 44759/98, ECHR 2001 VII, 12.07.2001; Maisto (2011), p. 373.

[833]  Baker (2001) p. 205; see also Attard (2011), p. 397 ff; Giusi De Flora (2011), p. 411; Lyal (2011), p. 444; Mauro (2011), p. 459; Bizioli (2011), p. 489; see also, notably, Cordeiro Guerra/Dorigo (2011), pp. 425, 426 (arguing in a convincing way that there is no ontological difference between an individual and a taxpayer and there is no reason why he should be regarded as a 'sui generis' individual, whose 'protection would be dependant, at the most, on the kind permission of the taxing sovereign state').

[834]  Maisto (2011), p. 372 with various references.

[835]  *Engel and Others v. the Netherlands*, No 5100/71; 5101/71; 5102/71; 5354/72; 5370/72, Series A n. 22, 8 June 1976, nn. 82–83; Maisto (2011), p. 375.

[836]  See in this respect Baker (2001), p. 205 ff.; Baker (2000), p. 298 ff.

[837]  Decision of May 3, 2001 *JB v. Switzerland* n. 31827/96.

[838]  *Ravon and Others v. France* No 1849/03, 21.02.2008.

The extent to which this right applies in the process of international exchange of information is however a matter of controversy. The Swiss Federal Supreme Court, notably in the context of the 'UBS saga', has judged that Art. 6 ECHR is in fact not applicable.[839] Under the reasoning of the Court, the rules of international exchange of information are similar to a gathering of facts, which is part of international assistance between states.

We do not share this view. First, in the context of international assistance in criminal tax matters, Art. 6 ECHR should be applicable. Criminal tax matters, in the framework of Art. 6 ECHR include notably tax evasion cases and penalties. Second, in the more general context of international assistance, Maisto admits that information exchange under either the EU Directive or a bilateral treaty may fall under the scope of Art. 6(1) ECHR because the gathering of information is by itself 'part of the investigation process that is functional to the issue of the act of assessment'.[840] In addition, the 'weak position of the taxpayer with the course of the information exchanged procedures is evident and the exorbitant discretionary power exercised by the tax authorities to request/ deny information'.[841] This means that adequate protection should be offered to the taxpayers involved. In order to be in a position to defend his or her case, the taxpayer should therefore at least be aware of the process, i.e. to be notified of the exchange of information procedure.[842]

# V. TAXPAYER PROTECTION RULES AT THE EU LEVEL

## A. Data Protection Rules

At the EU level, protection of personal data is guaranteed by various instruments, notably Art. 16 of the Treaty on the Functioning of the European Union (TFEU), the Charter of Fundamental Rights of the EU,

---

[839] See supra p. 43 ff.

[840] Maisto (2011), p. 386.

[841] Maisto (2011), p. 387.

[842] Same opinion Koppensteiner (2012), p. 251 (arguing that, in order to avoid risks of jeopardizing the process, the right of information should be granted, at least after the exchange of information has been completed).

and the European Convention for the Protection of Human Rights and Fundamental Freedoms, in particular Art. 8, which protects right to privacy.[843]

Article 7 of the Charter protects the right to respect for private and family life. In addition, according to Art. 8 of the Charter,

> Everyone has the right to the protection of personal data concerning him or her. Such data must be processed fairly for specified purposes and on the basis of the consent of the person concerned or some other legitimate basis laid down by law. Everyone has the right of access to data, which has been collected concerning him or her, and the right to have it rectified.

Limitations on these rights are possible but must be provided by law, in respect to the essence of those rights and freedoms, and in accordance with the principle of proportionality.[844]

The Data Protection Directive of 1995 (hereafter DPD) provides for an effective protection of the fundamental right to data protection in the EU.[845] Member States must provide that personal data must be processed fairly and lawfully, collected for legitimate purposes, adequate, accurate and kept in a form that permits the identification of the data subject for no longer than necessary (Art. 5).

First, where the data has not been obtained from the data subject, the latter has the right to specific information, and notably, the identity of the controller, the purpose of the processing, the categories of data concerned, and the recipient of such data (Art. 11 Directive). This implies that the taxpayer must be *informed* about the data processing or the transfer of data.[846] Second, the member state must guarantee every data subject the right to obtain from the controller, a) the right to *access*; b) the right to *rectification*, erasing or blocking of data if the processing does not comply with the Directive; c) notification to third parties to whom the data have been disclosed of any rectification, erasure, or blocking carried out (Art. 12 Directive). Those rights may however be restricted, in particular, if such a restriction constitutes a necessary measure to safeguard: 'an important economic or financial interest of a Member State or of the European Union, including monetary, budgetary and taxation matters' (Art. 13 par. 1 Directive). The combination of these

---

[843]   Rust (2012), p. 189 s.

[844]   Rust (2012), p. 190.

[845]   Directive 95/46/EC of 24 October 1995 on the protection of individuals with regard to the processing of personal data and on the free movement of such data, OJ L 281/31.

[846]   Rust (2012), p. 191.

rules has the effect that the notification to the taxpayer may be suspended if it could prevent the tax collection.[847]

In the landmark *Google* case,[848] the Court of Justice confirmed that Art. 12 of the Directive included a *'right to be forgotten'*, in the sense that under certain conditions, individuals had the right to ask a search engine, such as Google, to remove links with personal information, in particular where the information is inaccurate, inadequate, irrelevant or excessive. The Court however confirmed that this right is not absolute and needs to be balanced against other fundamental rights, in particular the freedom of expression and of the media.[849] In other words, a case-by-case analysis is required where the sensitivity for the private life of the individual at stake is balanced with the interest of the public to have access to the information. In this specific case, the Court ruled that the violation of the data protection rules could not be justified by the sole economic interest of the search engine.

Finally, according to Art. 25 of the Directive, the transfer of personal data to third countries is only allowed if the third country in question ensures an adequate level of protection.

The important technological developments and globalization have brought new challenges in the protection of personal data. A new legal framework for the protection of personal data in the EU is currently pending.[850] On 25 January 2012, the EU Commission presented a proposal for a new Directive of the European Parliament and of the Council on the protection of personal data.[851] The proposal is designed to ensure a high level of data protection of individuals with regard to the processing of personal data by Union institutions and by the Member States. It also covers the processing of personal data in the areas of judicial co-operation in criminal matters and police cooperation.

In addition, based on Art. 218 of the Treaty on the Functioning of the EU (TFEU), the EU has been negotiating with the United States on an international framework agreement in order to protect data transfer between the EU and the US for law enforcement purposes (Data

---

[847] Ibid.

[848] ECJ, 13 May 2014, Google Spain SL, Google Inc, Case C-131/12.

[849] Case C-131/12, n. 85.

[850] See Communication of the EU Commission, COM (2012) 9 final.

[851] EU Commission, Proposal for a Directive on the protection of individuals with regard to the processing of personal data by competent authorities for the purposes of prevention, investigation, detection or prosecution of criminal offences or the execution of criminal penalties, and the free movement of such data, 25 January 2012, COM (2012) 10 final.

Protection Umbrella Agreement). The negotiations are still pending but have reached a final phase.[852]

## B. EU Directives

### 1. Secrecy and data protection

The EU Directives in the area of exchange of information also include rules of secrecy and data protection. The same data protection rules apply in the EUSD and the Directive on administrative cooperation in tax matters (DAC).[853] Indeed, Art. 9 par. 3 EUSD refers to the rules of the mutual assistance Directive. Furthermore, as a matter of principle, the EU Data Protection Directive applies to all exchanges of information governed by the DAC.[854] However, according to Art. 25 DAC, the rights provided for in Art. 10, Art. 11 par. 2, Art. 12 and Art. 21 of the Data Protection Directive may be restricted in order to safeguard the collection of tax revenue as an important economic and financial interest. As such, this rule is also in line with the Data Protection Directive.[855]

Secrecy requirements are governed by Art. 16 DAC. According to Art. 16 par. 1 DAC, information exchange is subject to the same secrecy obligation in the requesting State as information obtained under domestic law (equality of treatment) but the requested State is no more entitled to ask for the application of its own secrecy standard.[856] In addition, the requested State may authorize the use by the requesting State for other purposes if this is in accordance with the law of the requesting State. Transfer of information to a third country is possible, under the conditions of Art. 16 par. 4 DAC, but, according to Art. 25 of the Data Protection Directive, only if the recipient country provides an adequate level of data protection.[857]

### 2. Procedural rights, notably right to be informed

In the interesting *Sabou* case, the ECJ had to examine the extent of the right to be informed and the right to be heard within the framework of an exchange of information under the Council Directive 77/799 of 19

---

[852]   See EU Commission, Factsheet EU-US Negotiations on data protection, June 2014.

[853]   Rust (2012), p. 192.

[854]   See DAC Recital at Preamble, par. 27 and 28; Rust (2012), p. 194.

[855]   In the same sense, see Art. 13 par. 1 lit. a of the Data Protection Directive.

[856]   Rust (2012), p. 194 (considering this change as a 'step backward' in the protection of the taxpayer).

[857]   Rust (2012), p. 195.

December 1977.[858] Mr. Sabou, a professional footballer resident in the Czech Republic, had claimed expenditure with a view to a possible transfer to one of the football clubs of several Member States. The Czech tax authorities, raising doubts on the truthfulness of the expenditure, sought notably assistance from the Spanish, French and United Kingdom tax authorities. It followed from the replies that none of the clubs approached knew either Mr. Sabou or his agent. The taxpayer then claimed: (i) that the tax authority should have informed him of their request for assistance to other authorities; (ii) that he had not been able to take part in formulating the questions addressed to those authorities; (iii) that he had not been invited to take part in the examination of witnesses in other Member States, in contrast to the right enjoyed under Czech law in similar proceedings.

The Czech Supreme Administrative Court referred three questions to the ECJ for a preliminary ruling, in summary: (i) whether under EU law a taxpayer had the right to be informed of a decision of the tax authorities to make a request for information in accordance with Directive 77/799 and whether the taxpayer has the right to take part in formulating the request or if not, whether domestic law can confer similar rights; (ii) whether the taxpayer has the right to take part in the examination of witnesses in the requested Member State and whether that State is obliged to inform the taxpayer beforehand; and (iii) whether the tax authorities of the requested Member State are obliged to observe a certain minimum content in their answers; may the taxpayer challenge the correctness of the information thus provided (for instance on procedural defects).

First, the ECJ considered that

> it is thus apparent from the examination of Directive 77/799, the purpose of which is to govern cooperation between tax authorities of Member States, that it coordinates the transfer of information between competent authorities by imposing certain obligations on the Member States. The Directive does not, however, confer specific rights to the taxpayer, and in particular does not lay down any obligation for the competent authorities of the Member States to consult the taxpayer.

---

[858] Council Directive 77/799/EEC of 19 December 1977 concerning mutual assistance by the competent authorities of the Member States in the field of direct taxation and taxation of insurance premiums, OJ 1977 L 336 p. 15, as amended by Council Directive 2006/98/EC of 20 November 2006, OJ 2006 L 363 p. 139. Although Directive 77/799 has been repealed by the DAC (2011/16) of 15 February 2011, see supra p. 104, proceedings were still governed by Directive 77/799, due to the date of the facts.

Second, the ECJ examined, whether the taxpayer may nevertheless derive from the right of the defence, which is a general principle of European Union Law, a right to participate in the exchange of information between the competent authorities. In accordance with that general principle, 'the addressee of decisions which significantly affect their interest must therefore be placed in a position in which they can effectively make known their views as regards the information on which the authorities intend to base their decision'. In addition, when EU Member States take decisions which are under the scope of EU laws, they must respect the right to be heard, even if EU law does not expressly provide for such a requirement.[859]

In the present case, however, the Court found that a request for information by one Member State sent to the tax administration of another Member State does not constitute an act giving rise to such an obligation. When the authorities gather information, they are not required to notify the taxpayer of this or obtain his point of view. The same applies to the reply made by the requested tax authorities and the inquiries carried out to that end, including the examination of witnesses.

It is interesting to mention that, in its reasoning, following observations from all of the Member States which submitted them, the Court mentions that,

> in tax inspection procedures, the investigation stage, during which the information is collected and which includes the request for information by one tax authority to another, must be distinguished from the contentious stage, between the tax authorities and the taxpayer, which begins when the taxpayer is sent the proposed adjustment'.[860]

In this respect, the Court seems to follow the view that exchange of information remains a 'fact gathering' process and that rights of tax-payers should be granted only at the later stage, after the decision in the requesting State is taken.

Third, the ECJ stated that Directive 77/799 does not address the taxpayer's right to challenge the accuracy of the information conveyed and it does not impose a particular obligation with regard to the content of the information conveyed. This issue is a question of national law. The taxpayer may challenge the information concerning him conveyed to the

---

[859]   C-276/12 at par. 37 ff.
[860]   C-276/12 at par. 40 f.

requesting Member State in accordance with the rules of the domestic laws of that Member State.[861]

Therefore, the ECJ, in its answer to the request for a preliminary ruling, on these three questions found that European law, as it results in particular from Directive 77/799 and the fundamental right to be heard, must be interpreted as not conferring on a taxpayer of a Member State either the right to be informed of a request for assistance from that Member State to another Member State, or the right to take part in formulating the request addressed to the requested Member State, or the right to take part in examinations of witnesses organized by the requested Member State. However, the Court mentioned that nothing prevents a Member State to extend the right to be heard in other stages of the investigations, by involving the taxpayer in various stages of the gathering of information. Finally, Directive 77/799 does not govern the question of the circumstances in which the taxpayer may challenge the accuracy of the information conveyed to the requested Member State, and it does not impose any obligation with regard to the content of the information conveyed.

It appears that the ECJ took a rather restrictive approach on the potential application of taxpayers' rights to exchange of information under EU law. Some commentators have already expressed dissenting views.[862] At least, it can be inferred from that judgment that the EU general principle of the right of defence is applicable but only when the *decision* affecting the taxpayer is taken, namely at the end of the administrative process. The Court also ruled that the Member States are free to extend the right to be heard to other stages of the investigation. It means at least that EU law does not preclude the development of participation rights at the domestic level at other stages of the international exchange of information.[863]

In any event, we share the criticism of Calderón and Quintas. Even if the taxpayer has the right of defence, notably the right to be heard, at the end of the process in the requesting Member State making the final tax assessment on the basis of information received from the requested State, this decision is based on a preliminary analysis by the requested State, which is based on documents, evidence, procedures, discretionary decisions and analysis in which the taxpayer should be able to participate and which have to be implemented in accordance with due process procedural

---

[861] C-276/12 ar par. 48 ff.
[862] Calderón Carrero/Quintas Seara (2014), p. 498 ff.
[863] Calderón Carrero/Quintas Seara (2014), p. 501.

protection rules. Only with the knowledge of details about 'sources, procedures and safeguards used in the requested Member State to obtain the information conveyed' will the taxpayer be in a position to exercise a 'real right of defense'.[864] It follows that denying the right of defence to the taxpayer during the mutual assistance procedure conducted in the requested Member State

> could seriously affect the legitimate rights and interests of those taxpayers (for example, the right to challenge the accuracy of the data provided, the right to informational self-determination, the right to prevent the transmission of sensitive information (trade secrets) unless strictly necessary and under specific conditions of confidentiality, or the right to suspend the transmission of the information if there is a serious risk of irreparable harm to the taxpayer).[865]

## VI.  CONSTITUTIONAL RULES

According to Rust, in its famous 'population census' judgment, the German Constitutional Court held that

> Articles 1 and 2, when construed together, guarantee a right to informational self-determination, meaning that every person has the right to decide for himself/herself when and to what extent about his/her personal life is to be revealed to others.[866]

A justification is only possible, if the following cumulative conditions are met: (i) the restriction follows a legitimate goal; (ii) is capable of achieving that goal; (iii) it does not go beyond what is necessary to achieve that goal and (iv) the goals achieved are more important than the damaged caused by the measure.[867]

Similar principles may be found in many other countries. For instance, Art. 13 of the Swiss Constitution guarantees the right to privacy and more particularly the right to be protected against abusive use of personal data. The Spanish Constitution also provides for similar rights.

---

[864]  Calderón Carrero/Quintas Seara (2014), p. 501.
[865]  Ibid.
[866]  Rust (2012), p. 178.
[867]  Ibid.

# VII. IMPLEMENTATION OF THE LEGAL PROTECTION OF THE TAXPAYER

## A. Substantive and Procedural Rights

The development of international assistance in tax matters and the movement towards global transparency raise new challenges for the protection of the persons involved in this process, and notably require adequate protection of the taxpayer. We have seen so far that, in general, the principles governing exchange of information in the various international instruments tend to protect the interest of the Contracting States. The interest of the taxpayer has however to be taken into account, at least in cases where the state has a discretionary power of decision in the process. In other words, in the balance of interests, the protection of the taxpayer has to find its place.[868]

We then have identified which rights (human rights, constitutional guarantees, procedural rights) serve as protection to the taxpayers within the exchange of information process between states. In this context, we may draw a distinction between what we call *substantive* rights (protection of privacy, data protection, secrecy), on the one hand, and *procedural* rights, such as due process, the right to be heard, the right to participate in the investigations and the right to appeal, on the other hand.[869] Contrary to substantive rights, based on human rights or constitutional law, which tend to protect essential elements of the taxpayer as a human being, procedural rights have the function to guarantee the proper functioning of the tax assessment and exchange of information process according to fundamental guarantees (due process and fair trial).

---

[868] See also Schenk-Geers (2009), p. 109 ff.

[869] See also Brokelind (2011), who tends to distinguish substantive rights, i.e. rights directed mostly against 'arbitrary taxation', from procedural rights, that is guarantees for taxpayers in tax audits. We tend to use a slightly different distinction based on administrative law. In this sense procedural rights are designed to protect the taxpayer during the course of tax procedure, including exchange of information, such as the right of defence and due process of law, while substantive rights are human or constitutional rights protecting fundamental rights, such as rights to ownership, privacy, family or data protection.

## B.   Taxpayer protection in the exchange of information process

### 1.   The exchange of information process as an independent administrative procedure

We now need to analyse in more detail how the rights of the taxpayers may be protected during the various steps of an information exchange. In practice, exchange of information may occur in situations concerning taxpayers resident either in the requesting State or in the requested State, or in both.

In the first, and most frequent case, such as in the *Sabou* case described above,[870] the state of residence asks for assistance in the requested State, typically in order to check whether the global tax situation of the taxpayer (fully tax liable in the requesting State) corresponds to his or her tax declaration. For instance, the requesting State may want to discover undisclosed assets sited in the requested States (bank accounts, mobile goods, etc.). Such a request may also frequently occur for corporate taxation, typically in the transfer pricing area, or in order to ascertain the international allocation of profits between a foreign branch (sited in the requested State) and the resident head office. In this case, so far, notification rights are rare.[871]

In the second case, the requesting State usually does not know the global position of the taxpayer and needs the assistance of the requested State where the taxpayer is resident. For instance, the requesting State may want to verify if the foreign resident taxpayer may benefit from a reduced tax at source, based on the applicable DTC. In a case where the resident is a UK resident but non-domiciled, the source state may want to check the amount of income 'remitted' in the UK. In the area of taxation of groups of companies, exchange of information may also occur in this context in order to better evaluate the legal or economic relations between companies or to allocate profits of a branch in the requesting State.

Finally, there are also mixed cases where both requesting and requested States use exchange of information to ascertain the effective residence of individuals or companies, under Art. 4 par. 2 or 3 of the applicable DTC (conflict of residence). Another example of exchange of information in the context of a conflict of double unlimited tax liability would be a request from the IRS to verify the tax position of a US national, resident in the requested State.

---

[870]   See supra p. 230 ff.
[871]   Seer/Gaber (2011), p. 96.

As demonstrated by the two IFA General Reports of 1990 and 2013 on the international exchange of information in tax matters,[872] differences of practice among states do exist. Some states tend to inform the taxpayers involved in the request and, although under different conditions, to grant them the right to participate and to defend themselves in the process. Other states offer much fewer participation rights, if any.

Behind these differences, we have identified two different schools of thought pertaining to the application of procedural rights to the taxpayers within the framework of international administrative assistance.[873]

On the one hand, some states consider that administrative assistance is in fact similar to a fact-gathering process. Under this line of reasoning, assistance in tax matters belongs to the usual cooperation or assistance between two states and no specific procedural rights should be granted at this level. Under EU law, as we have seen, the ECJ seems to follow this approach. Following the observations submitted by Member States, the request for information belongs to the *investigation* stage, during which information is collected, which should be distinguished from the *contentious* stage, involving both the taxpayer and tax authorities.[874] At this later stage, the person involved is however granted all the potential rights in the requesting State's jurisdiction.

On the other hand, many states tend to view the assistance process as an *independent* administrative procedure, under which the person involved is granted all the relevant procedural rights during the procedure. In our view, this second approach should prevail. It is more consistent with the modern process of international assistance in tax matters. Indeed, as we have demonstrated, the secrecy rules and the limits to the exchange of information granted under international instruments (DTC, EU Directives, CMAAT, IGAs, or TIEAs) are also in the interest of the taxpayer. When the requested State is in the process of an information exchange it also has to balance the interests of the proper conduct of the administrative assistance process, and to make a *substantive choice* about the content and the extent of the exchange. This decision, in other words, like any administrative decision with substance, may affect the rights of the taxpayer involved.

The independent administrative nature of the exchange of information process in the requested State is reflected both on the substantive and procedural side. On the *substantive* side, the requested State has to

---

[872] See Oberson (2013) p. 28 ff; Gangemi (1990), p. 69 ff.
[873] Oberson (2013), p. 57 ff.
[874] *Sabou*, C-276/12, at par. 40 f.

exercise its power of discretion in the exchange, to observe and preserve secrecy and confidentiality rules and to decide the extent to which ground for refusals (and other limitations) to the exchange have to be observed, such as business secrecy, reciprocity, or public order. On the *procedural* side, the gathering of information may involve hearing witnesses, and analysis of reports, documents or other information, which should occur under due process rules. The authenticity and 'probative value'[875] of those documents should be checked and challenged by an independent Court, in accordance with respect for the right of defence.

It follows that the exchange of information is much more than a simple 'fact gathering' process, and that the taxpayer should be in a position to defend his or her interest already at this stage.

## 2.  Substantive rights

In this context we have seen that an information exchange may constitute an infringement of taxpayer's rights, notably of human or constitutional rights.[876] Relevant rights that are concerned are, notably, the right of privacy or the right of data protection. In any event, even if an infringement occurs, it does not imply that the rights of taxpayers are violated because such infringement could be justified, following the conditions provided for by constitutional or case law, such as the rule of law, a legitimate purpose and the principle of proportionality. The scope of protection will however differ considerably between each state.

What is however crucial is that the taxpayer, during the exchange of information process, should be in the position to effectively protect those substantive rights. This in fact requires the granting of basic procedural rights during this process.

## 3.  Procedural rights

*i) In general*    According to the OECD, the taxpayer protection rights can be divided into three categories:[877] (i) right to be informed of an information request and of its essential content (notification); (ii) right to participate in the process of gathering information (consultation); and (iii) right to appeal and to control the legitimacy of the request (intervention).

---

[875]    See, in this respect, the interesting comments of Calderón Carrero/ Quintas Seara (2014), p. 502 (defending a 'principle of probative value').

[876]    Koppensteiner (2012), p. 240.

[877]    Tax Information exchange between OECD Member countries, Paris 1994, par. 65 ff. See also Calderón Carrero/Quintas Seara (2014), p. 502.

These basic rights can be found in the domestic (typically constitutional) rules of the various states. We have however seen that Art. 26 paras 2 and 4 of the OECD Model, and comparable provisions in the CMAAT, even if they are targeted at competent authorities of the states, also protect the taxpayers.[878] However, no specific rights are granted in the text of these provisions. It seems as if the taxpayers should trust that the Contracting States would respect the rules they have implemented themselves.[879]

In addition, the right to a fair trial, granted by Art. 6 ECHR, offers an important safeguard. Even if, according to the *Ferazinni* ruling, the scope of application of this provision to tax procedure is quite disputed, this rule should in our view be applicable during the exchange of information process, which goes beyond a mere 'fact gathering' procedure.[880] At the EU level, the fundamental rights of defence (including the right to be heard) are also applicable. In this respect, the ECJ has ruled that at least after the fact gathering process of exchange of information, the rights of defence apply in the requesting State.[881]

*ii) Right to be informed of the information exchange*   In order to ensure that taxpayers in practice benefit from an effective protection, a crucial first issue is the extent to which the taxpayer is informed of the information exchange. Indeed, taxpayers may only effectively protect their rights if they are informed of the request, and in fact before the information is transmitted to other states.[882] As various jurisprudences have demonstrated, a 'fair balance' should be found between the legitimate need of the state to obtain information, notably for the fight against tax avoidance, and the protection of the taxpayers' rights.

At the EU level, in the *Sabou* case described above, the ECJ confirmed that the right of defence, as a fundamental principle of EU law, is applicable but as a 'minimal standard' and only at the end of the process, namely during the tax assessment by the requesting State. In other words, the ECJ has considered that EU law does not require that the taxpayer should be informed of the request of information. Member States are however free to grant more extended rights. Article 6 ECHR also guarantees the right of a fair trial but only in cases of criminal tax proceedings. The application of such principles during the exchange as

---

[878] Schenk-Geers (2009), p. 109.
[879] Koppensteiner (2012), p. 239.
[880] See supra p. 227.
[881] See supra p. 231.
[882] Seer/Gaber (2011), p. 96; compare Koppensteiner (2011), p. 252.

such and the tax investigations implemented by the requested State are however highly controversial, even if the ECHR tends to accept that pre-trial investigations are part of tax proceedings.[883]

It follows that, beyond the minimal standard described above, the implementation of procedural protection rights remains until today mostly in the competence of the domestic law of the states. Some states, like Germany, Switzerland or Luxembourg grant the right to notification, while many other states don't. As the ECJ has confirmed, even under EU law, nothing prevents EU Member States to grant extended participation rights but EU law, as such, does not go beyond the 'minimum standard'.

The rule of law however requires that the taxpayer should be in a position to defend his/her right and, at least, have a legal means to ask for an independent review whether the request is legitimate or not. This requires that the taxpayer be *informed* of the process.

In our view, as a matter of principle, the taxpayer should be informed of the process of exchange of information and have a possibility to challenge and claim protection of his or her legitimate rights (for example, privacy, business secrets).[884] As a matter of principle, the taxpayer should therefore be informed; more precisely receive *notification* of the request for exchange of information.

In the balance of interests, it is also true that such a right to information should not be used to jeopardize in advance the success of the request, so that in cases of emergency, such a right of notification could then only be granted at a later stage. This corresponds to the position of the Global Forum, which considers that rights of notification, which as such are governed by domestic law, may be granted, but some exceptions should be possible in cases of emergency where the notification could notably harm the investigation process.[885] But this emergency clause should remain as an exception to the rule in favour of granting notification rights at the beginning of the process, and be taken following a balancing of the interests between the efficiency of the exchange and the rights of the taxpayers.

For example, in order to implement the rules of exchange of information in tax treaties, Switzerland issued an application ordinance (Ordinance on administrative assistance according to tax treaties), which entered into force on 1 October 2010 and was later replaced, as of 1 February 2013, by the Federal Act on International Administrative Assistance in Tax Matters (IAAT). In the meantime, the IAAT has

---

[883]   Maisto (2011), pp. 376, 386; see supra p. 226 ff.
[884]   Koppensteiner (2012), p. 252.
[885]   See Calderón Carrero/Quintas Seara (2014), p. 505.

already been subject to a partial revision, which entered into force on 1 August 2014. The amendment includes notably, in addition to more precision regarding group requests, a new provision that envisages a procedure with, in exceptional cases, *deferred notification* of persons entitled to appeal. This modification has been adopted precisely in order for Switzerland to comply with the applicable international standard for administrative assistance of the Global Forum on Tax Transparency.

Therefore, and following the various views on this rule among states, the '*minimum* standard' should correspond to a right of information of the taxpayer involved of the request for information exchange, subject to exceptions under the emergency clause. This implies that in any case the taxpayer should at least have the possibility of challenging the decision made by the requesting State, before the tax assessment, and to understand on which grounds the decision is founded, which requires that he or she should be aware of the exchange of information process and be in a position to know the 'main content' of the information transferred.

*iii) Right to participate to the investigations in the requested State* Protection of taxpayers' rights during the information exchange may only be effective if the taxpayer is informed of the process. In states without notification rights, taxpayers may however still be in a position to intervene, if they become aware of the request, in particular when the tax authorities are not in possession of the information and have to ask for it.[886] The tax authorities, in this case, may indeed ask the taxpayer for the information or ask the information holder who then passes the information to him.

When the taxpayer is informed, or officially notified, various rights may apply, depending on the relevant domestic law. It follows from the *Sabou* case that EU law does not entail rights to take part in the investigation process, notably to participate to the examination of witnesses in the requested EU Member State. But nothing prevents EU Member States to confer extended rights in domestic law.

In practice, depending on the domestic legislation, two distinct procedural rights could be applicable. First, the taxpayer may in particular have the right to be *heard*, which implies the right of consultation of the file (subject to limitation) and, at least in writing, to make comments about the request and also during the investigation stages (hearing of witnesses, expert opinions about authenticity and validity of documents, legal opinion, etc.).

---

[886] Seer/Gaber (2011), p. 96.

Second, the taxpayer is also sometimes granted, after the decision to transfer the information is taken by the requested State, the right to *appeal* to an independent Court. In this case, a relevant issue is the extent to which such appeal has or does not have a suspending effect. This possibility, in the author's view, is an essential safeguard for the protection of the taxpayer's right. Indeed, during this appeal in the requested State, the taxpayer would be offered the possibility to challenge the conditions of the exchange of information under the international instrument (secrecy, reciprocity, limits) and also the possibility to use the information gathered (for instance in the case of illegal data) and its authenticity. This appears to be crucial because, once this information is transferred, the taxpayer may no longer be in a position to challenge or ask for a remedy against violation of these rules under the domestic law of the requesting State. At least the taxpayer should have the possibility, in the requested State, to stop the transfer of sensitive information or protected secrets to the requesting State, or have the right to suspend such transmission in case of 'serious risks of irreparable harm'.[887]

*iv) Right to challenge the assessment decision in the requesting State*
Under EU law, according to the Sabou case, the taxpayer should be granted, as a minimum standard, the right of defence in the requesting State during the tax assessment phase. At this level, the taxpayer has all the protection rights granted under the domestic law of the requesting State. The level of protection will however depend on the possibilities offered by the domestic law of the requested State.

If the taxpayer enjoys extended procedural rights under the domestic law of the requested State, no specific problem should occur. But as we have seen, absent rights of defence in the requested State, based for instance on the 'fact gathering' doctrine, the taxpayer will in our view not enjoy an effective right of protection. He or she should then, at least, be in a position to challenge in the requesting State the grounds of decision-making process, and, following Calderón and Quintas, the 'probative value' of the documentation used in the requesting State. In our view, this requires that the taxpayer be in a position to understand the grounds on which the requesting State has founded its assessment. On this occasion, the legal value, authenticity and quality of the information transferred should be determined. At least, the taxpayer should receive the 'essential elements' of the information transmitted.

---

[887]    In the same vein, Calderón Carrero/Quintas Seara (2014) p. 507.

Another (indirect) way to challenge *ex post* the exchange of information is to contest the use of some information obtained during the process, in violation of legal rules.[888] For instance, the use of stolen data or of information obtained illegally might be challenged.[889] This possibility is however highly controversial. The taxpayer could still try to contend in the subsequent tax assessment procedure in the requesting State that it is based on illegal proofs, or a forbidden data collection mechanism. Indeed, the exchange of illegal data between states could be characterized as a violation of the good faith principle embodied in Arts 24 and 31 of the Vienna Convention.[890]

*v) Rules of conduct of states in the exchange of information process*　A transfer of information in clear violation of treaty conditions, notably secrecy rules, could result in the state being held responsible, provided the conditions in the applicable law are met. The practical difficulties of ascertaining the presence of a damage are however very important, so that the relevance of this legal means is to be questioned.[891]

In addition, according to the rules of international law, violations of the conditions of the exchange of information, notably secrecy rules, could also be characterized as a violation of an international agreement, which could lead to a termination of the treaty or at least its suspension.[892]

The Model CAA of the OECD CRS also provides for suspension in case of non-compliance with the agreement, notably non-compliance with the confidentiality and data safeguarding provisions of this Agreement and the instrument (see Section 7 par. 2 Model CAA). In the context of the CAA, at least, the relevant taxpayer could disclose to their resident state any violation of the rules of exchange of information based on the treaty of the relevant international instrument. This does not give the taxpayer a firm right to get an intervention from its residence state, but it represents at least another indirect way for the taxpayer to influence the proper implementation of the exchange of information rules. Indeed, reciprocal assistance between competent authorities is only possible if each administration 'is assured that the other administration will treat with proper confidence the information which it will receive in the course

---

[888]　Koppensteiner (2012) p. 263.

[889]　See Marchgraber (2012), p. 271 ff; See also supra pp. 35, 223.

[890]　See supra p. 222.

[891]　Koppensteiner (2012), p. 261.

[892]　See, in the context of the limits rules of Art. 26 par. 3 OECD Model DTC, Pistone/Gruber (2011), p. 113.

of their cooperation'.[893] While this rule is intended to protect the interests of the Contracting States, it is also in the interest of the taxpayer and it is essential that confidence in the respect for confidentiality and data protection rules is not only based on the goodwill of the Contracting States.

---

[893]   OECD Model DTC Commentary, n. 11 ad Art. 26.

# 15. Conclusion

The past seven years have seen an unprecedented development in the area of international information exchange in tax matters. More has been accomplished in the last decade than in the preceding century.

The movement started to accelerate around 2007, and notably in 2008, following the financial crisis and a series of scandals. 13 March 2009 will probably remain as the first turning point, the 'big bang', during which the competing financial centres agreed to a minimum global standard for exchange of information, upon request, of information foreseeably relevant to carrying out the domestic tax laws of the requesting State. Under this standard, domestic bank secrecy is no longer a valid reason to refuse to supply information. From that moment, following notably the works of the G20, the OECD and the Global Forum, a worldwide network of double taxation treaties, TIEAs, or ratifications of the CMAAT emerged. Important practices, cases and jurisprudence started also to develop and address, sometimes in controversial ways, new specific legal issues of this growing legal environment, such as the scope of exchange, the concept of 'group requests', the limits of fishing expeditions, and the use of stolen or illegal data in the process.

After 2010, notably with the enactment of FATCA in the United States, a new phase started. What was first seen as mere domestic legislation designed to fight against offshore tax avoidance of US taxpayers came to be transformed into a global model. The decisive moment, retrospectively, may be seen in the Joint Declaration of the G5 and the United States, of February 2012, to develop a common intergovernmental agreement (IGA), on a reciprocal basis. This so-called Model 1 IGA, later adopted by more than a hundred states, combined, but to a limited extent, with the Model 2 IGA, includes the foundation of a global system of automatic exchange of information.

In parallel, the EU played a major role in the implementation of various systems for exchange of information. They had already started in the late 1970s, more precisely in 1977, with a first Directive on exchange of information, which was modified and later repealed. But the EUSD, which entered into force on 1 July 2005, represents one of the first comprehensive models of automatic exchange of information, even if the scope is still limited to interest on savings. In 2011, the EU also adopted the DAC, which gave further impetus to the automatic exchange. Many important rules of exchange of information also exist and are constantly developed and improved on the indirect tax side, notably in the area of VAT and excise duty.

As of 2012, Switzerland tried to introduce an alternative approach, the so-called 'Rubik' system. The idea is to levy a withholding tax at the paying agent level at a rate which should correspond to the applicable rate in the state of residence of the taxpayer, while keeping confidentiality. The model offers an interesting system but could not serve as a long-term alternative to automatic exchange of information.

In fact, a second turning point occurred in 2013, roughly four years after the big bang. On 19 April 2013, in particular, the G20 Finance Ministers and Central Bank Governors endorsed the automatic exchange of information (AEOI), which emerged as the global standard. This decision appears to have been strongly influenced by the joint declaration of the so-called G5 and the United States to develop a multilateral system of information exchange based on FATCA (IGA). Following that date, joint efforts were made by the G8, the G20, the OECD and the EU to develop the global standard. This approval was achieved following various meetings of the G20 and in the mandate to the OECD. The OECD published the global common reporting standard in July 2014. Countries around the world, so-called 'early adopters' and others, are on the way to implementing these regimes globally. At the meeting of the Global Forum in Berlin, on 29 October 2014, 51 countries signed (or committed to sign) a multilateral competent authority agreement implementing the CRS standard. The first exchanges of information under this global standard are expected as of 2017. A second group of around 60 countries should follow one year later. In the EU, on 14 October 2014 the European Council also agreed to implement, within the EU, the new global standard on automatic exchange of information developed by the OECD and endorsed by the G20.

This global acceptance of a general standard should however just be the beginning of a new area where many issues still have to be resolved. Indeed, the standard of AEOI will gain in worldwide acceptance, to the extent that it is applied consistently and under equivalent due diligence rules by participating states. In addition, the standard, in order to be considered as fair, should be based on balanced implementation rules taking sufficient account of secrecy, data protection and rights of the taxpayers and information holders involved in the process. More precisely, five issues seem essential to us in this context.

First, there is a question of *coordination* of the models. It is not conceivable that different systems or models of AEOI would be applied simultaneously or in conflicting ways. The OECD standard, in this respect, suggests using existing treaties, including the CMAAT, or IGAs as a legal basis on which AEOI would be implemented, in accordance with the OECD CRS or equivalent rules (FATCA for example). The EU is also working in this direction. According to the decision of the EU Council of 14 October 2014, a new extended version of the DAC would implement a more global system of AEOI and at the same time trigger the repeal of the EUSD, which would in fact become obsolete in a system of AEOI.

While the OECD CRS has been strongly influenced by the FATCA regime, differences between the two remain. The devil is in the detail and discrepancies between the two systems during the implementation phase should, to the maximum extent possible, be avoided. In fact, it would be quite complex and costly for financial intermediaries to implement and apply simultaneously different mechanisms (including IT systems) depending on the participating country.

Second, there is an issue of *reciprocity*. The global system of AEOI will only achieve global acceptance if not only its concept but also the implementation are effective and applied in a similar way by partner states. The OECD CRS already provides a potential suspension of the system, implemented by a CAA, should one of the Contracting States not respect the rules, notably secrecy rules or identification of controlling persons. Another key issue in this respect will be the implementation of reciprocity rules in the United States according to the IGA Model 1. We recall that already in the OECD Model CRS, an exception to the look-through treatment for investment authorities in non-participating jurisdictions is granted to the United States, taking into account the IGA's approach, as a pre-existing system with close similarities to the CRS and 'the anticipated progress towards widespread participation in the CRS'.[894]

Third, there is the requirement of a *'level playing field'*. One of the crucial issues will be to ensure that participating countries do effectively apply the system and include secrecy and data protection rules in an equivalent way. In this respect, each participating state should have sufficient domestic rules to identify the taxpayer and in case of entities (companies, foundations, trust, partnership) determine who is the controlling person, in accordance with the global standard. After all, a state can

---

[894]   OECD, Standard AEOI, n. 5 ad Introduction.

only provide, upon request, spontaneously or automatically, information that it has or can effectively obtain domestically. For that purpose, the level of implementation of KYC/AML rules in the domestic law of the participating states for the identification of beneficial owners will be essential because the OECD CRS rules of due diligence clearly refer to them.

Fourth, in accordance with general principles of administrative and tax rules, the principles of *proportionality, subsidiarity* and *specialty* should apply. It means that, in the balancing of interests, the state should enforce exchange of information in a way that only affects the involved taxpayers and information holders to the extent necessary. When rights of taxpayers are infringed a fair balancing of interests involved should occur (proportionality). In addition, before entering into the process of exchange of information, the requesting State should have used in the first place all potential domestic means to obtain the information (subsidiarity). Finally, information exchange should in principle only be used for the specific purposes of the request and be transferred only to the authorities defined under the instruments providing for the exchange (subsidiarity).

Finally, in the last part of the book, we have tried to identify the various rights which are relevant in the context of information exchange. In a nutshell, we may distinguish between substantive rights and procedural rights. *Substantive* rights, on the one hand, are based on international instruments or domestic constitutions (human rights, constitutional rights) and protect the essential sphere and elements of human beings (privacy, right of ownership, protection of family or data protection). *Procedural* rights, on the other hand, focus on the process of the exchange and ensure that the rights of defence of the taxpayers involved, notably the right to be informed, right to participate and right of appeal, are duly respected, in accordance with a due process of law and fair trial procedure.

*Substantive* rights may be infringed in the area of exchange of information. It implies that, according to case law, any infringements of human or constitutional rights effected in the exchange of information process should be based on the fundamental conditions granted by the respective courts, which are subject to variations according to domestic law but, in essence, require: a legal basis, that the infringement is justified by objective grounds, the respect of the principle of proportionality and the rule of law. In other words, a *fair balance* should be found between the legitimate interest of the state to obtain information, and fight against tax crimes and evasion, and the interest of the taxpayers involved in the process.

The scope of application of *procedural* rights, despite major developments notably under EU law and ECHR jurisprudence, remains so far mainly in the hands of domestic law. There is a distinction in practice between two schools of thoughts. For some, exchange of information belongs to the 'fact-gathering' process. As a consequence, the taxpayer may benefit from procedural rights but only at the end of the process during the tax assessment decision in the requesting State. For others, the exchange of information is an independent administrative and tax procedure, which should also protect as such the procedural rights of the taxpayers. In the *Sabou* case, the ECJ seem to have endorsed the first school of thought by confirming, at least in the context of the old Directive for exchange of information, that neither the directive nor the EU right of defence could grant a right to be heard to the taxpayer on the request of information and to participate in the investigations in the requested States.

There are however some improvements. First, the EHCR has already recognized that the right of fair trial, granted by Art. 6 ECHR, is applicable in proceedings for criminal taxes. This includes pre-trial measures. In our view, although the issue remains controversial, there is no reason why Art. 6 ECHR should not apply in the context of exchange of information, at least when the process pertains to tax evasion cases, which correspond to 'criminal penalties' according to Art. 6 ECHR. Second, in the *Sabou* case, the ECJ has however tried to define a sort of 'minimum standard' of application for the rights of defence of taxpayers. In particular, the ECJ has confirmed that the taxpayer had rights of defence, and notably the right to be heard, at the level of the requesting State issuing the final assessment after the exchange of information process.

In our view, the exchange of information procedure is more than a 'fact gathering' process but is characterized as an independent administrative and tax procedure, which can affect the rights of defence of the taxpayers involved. According to the *Sabou* case, the state remains free to define more extended participation rights. We tend to believe that a modern and effective standard of protection should be to grant to the taxpayers a right to be informed of the information process, the right to be heard and participate in it and the right to appeal. Following the 'self-determination' jurisprudence in Germany, the taxpayer should also have the right of data protection with all the relevant control and correction possibilities attached to it. It appears however that the views of various states are quite divergent in this respect and at this stage it would be rather difficult to obtain a global consensus.

Therefore, a '*minimum* standard' should correspond to a right of information for the taxpayer involved, in principle at the beginning of the process, subject to the exceptions under the emergency clause. In any event, at least, the taxpayer should be informed of the exchange of information process and have the possibility to challenge the decision made by the requesting State, before the tax assessment, and to understand on which grounds the decision has been founded, which requires that he or she should be in a position to know the 'main content' of the information transferred.

This would be the minimum standard and states should be free to grant more extended procedural rights, and in particular the right to be notified of the information exchange, already at the level of the requested State receiving a request, and to challenge such exchange. In this case, following the Global Standard, the notification could however be postponed in case of emergency or if this could jeopardize the result of the process, but this rule should correspond to an exception. In addition, in such a case, the taxpayer should in any event still be in a position to present his or her case at the level of the requesting State, following the minimum standard described above.

In the long run, the implementation of the rules of exchange of information by participating states in a fair and equivalent way will be decisive for their global recognition and acceptance. In the absence of a worldwide controlling body, such as an International Tax Court, the peer reviews of the Global Forum could play a key role in promoting, not only the efficiency of the process for the benefit of the participating states but also the respect of implementation rules by each participant, and of the substantive and procedural rights of the taxpayers. Perhaps one day, the peer review process will then also analyse the extent and effective implementation of protection rules for the taxpayers, notably secrecy and data protection rules, in the various states.

# General bibliography

## BOOKS

Aubert M./Béguin P.-A./Bernasconi P./Graziano von Burg J./Schwob R./Treuillaud R., Le secret bancaire suisse, 3rd edn, Bern 1995.

Danon R./Gutmann D./Oberson X./Pistone P. (eds), Modèle de Convention OCDE concernant le revenu et la fortune, Commentaire, Helbing & Lichtenhan/Editions Francis Lefebvre, Lausanne/Paris/Geneva/Vienna 2014.

EATLP, Mutual Assistance and Information Exchange, Santiago de Compostela Congress, EATLP International Tax Series, volume 8, 2009.

Grau Ruiz M.-A., Mutual Assistance for the Recovery of Tax Claims, The Netherlands 2001.

Günther O.-C./Tüchler N. (eds), Exchange of Information for Tax Purposes, Vienna Linde 2013.

Helminen M., EU Tax Law Direct Taxation, 3rd. edn, IBFD Amsterdam, 2013.

IFA, Exchange of information and cross-border cooperation between tax authorities, Volume 98b (Copenhagen Congress), La Haye 2013.

IFA, International Mutual Assistance through exchange of information, CDFI, vol 75b (Stockholm Congress) 1990.

Kofler G./Poiares Maduro M./Pistone P. (eds), Human Rights and Taxation in Europe and the World, IBFD, Amsterdam 2011.

Kristoffersson E./Lang M./Pistone P./Schuch J./Staringer C./Storck A. (eds), Tax Secrecy and Tax Transparency, Part 1, Part 2. Frankfurt am Main 2013.

Lang M., Introduction to the Law of Double Taxation Conventions, 2nd edn, Linde, Vienna 2013.

Lang M./Pistone P./Schuch J./Staringer C. (eds), Introduction to European Tax Law on Direct Taxation, 3rd edn, Vienna 2013.

Lang M./Schuch J./Staringer C. (eds), Internationale Amtshilfe in Steuersachen, Vienna 2011.

Maitrot de la Motte A., Droit fiscal de l'Union européenne, Bruylant, Brussels 2012.

Oberson X., Précis de droit fiscal international, 4th edn, Stämpfli, Bern 2014.

Oberson X./Hull H.R., Switzerland in International Tax Law, 4th edn, IBFD, Amsterdam 2011.

Popp P., Grundzüge der internationalen Rechtshilfe in Strafsachen, Basle 2001.

Rust A./Fort E. (eds), Exchange of Information and Bank Secrecy, Wolters Kluwer 2012.

Schenk-Geers T., International Exchange of Information and the Protection of Taxpayers, Wolters Kluwer 2009.

Terra B.J.M./Wattel P.J., European Tax Law, 6th edn, Wolters Kluwer 2012.

Vogel K., Klaus Vogel on Double Taxation Conventions, 3rd edn, Kluwer 1997.

Vogel K./Lehner M., Doppelbesteuerungs-abkommen Kommentar, 5th edn, Verlag Beck, Munich 2008.

## ARTICLES

Afandi R., The Role and Work of the Global Forum on Transparency and Exchange of Information for Tax Purposes, in: Günther/Tüchler (2013), p. 35.

Amatucci F./Herrera P.M., Burden of Proof, in: Mutual Assistance and Information Exchange, EATLP 2009, p. 91.

Attard R., The Classification of Tax Disputes, Human Rights Implications, in: Kofler/Poiares Maduro/Pistone (2011), p. 397.

Aumayr E., Der Umfang des Informationsaustausches nach Art 26 OECD-MA, in: Lang/Schuch/Staringer (2011), p. 47.

Avi-Yonah R., Globalization, Tax Competition, and the Fiscal Crisis of the Welfare State, 113 Harvard Law Review 2000, p. 1575.

Avi-Yonah R., IGAs vs. MAATM: Has Tax Bilateralism Outlived Its Usefulness?, Public Law and Legal Theory Research Paper Series, paper no 384, February 2014.

Avi-Yonah R., The Structure of International Taxation: A Proposal for Simplification, 74 Texas Law Review, 1996, p. 1303.

Azoulai L., EU Human Rights and the Reserved Powers of the Member States, in: Kofler/Poiares Maduro/Pistone (2011), p. 75.

Baker P., Should Article 6 EHCR (Civil) Apply to Tax Proceedings?, Intertax 2001, p. 205.

Baker P., Taxation and the European Convention on Human Rights, European Taxation 2000, p. 298.

Bal, Extraterritorial Enforcement of Tax Claims, IBFD Bulletin for International Taxation, October 2011, p. 600.

Barnard J., Former Tax Havens Prepared to Lift Bank Secrecy, Bulletin IBFD, January 2003, p. 9.

Behnisch U., Amtshilfe der Schweiz in Steuer(straf)sachen, insbesondere an die USA: Durcheinandertal, Archives 77 (2008/2009), p. 737.

Behnisch U., Schweizer Amtshilfe – quo vadis?, in: Steuern und Recht – Steuerrecht!, Liber amicorum für Martin Zweifel, Basel 2013, p. 247.

Belloni M., Exchange of Information and Availability of Bank, Ownership, Identity and Accounting Information, in: Günther/Tüchler (2013), p. 521.

Besson S., The Human Rights Competence in the EU – The State of the Question after Lisbon, in: Kofler/Poiares Maduro/Pistone (2011), p. 37.

Bizioli G., The Impact of the Right to a Fair Trial on Tax Evidence: An EU Analysis, in: Kofler/Poiares Maduro/Pistone (2011), p. 48.

Blank J./Mason R., Exporting FATCA, Law & Economics Research Paper Series, Working Paper n. 14-05, February 2014, p. 1246.

Böckli P., Zahlensteuer. Konzepte und Problem der geplanten EU-Zinsabzugsteuer am Schweizer Sicht, Archives 68 (1999/00), p. 529.

Bonnard Y./Grisel G., L'Accord UBS: spécificités, validité, conformité aux droits de l'homme, RDAF 2010 II p. 361.

Bovet Ch./Liégeois F., Cross-Border Tax Administrative Assistance: 'For The Times They Are A-Changin'', RSDA 2013, p. 25.

Braum S./Covolo V., European Criminal Law and the Exchange of Tax Information: Consequences for Luxembourg's Bank Secrecy Law, in: Rust/Fort (2012), p. 31.

Briffa B., Exchange of Information and Professional Privileges, in: Günther/Tüchler (2013), p. 545.

Brokelind C., The Role of the EU in International Tax Policy and Human Rights: Does the EU Need a Policy on Taxation and Human Rights? in: Kofler/Poiares Maduro/Pistone (2011), p. 113.

Calderón Carreo J. M., Taxpayer Protection within the Exchange of Information Procedure Between State Tax Administrations, Intertax 2000, p. 462.

Calderón Carreo J./Quintas Seara A., The Taxpayer's Right of Defense in Cross-Border Exchange-of-Information Procedures, Bulletin for International Taxation 2014, p. 498.

Cannas F., The Historical Development of the Exchange of Information for Tax Purposes, in: Günther/Tüchler (2013), p. 15.

Carelli F., The New Tax Agreement between Switzerland and the United Kingdom – An Analysis, European Taxation 2012, p. 301.

Carra Richter F., Exchange of Information for the Assistance in the Collection of Taxes under Art. 27 OECD Model, in: Günther/Tüchler (2013), p. 131.

Cavelti L., Automatic Information Exchange versus the Withholding Tax Regime Globalization and Increasing Sovereignty Conflicts in International Taxation, World Tax Journal 2013, p. 172.

Chirinos Sota C., Confidentiality Rules under Article 26 OECD Model (Art 26(2) OECD Model), in: Günther/Tüchler (2013), p. 93.

Cockfield A., Protecting Taxpayer Privacy Rights Under Enhanced Cross-Border Tax Information Exchange: Toward a Multilateral Taxpayer Bill of Rights, 42 U.B.C. Law Review 2010, p. 419.

Cordeiro Guerra R./Dorigo S., Taxpayer's Rights as Human Rights During Tax Procedures, in: Kofler/Poiares Maduro/Pistone (2011), p. 425.

Cosentino S., The Council Directive on Taxation of Savings Income in the Form of Interest Payments (2003/48/EC), in: Günther/Tüchler (2013), p. 281.

Cottier T., Tax fraud or the like: Überlegungen und Lehren zum Legalitätsprinzip im Staatsvertragsrecht, Revue de Droit Suisse (RDS) 2011 I, p. 97.

Cottier T./Matteotti R., Das Abkommen über ein Amtshilfegesuch zwischen der Schweizerischen Eidgenossenschaft und den Vereinigten Staaten von Amerika vom 19. August 2009 – Grundlagen und innerstaatliche Anwendbarkeit, Archives 78 (2009/10), p. 349.

Czakert E., Exchange of Information: The German Perspective, in: Rust/Fort (2012), p. 163.

Daniels A.H.M., Council of Europe/OECD Convention on Mutual Administrative Assistance in Tax Matters, Intertax 1988, p. 101.

Daurer V., Die Amtshilfe in Steuersachen auf unionsrechtlicher Grundlage, in: Lang/Schuch/Staringer (2011), p. 13.

Dean S., The Incomplete Global Market for Tax Information, 49 Boston College Law Review 2008, p. 1.

Deborah, The Legal Relevance of the OECD Standard, in: Günther/Tüchler (2013), p. 53.

de Goede J.J.P./Selicato P., Efficiency, in: Mutual Assistance and Information Exchange, EATLP 2009, p. 121.

De Troyer I., Tax Recovery Assistance in the EU: Analysis of Directive 2010/24/EU, EC Tax Review 2014, p. 135.

del Federico L., The ECHR Principles as Principles of European Law and their Implementation through the National Legal Systems, in: Kofler/Poiares Maduro/Pistone (2011), p. 83.

Dizdarevic M., The FATCA Provisions of the Hire Act: Boldly Going Where No Withholding Has Gone Before, 79 Fordham Law Review 2011, p. 2968.

Dourado A.P., Exchange of Information and Validity of Global Standards in Tax Law: Abstractionism and Expressionism or Where the Truth Lies, European University Institute, Working Paper, RSCAS 2013/11.

Dourado A-P./Silva Dias A., Information Duties, Aggressive Tax Planning and nemo tenetur se ipsum accusare in the light of Art. 6(1) of ECHR, in: Kofler/Poiares Maduro/Pistone (2011), p. 131.

Drüen K.-D., Implementation of Provisions of Mutual Assistance in Tax Affairs, in: Mutual Assistance and Information Exchange, EATLP 2009, p. 55.

Drüen K.-D., Internationale Amtshilfe in Steuersachen im Lichte des deutschen Steuerhinterziehungsbekämpfungsgesetzes, in: Lang/Schuch/Staringer (2011), p. 13.

Drüen K.-D., The Mutual Assistance Directives, in: Rust/Fort (2012), p. 77.

Engelschalk, Commentary to Art. 26 OECD MC, in: Vogel (1997).

Engelschalk, Commentary to Art. 26 OECD MC, in: Vogel/Lehner (2008).

Englisch J., The Impact of Human Rights on Domestic Substantive Taxation – The German Experience, in: Kofler/Poiares Maduro/Pistone (2011), p. 285.

Ennio La Scala A., The Fundamental Human Rights as European Law Principles: Their Development through the ECHR Principles and the Constitutional Traditions Common to the Member States, in: Kofler/Poiares Maduro/Pistone (2011), p. 199.

Fort E./Hondius P./Neugebauer J., Development of the International Information Exchange and Domestic Implementation, in: Rust/Fort (2012), p. 87.

Fortsakis T., The Role of Individual Rights in the Europeanization of Tax Law, in: Kofler/Poiares Maduro/Pistone (2011), p. 95.

Gabert I., Council Directive 2011/16/EU on Administrative Cooperation in the Field of Taxation, European Taxation 2011, p. 342.

Gabert I., Outlook: Comparison on Council Directive 77/799/EEC and COM (2009) 29 in: Mutual Assistance and Information Exchange, EATLP 2009, p. 145.

Gangemi B., General Report in: IFA, International Mutual Assistance through exchange of information, CDFI, vol 75 b (Stockholm Congress) 1990.

Garcia Prats F.A., Exchange of Information under Art. 26 UN Model Tax Convention, Bulletin Tax Treaty Monitor 1999, p. 541.

Giusy De Flora M., A New Vision on Exercising Taxing Powers and the Right to Fair Trial in Judicial Tax Procedures under Art. 6 ECHR, in: Kofler/Poiares Maduro/Pistone (2011), p. 411.

Grau Ruiz M.A., Convention on Mutual Administrative Assistance in Tax Matters and Community Rules: How to Improve their Interaction?, EC Tax Review 2006, p. 196.

Grinberg I., Taxing Capital Income in Emerging Countries: Will FATCA Open the Door? World Tax Journal 2013, p. 325.

Grinberg I., The Battle Over Taxing Offshore Accounts, 60 UCLA Law Review 2012, p. 304.

Grüniger H./Keller A., Exchange of Information in Fiscal Matters, Archives 65 (1996/97), p. 107.

Gupta A., The Foreign Account Tax Compliance Act (FATCA), in: Günther/Tüchler (2013), p. 221.

Gusmão de Oliveira A., Exchange of Information on Request, in: Günther/Tüchler (2013), p. 463.

Gutmann D., Taking Human Rights Seriously: Some Introductory Words on Human Rights, Taxation and the EU, in: Kofler/Poiares Maduro/ Pistone (2011), p. 105.

Guttentag J./Avi-Yonah R., Closing the International Tax Gap, in: Sawicky M. ed, Bridging the Tax Gap, Washington 2005, p. 99.

Harvey R.'D.' Jr., Offshore Accounts: Insider's Summary of FATCA and Its Potential Future, 57 Villanova Law Review 2011, p. 1.

Heiberg J., FATCA: Toward a Multilateral Automatic Information Reporting Regime, 69 Washington and Lee Law Review 2012, p. 1685.

Heidenbauer S., The Savings Directive, in: Lang/Pistone/Schuch/ Staringer (2013), p. 193.

Hemels S.J.C./Pita Grandal A.M., The Use of the Mutual Assistance in Tax Affairs by the Member States and the ECJ, in: Mutual Assistance and Information Exchange, EATLP 2009, p. 63.

Hess E., Die Möglichkeiten und Grenzen der Schweiz auf dem Gebiete der internationalen Zusammenarbeit in Steuersachen, Archives 70 (2001/02), p. 125.

Hess M., Exchange of Information: The Swiss Perspective, in: Rust/Fort (2012), p. 169.

Hufschmid D., 'Tax Fraud and the like' Die Voraussetzungen der Aufhebung des Bankgeheimnisses im Rahmen der Amtshilfe bei Steuerdelikten gemäss DBA-USA, Archives 72 (2003/04), p. 433.

Jeong Y., Spontaneous Exchange of Information, in: Günther/Tüchler (2013), p. 445.

Joosen M., Rubik Agreements, in: Günther/Tüchler (2013), p. 241.

Kofler G./Pistone P., General Report, in: Kofler/Poiares Maduro/Pistone (2011), p. 3.

Kofler G./Tumpel M., Tax Information Exchange Agreements, in: Lang/ Schuch/Staringer (2011), p. 181.

Koppensteiner F., Internationale Amtshilfe in Steuersachen: Rechtsschutz des Steuerpflichtigen im ersuchten und ersuchenden Staat, in: Lang/ Schuch/Staringer (2011), p. 237.

Kristoffersson E./Pistone P., General Report, in: Kristoffersson/Lang/ Pistone/Schuch/Staringer/Storck (2013), p. 1.

Lang M., Introduction, in: Lang/Pistone/Schuch/Staringer (2013).

Langer M., Liechtenstein Report, in: IFA, Exchange of Information and Cross-border Cooperation between Tax Authorities, Vol 98b, The Hague 2013, p. 449.

Lao J., The Council Directive concerning Mutual Assistance for the Recovery of Claims (2010/24/EU), in: Günther/Tüchler (2013), p. 303.

Le Mentec F., Exchange of Information: The French Perspective, in: Rust/Fort (2012), p. 153.

Lieja Carrasco A., Exchange of Information and the Legal Protection of the Taxpayer, in: Günther/Tüchler (2013), p. 565.

Lissi A./Bukara D., Abkommen mit Deutschland und Grossbritanien über die Zusammenarbeit im Steuerbereich (parts 1 and 2), FStR 2012, pp. 42 (part 1), 103 (part 2).

Locher P., Die schweizerische Haltung zur internationalen Amtshilfe bei den direkten Steuern in einem veränderten Umfeld, in: Mélanges Ryser 2005, p. 271.

Lüthi D., Informationsaustausch im Internationalen Steuerrecht der Schweiz; in: Höhn (ed.), Handbuch 1993, p. 438.

Lyal R., Tax and Fundamental Rights in EU Law: Procedural Issues, in: Kofler/Poiares Maduro/Pistone (2011), p. 445.

Maier H.F., Exchange of Information on Tax Matters in the Jurisprudence of the ECJ in respect to Primary Law, in: Günther/Tüchler (2013), p. 345.

Maisto G., The Impact of the European Convention on Human Rights on Tax Procedures and Sanctions with Special Reference to Tax Treaties and the EU Arbitration Convention, in: Kofler/Poiares Maduro/Pistone (2011), p. 373.

Malherbe J., General Report, Protection of Confidential Information in Tax Matters, Cahiers de Droit Fiscal International, Vol LXXVIb (IFA) 1991.

Malherbe P./Beynsberger M., 2011: The Year of Implementation of the Standards?, in: Rust/Fort (2012), p. 119.

Marchgraber C., Internationale Amtshilfe in Steuersachen und Beweis-verwertungsverbote, in: Lang/Schuch/Staringer (2011), p. 271.

Matteotti R., Das Abkommen über ein Amtshilfegesuch zwischen der Schweizerischen Eidgenossenschaft und den Vereinigten Staat von Amerika von 19 August 2009, Archives 78 (2009/10), p. 349.

Mauro C., The Concept of Criminal Charges in the European Court of Human Rights Case Law, in: Kofler/Poiares Maduro/Pistone (2011), p. 459.

McIntyre J., How to End the Charade of Information Exchange, Tax Notes International 2009, p. 254.

Michel D.S./Matthews M., The Justice Department and Swiss Banks: Understanding the Special Disclosure Program, Bloomberg BNA's Banking Report, 101 BBR 489, 24 September 2013, p. 1.

Morse S., Ask for Help, Uncle Sam: The Future of Global Tax Reporting, 57 Villanova Law Review, p. 529, 2012.

Muñoz Forner A., The Council Directive on Administrative Cooperation in the Field of Taxation (2011/16/EU), in: Günther/Tüchler (2013), p. 261.

Novis K., The Limits of Exchange of Information under Article 26 OECD Model (Article 26(3) to (5) OECD Model), in: Günther/Tüchler (2013), p. 115.

Oberson X., Agreement between Switzerland and the European Union on the Taxation of Savings – A Balanced 'Compromis Helvétique', Bulletin for International Fiscal Documentation 2005, p. 108.

Oberson X., General Report in: IFA, Exchange of Information and Cross-border Cooperation between Tax Authorities, Volume 98b (Copenhagen Congress), La Haye 2013.

Oberson X., La mise en oeuvre par la Suisse de l'art. 26 MC OCDE, FStR 2012, p. 4.

Oberson X., 'Tax fraud or the like', selon l'art. 26 de la CDI de 1996 entre les Etats-Unis d'Amérique et la Suisse, Archives 81 (2012/13), p. 101.

Oberson X., The Development of International Assistance in Tax Matters in Switzerland: From Evolution to Revolution, European Taxation 2013, p. 368.

Oberson X., The OECD Model Agreement on Exchange of Information – a Shift to the Applicant State, Bulleting IBFD 2003, p. 14.

Öner C., Using Exchange of Information in regard to Assistance in Tax Collection, IBFD, European Taxation, vol. 51, 2011, p. 124.

Pankiv M., Tax Information Exchange Agreements (TIEAs), in: Günther/Tüchler (2013), p. 153.

Parida S., Automatic Exchange of Information, in: Günther/Tüchler (2013), p. 421.

Perdelwitz A., The New Tax Agreement between Germany and Switzerland – Milestone or Selling of Indulgences? European Taxation 2011, p. 496.

Pistone P., Exchange of Information and Rubik Agreements: The Perspective of an EU Academic, Bulletin for International Taxation, Vol 67, 2013 p. 216.

Pistone P./Gruber M., Die Möglichkeiten der Verweigerung des Informationsaustausches nach Art 26 OECD-MA, in: Lang/Schuch/Staringer (2011), p. 75.

Pratz G., Exchange of Information under Article 26 of the UN Model Tax Convention, in: Bulletin Tax Treaty Monitor 1999, p. 541.

Pross A./Russo R., The Amended Convention on Mutual Administrative Assistance in Tax Matters: A Powerful Tool To Counter Tax Avoidance and Evasion, Bulletin for International Taxation 2012, p. 361.

Radcliffe P., The OECD's Common Reporting Standard: The Next Step in the Global Fight against Tax Evasion, IBFD Derivatives & Financial Instruments 2014, p. 160.

Reich M., Das Amtshilfeabkommen in Sachen UBS oder die Grenzen der Staatsvertragskompetenz des Bundesrats, FStR 2010 p. 111.

Richter Filipe C., Exchange of Information for the Assistance in the Collection of Taxes, in: Günther/Tüchler (2013), p. 131.

Rivolta A., New Switzerland-Germany and Switzerland-United Kingdom Agreements: Does Anyone Offer More than Switzerland?, 66 Bulletin for International Taxation 2012, p. 138.

Roncarati A., Other Forms of Administrative Cooperation than the Traditional Forms of Exchange of Information (Automatic, Spontaneous and on Request), in: Günther/Tüchler (2013), p. 503.

Rosenbloom H. D., The Foreign Account Tax Compliance Act and Notice 2010-60, in: Kofler/Poiares Maduro/Pistone (2011), p. 211.

Ruiz Jimenez C. A., Fair Trial Rights on Taxation: The European and Inter-American Experience, in: Kofler/Poiares Maduro/Pistone (2011), p. 521.

Rust A., Data Protection as a Fundamental Right, in: Rust/Fort (2012), p. 177.

Sarmiento D., Fundamental Rights and Fundamental Boundaries in EU Law, in: Kofler/Poiares Maduro/Pistone (2011), p. 65.

Schenk-Geers T./Sacchetto C., Legal Protection, in: Mutual Assistance and Information Exchange, EATLP 2009, p. 103.

Schilcher M./Spies K., The Directives on Mutual Assistance in the Assessment and in the Recovery of Tax Claims in the Field of Direct Taxation, in: Lang/Pistone/Schuch/Staringer (2013), p. 207.

Schröder J., Savings Taxation and Banking Secrecy, in: Rust/Fort (2012), p. 59.

Schuch J./Titz E., Die Bedeutung der internationalen Amtshilfe in Steuersachen für die Mitwirkungspflicht im Abgabenverfahren, in: Lang/Schuch/Staringer (2011), p. 343.

Seer R., Recent Development in Exchange of Information within the EU for Tax Matters, EC Tax Review 2013, p. 66.

Seer R./Gabert I., European and International Tax Cooperation: Legal Basis, Practice, Burden of Proof, Legal Protection and Requirements, Bulletin for International Taxation 2011, p. 88.

Seer R./Gabert I., General Report, in: Mutual Assistance and Information Exchange, EATLP 2009, p. 23.

Simader K., Die Bedeutung der internationalen Amtshilfe in Steuersachen in der Rechtsprechung des EuGH zu den Grundfreiheiten, in: Lang/Schuch/Staringer (2011), p. 309.

Somare M./Wöhrer V., Two Different FATCA Model Intergovernmental Agreements: Which is Preferable?, Bulletin for International Taxation 2014, p. 395.

Staringer C./Günther O.-C., Bankgeheimnis und internationale Amtshilfe in Steuersachen, in: Lang/Schuch/Staringer (2011), p. 203.

Steichen A., Information Exchange in Tax Matters: Luxembourg's New Tax Policy, in: Rust/Fort (2012), p. 9.

Stewart M., Transnational Tax Information Exchange Networks: Step towards a Globalized, Legitimate Tax Administration, World Tax Journal, June 2012, p. 152.

Tanzi V./Zee H.H., Taxation in a Borderless World: The Role of Information Exchange, in: International Studies in Taxation: Law and Economics (Liber Amicorum Leif Muten), Stockholm 1999, p. 321.

Tello C.P., FATCA: Catalyst for Global Cooperation on Exchange of Tax Information, Bulletin for International Taxation 2014, p. 88.

Tello C.P./Malherbes J., Le Foreign Account Tax Compliance Act (FATCA) américain: un tournant juridique dans la coopération sur l'échange d'informations fiscales, Revue de droit fiscal, January 2014, p. 1.

Toifl G., Internationale Amtshilfe in Finanzstrafsachen, in: Lang/Schuch/Staringer (2011), p. 141.

Torres Jimenez M.-A., The Extent of Exchange of Information under Article 26 OECD Model (Article 26(1) OECD Model), in: Günther/Tüchler (2013), p. 73.

Torres-Richoux J., The Council Regulation on Administrative Cooperation and Combating Fraud in the Field of Value Added Tax (904/2010), p. 327, in: Günther/Tüchler (2013), p. 327.

Tüchler N., Die Amtshilfe bei der Erhebung von Steuern nach Art 27 OECD-MA, in: Lang/Schuch/Staringer (2011), p. 117.

Untersander O., The Exchange of Information Procedure According to Double Tax Conventions: The Swiss Approach or How Taxpayer Rights Are Protected under Swiss Procedural Rules, in: Rust/Fort (2012), p. 197.

Valdes Zauner A.C., Exchange of Information through Group Requests, in: Günther/Tüchler (2013), p. 483.

Valkama M., The Nordic Mutual Assistance Convention on Mutual Administrative Assistance in Tax Matters, in: Günther/Tüchler (2013), p. 197.

van Thiel S., Is there a Need for International Enforcement of Human Rights in the Tax Area?, in: Kofler/Poiares Maduro/Pistone (2011), p. 153.

Van West J.-P., Exchange of Information in the Jurisprudence of the ECJ in respect to Secondary Law, in: Günther/Tüchler (2013), p. 381.

Vanistendael F., Global Law and the Search for Constitutional Pluralism, in: Kofler/Poiares Maduro/Pistone (2011), p. 185.

Vanistendael F., The European Interest Savings Directive – An Appraisal and Proposals for Reform, Bulletin for International Taxation 2009, p. 152.

Vanistendael F., The Interest Savings Directive: European Hide and Seek, in: A Tax Globalist, Essays in Honour of Maarten J. Ellis, Amsterdam 2005, p. 326.

Vanistendael F. The International Information Exchange Puzzle, Tax Notes International 2014, p. 1149.

Vascega M./Van Thiel S., Council Adopts New Directive on Mutual Assistance in Recovery of Tax and Similar Claims, European Taxation 2010, p. 231.

Vinnitskiy D.V., The Protection of Human Rights and its Impact on Tax Litigation from a Russian Perspective, in: Kofler/Poiares Maduro/ Pistone (2011), p. 505.

Waldburger R., Abgeltungs-steuern im Konflikt in dem EU-Zinsbesteuerungs-abkommen?, FStR 2012, p. 169.

Waldburger R., Das Amtshilfeverfahren wegen 'Steuerbetrugs und dergleichen mit den USA', FStR 2009, p. 91.

Waldburger R., Entraide administrative et judiciaire internationale en matière fiscale, in: OREF (ed.), Les procédures en droit fiscal, 2nd edn., Berne 2005, p. 293.

Walker B., Exchange of Information for Criminal Tax Matters, in: Günther/Tüchler (2013), p. 583.

Weidmann M./Suter C., Sicherstellung des Abkommenszwecks, FStR 2012, p. 127.

Winandy J.-P., Legal Protection against the Transfer of Information (Luxembourg), in: Rust/Fort (2012), p. 221.

Wittmann K., The CoE/OECD Convention on Mutual Administrative Assistance in Tax Matters, in: Günther/Tüchler (2013), p. 175.

Wouters J./Meuwissen K., Global Tax Governance: Work in Progress?, in: Kofler/Poiares Maduro/Pistone (2011), p. 221.

Zagaris B., Information Exchange between the U.S. and Latin America: The U.S. Perspective, Parts 1 and 2, Tax Notes International 2014, p. 955 (Part 1), p. 1051 (Part 2).

## REPORTS, OFFICIAL DOCUMENTS, ETC.

FATF/OECD, International Standards on Combating Money Laundering and the Financing of Terrorism and Proliferation, The FATF Recommendations, February 2012.

OCDE, Echange de renseignements fiscaux entre les pays Membres de l'OCDE – une vue d'ensemble des pratiques actuelles, Paris 1994.

OECD, Agreement on Exchange of Information on Tax Matters, Paris 2002.

OECD, Harmful Tax Competition – An Emerging Global Issue, 1998.

OECD, Improving Access to Bank Information for Tax Purposes, Paris 1998.

OECD, Keeping it Safe – The OECD Guide on the Protection of Confidentiality of Information Exchanged for Tax Purposes, Paris, July 2012.

OECD, Manual on the Implementation of Exchange of Information, 2006.

OECD, Report to the G20: 'Automatic Exchange of Information: What it is, How it works, Benefits, What remains to be done', Paris 2012.

OECD, Standard for Automatic Exchange of Financial Account Information, Common Reporting Standard, 13, 2, 2014.

OECD, Standard for Automatic Exchange of Financial Account Information in Tax Matters, July 2014.

United States Government Accountability Office, GAO, Tax Administration, IRS's Information Exchanges with Other Countries Could Be Improved through Better Performance Information, September 2011.

# Index

administrative cooperation
  CMAAT *see* OECD, Convention on
    Mutual Administrative
    Assistance in Tax Matters
    (CMAAT)
  EU Directive 104–18, 139–40, 164,
    165–6, 171–2
  in indirect taxes 7, 126–42
admissibility of evidence in criminal
    proceedings 25, 35, 59–60, 65–6,
    98, 106, 159–60, 207, 227
  *see also* criminal offences
agreements
  bilateral 88–9, 90, 111, 139, 169, 197
  intergovernmental *see* IGA
    (intergovernmental agreement)
  OECD Competent Authority
    Agreement (CAA) 12, 46,
    167–8, 184–5, 187–8, 197, 219,
    246
  'Qualified Intermediary' (QI)
    agreement 9, 44, 150–51, 173,
    174
  Swiss Rubik agreements 10, 143–9,
    165–6, 174–9, 204–5
  Tax Information Exchange
    Agreements (TIEAs) 7, 16,
    56–66, 167–8
  with third countries *see* third
    countries
anti-money laundering legislation *see*
    *under* money laundering
assistance in the collection of taxes 17,
    49–55, 109, 119–20, 177
automatic exchange of information *see*
    exchange of information,
    automatic

bank secrecy
  EU Directive on Administrative
    Cooperation (DAC) 107, 115
  EU Savings Directive 81, 90, 161
  and FATCA 157, 161, 166
  OECD DTC (Double Taxation
    Convention) 36–7
  OECD TIEA (Tax Information
    Exchange Agreement) 59, 61–2
  Switzerland-United States Income
    Tax Convention 40
  VAT regulation 130, 142
  *see also* secrecy
beneficial owner
  as controlling person 196
  EU Savings Directive 83–5, 86–8, 89,
    92, 103, 169, 171
  FATCA system 173, 181–2
  identification of 180–82
  individual is 95–7
  legal owner not same person 38
  limited liability companies 162
  and paying agent 85–6, 92, 94, 177
  and tax fraud 44–5
  withholding tax 153–4
big bang 8–11, 36, 58, 166
bilateral agreements 88–9, 90, 111, 139,
    169, 197
black lists 8
burden of proof 152
business secret 33–4, 38, 64, 74, 116,
    125, 138, 142, 221
  *see also* secrecy

CAA (competent authority agreement)
    12, 46, 167–8, 184–5, 187–8, 190,
    197, 201–2, 219, 246

*263*

special scheme 133, 135–6
spontaneous exchange of information
  *see* exchange of information,
  automatic
standards' implementation *see*
  implementation of standards
stolen data 35, 45, 148, 222–3, 243
  *see also* data protection
subsidiarity principle 19, 27, 31, 54, 73,
  115, 122, 137, 212, 213
substantive rights 235, 237–8, 248, 250
Switzerland
  administrative assistance and
    exchange of information with
    US 39–48
  anonymous withholding alternative
    approach 174–6
  EU Directive on administrative
    assistance (EUDAC) 118
  EU Savings Directive 82, 88–9, 169
  EU-Swiss Agreement on the Taxation
    of Savings 89–104
  exchange of information 5, 6, 18–19,
    20–21, 35, 36, 38, 82, 227,
    240–41
  group requests 22
  IGA (intergovernmental agreement),
    Model 2 48, 157–8, 159–60,
    218, 245
  paying agent 177
  right to privacy 234
  'Rubik' agreements 10, 143–9,
    165–6, 174–9, 204–5
  savings income taxation 7
  stolen data use 223
  Switzerland-United Kingdom
    Agreement 146
  Switzerland-United States Income
    Tax Convention 40
  Tax Information Exchange
    Agreements (TIEAs) 56, 59, 65
  US DoJ program for Swiss banks
    involved in tax evasion with US
    taxpayers 206–8
  US-Swiss double taxation treaty 20,
    22, 23, 159, 176

tax avoidance 14, 17, 21, 49, 67, 85–6,
  99, 148, 176, 212, 239, 245
tax collection assistance 17, 49–55, 109,
  119–20, 177
tax coordination 117–18, 126, 247
tax evasion 4, 7, 14, 17, 21, 58, 212
  anonymous withholding system
    174–6
  anti-money laundering legislation
    152, 171, 180–83, 195
  EU Directive on administrative
    cooperation in the field of
    taxation (DAC) 109, 139–40,
    171–2
  EU Savings Directive 169–72
  FATCA 150, 173
  and international tax treaties 212
  OECD Convention on Mutual
    Administrative Assistance in Tax
    Matters (CMAAT) 67–8, 174
  UBS 8, 9–10, 12, 22–3, 38–40, 43–8,
    151, 206–7, 213, 227
  US DoJ program for Swiss banks
    involved in tax evasion with US
    taxpayers 206–8
tax examination abroad 27, 68, 70, 71
tax fraud 6, 8, 12, 20, 25, 58, 181
  anti-money laundering legislation
    181
  and beneficial owner 44–5
  dual criminality principal 66
  EU Directive on administrative
    cooperation in the field of
    taxation (DAC) 165–6
  EU Savings Agreement 97, 98–9,
    100, 101
  exchange of information 89, 97, 109,
    142, 216
  FACTA 163–4
  relationship of trust 44
  Switzerland-United States Income
    Tax Convention 40, 41–2, 43
  VAT 127, 128–40
tax fraud and the like 23, 40, 41, 43,
  44–8, 89, 91, 98, 99, 208
tax haven 6, 8, 9, 58, 59, 61, 63, 181,
  197